THE NEW STRUGGLE FOR DEMOCRACY IN AFRICA

This book is dedicated to my son Robin,
fellow devotee of Gateshead F.C. and the music of Jimi Hendrix

The New Struggle for Democracy in Africa

JOHN A. WISEMAN
Department of Politics
University of Newcastle upon Tyne

Ashgate

Aldershot • Brookfield USA • Singapore • Sydney

Published by
Ashgate Publishing Limited
Gower House
Croft Road
Aldershot
Hants GU11 3HR
England

Ashgate Publishing Company
Old Post Road
Brookfield
Vermont 05036
USA

Reprinted 1997, 1998

British Library Cataloguing in Publication Data

Wiseman, J. A.
    New Struggle for Democracy in Africa
    I. Title
    321.8096

Library of Congress Catalog Card Number : 95-83288

Typeset by The Setting Studio
121 Newbridge Street
Newcastle upon Tyne

ISBN 1 85972 332 2

Printed in Great Britain by
Antony Rowe Ltd, Chippenham, Wiltshire

Contents

Acknowledgements

Although the focus of this book is clearly on the most recent period in African politics its writing has inevitably been affected by a vast range of influences on my understanding of the subject going back over the twenty five years or so I have been involved in this compulsively fascinating field of study. It is probably invidious to single out a handful of individuals from the huge number of teachers, colleagues, and personal friends in the UK and in Africa who have assisted me in so many different ways over such a long period but at the risk of upsetting the majority I would like to record my special thanks to Roger Charlton, Christopher Clapham, Dick Crook, J. Isawa Elaigwu, Ade Fowlis, Eleanor Gabaake, Arnold Hughes, Ba Tarawale, and Bill Tordoff.

In the Department of Politics here in Newcastle I am especially indebted to Tim Gray, Martin Harrop and Peter Jones who generously took over my departmental duties in order that I should have the time to complete the writing of this book. At Avebury Sarah Markham has been a delight to work with. My wife and children have been understanding about the way I have neglected them in order to sit at the word-processor, and have helped in many other ways as well.

It is not very likely that any of the above are responsible for any errors or ommissions which may have crept into the following pages but even if they are I will be happy to take the blame.

John A. Wiseman
University of Newcastle upon Tyne

1 Introduction: 'New', 'Struggle', and Democracy

As Africa entered the final year of the 1980s only five states could seriously claim to be democratically governed even if the relatively minimalist definition of democracy, involving free elections with competing political parties, was used. Botswana, The Gambia, Mauritius, Senegal, and Zimbabwe did meet these less than stringent conditions but even this short list appeared to be in danger of becoming shorter as President Mugabe had declared his intention to introduce a Marxist-Leninist single-party state in Zimbabwe in 1990[1]. Some observers would have expressed doubts over the democratic credentials of the remaining four, not least because only Mauritius had ever witnessed a change of government through the ballot box. The Republic of South Africa had had a long and continuing experience of competitive elections, which included change of government through the ballot box (although this had not occurred since 1948), but the denial of the franchise to the majority of the population excluded it from a list of democracies. At the beginning of 1989 Nelson Mandela was still a political prisoner, the African National Congress (ANC) and the other main anti-apartheid groups were legally banned and forced to operate underground and/or in exile, and the hardliner P. W. Botha was still President. Over the rest of Africa competitive party systems were absent at that point in time. The majority of the rest of the states were governed through the authoritarianism of single-party or military rule whilst a minority could hardly be described as being governed at all and were engaged in civil wars of varying intensity.

Six years later the situation had been transformed[2]. To say that democratic systems predominated in Africa would be an exaggeration but to say that there had been a quite remarkable movement in that direction was incontestable, notwithstanding the existence of a number of states (most notably Angola, Rwanda, and Burundi) where the initial momentum had been reversed. By 1995 there was not one fully fledged single-party state[3] left in Africa: the type of political system which had previously predominated had completely disappeared. For the first time in decades it was easier and quicker to list those states which had not experienced at least some progress towards multi-partyism than those which had. The situation in this latter group of states varied considerably from one to another.

In Nigeria and Sierra Leone the military were still in power. In the latter the government of Captain Valentine Strasser was promising a return to democratic civilian rule by 1996[4] but with the country collapsing into civil war and anarchy this was looking increasingly improbable. In Nigeria the situation was more complicated[5] because the country had already had relatively democratic elections in 1992 and 1993 but the military had refused to accept the results and remained in power albeit under a different leader, General Sanni Abacha having replaced General Ibrahim Babangida following a brief period when the government was nominally headed by an unelected civilian, Chief Ernest Adegunle Shonekan, who had been installed by military decree. In The Gambia a coup d'etat in July 1994 had replaced the democratic political system with military rule.

In three states a non-party political system was in operation. In Swaziland a version of the traditional Swazi monarchy was still in place. The government was willing to accept a variety of reform measures but not to countenance a multi-party system in spite of increasing pressure to do so from a variety of Swazi political movements, most prominent amongst which was the People's United Democratic Movement (PUDEMO)[6]. In Uganda the government of President Yoweri Museveni was still insisting that what it described as 'no-party democracy' should remain in place until the end of the century[7]. In Eritrea, which in May 1993 had become Africa's newest state following independence from Ethiopia, a transitional government of the Eritrean People's Liberation Front (EPLF) had pledged itself to proceed in the direction of a multi-party system.

In addition to these states there was another small group where civil war precluded the establishment of effective national government, democratic or otherwise[8.] This group included Angola, Liberia, Rwanda, Somalia, Sudan and, perhaps more arguably, Chad. Angola was experiencing renewed civil war after a temporary cessation of fighting which followed a peace agreement and competitive elections[9].

Thus, by 1995 these twelve states where party pluralism was absent represented the exception rather than the rule in Africa. In the remaining thirty six states competitive party systems existed: in six years the proportion of African states in this category had gone from 10% to 75% with, as we have seen, some

2

of the rest declaring their intention of doing so in the future. At this point the reader would be entitled to ask 'so what?'. The above figures represent merely a fairly superficial statistical statement about the formal characteristics of African political systems which by itself tells us little or nothing about how those systems operate and the extent to which apparent change over half a decade has or has not altered their actual modes of operation. Democracy starts with the possibility of political competition between those who would be leaders for the support of their fellow citizens but it certainly does not end there. It would be nonsense to suggest that all political systems which formally make allowance for the existence of more than one party could be regarded as constituting a single type of system and nonsense on stilts to suggest that all such systems could automatically be described as democratic, even in the minimalist sense of the term. I am suggesting neither. What I am doing is taking these developments as a starting point in the examination of political change in Africa in a particular period. Fundamental to this is the awareness of the importance of paying particular attention to the very different experiences of the different African states. Broad surface similarities in the changes taking place over so many states certainly hide crucial differences in what the change has meant.

Because I have chosen to describe what has taken place in Africa in recent years as constituting a 'new struggle for democracy' it is relevant at this point to say something about this terminology and to suggest why it is appropriate.

New

As the political developments, here identified as a struggle for democracy, which provide the primary focus for this study have occurred since around the beginning of 1989 there can be no argument about them being 'recent' but this is not quite enough to justify describing them as being 'new'. In many ways the struggle for democracy in Africa has been going on for a long time. Certainly the struggle of the African nationalist movements towards the end of the colonial period can be seen, at least in part, as constituting a struggle for democracy and an end to undemocratic colonial rule. As things turned out this struggle tended to be more successful in indigenising political control than it was in democratising it. Although, as indicated earlier, relatively democratic systems survived in a limited number of states a marked swing to authoritarianism took place in a majority of states as opposition parties were banned and/or unelected soldiers replaced civilian leaders. This did not mean that the struggle for democracy disappeared because throughout the entire post-independence period large numbers of supporters of democracy in Africa continued to work for a redemocratisation of their political systems[10]. In some cases their efforts met with success as some

3

political systems were, for a time at least, restructured along more democratic lines. The limited nature of the success of African democrats in the period before 1989 cannot be allowed to conceal the efforts and sacrifices that were made prior to that. This 'persistence of the democratic alter ego' (to resurrect a phrase I coined in my earlier book) remains a crucial factor in explaining more recent change. Although authoritarian rule was very common it had failed to extinguish the underlying belief of many Africans that a more democratic Africa was both attainable and desirable. As in most examples of historical change, closer inspection reveals significant elements of continuity.

Having given due recognition to this continuity in the struggle for democracy attention can now be focussed on aspects of change. I would suggest that the new features could be categorised in terms of three, empirically interlinked, groups. These groups of features are identified in terms of (1) *environment*, (2) *participation*, and (3) *outcomes*. All of these are discussed at greater length in subsequent chapters but a synopsis of the most important features will be useful here.

By *environment* I refer mainly to the new global political environment in which change in Africa has taken place. Although the application of a precise date is difficult, if not impossible, it can be said that the end of the 1980s marked the end of the essentially bi-polar competition of the Cold War. Retrospectively it could be argued that the Cold War had been winding down since the succession of the reformist Mikhail Gorbachev to the post of General Secretary of the Communist Party of the Soviet Union (CPSU) in 1985 but the profound changes which followed this were not instant or automatic. In the past the competitive nature of the Cold War had been antipathetic to the prospects for democracy in Africa because the competing super-powers had been willing to offer support to highly authoritarian regimes as a means of gaining strategic influence. Authoritarian African political leaders were more strongly placed to resist the pressures of African democrats when they could turn to outside powers to help them stay in power. Related to events in Eastern Europe this period also saw the almost total worldwide collapse of the legitimacy of Marxism-Leninism as a guide to organising systems of government. Whilst I do not completely share Francis Fukuyama's beliefs in the total victory of liberal democracy as a global ideology[11] the erosion of the Marxist-Leninist alternative appears fairly advanced. Of course by no means all of Africa's authoritarian regimes had claimed adherence to Marxism-Leninism[12]: indeed there were some (eg. Zaire, South Africa and Malawi) which incorporated opposition to Marxism-Leninism and the 'spread of international communism' into their justifications for authoritarian rule. Undemocratic regimes claiming legitimacy on the basis of the ideology or on opposition to it were simultaneously deprived of justification.

To these changes in the strategic and ideological aspects of the world political environment we can add a third factor. This is what Samuel Huntington refers to as the 'third wave of democratization'[13] which saw democratic regimes replacing authoritarian ones in some thirty countries of Southern Europe, Asia, and Latin America between 1974 and 1990. The timing of the publication of Huntington's study precludes the possibility of the consideration of the African case studies with which this book is concerned, but the high incidence of democratisation which he describes elsewhere in the world provides a further new factor in the global political environment of the struggle for democracy in Africa. The fact that a large proportion of these instances of democratisation occurred in the Third World underscores their relevance.

The second new feature in the struggle for democracy relates to *participation.* Although elites, of various types, have been important in the struggle, as they had been in the past, the later period has been marked by a much higher level of mass participation. In state after state thousands, tens of thousands, and hundreds of thousands have taken to the streets to demand an end to authoritarianism. Politicians and academics alike often tend to talk rather glibly about 'mass struggle' but the recent evidence from Africa tends to confirm that in this case the term is accurate. Later chapters provide detailed evidence of this phenomenon in large numbers of African states but at this point one example might suffice to give a flavour of events. In 1991 the military dictatorship of Moussa Traore was overthrown in the West African state of Mali, a development which paved the way for democratic elections the following year. One scholar describing the events which produced this change describes how 'tens of thousands of Malians took to the streets over three consecutive days to demonstrate for democracy and multi-partyism...the collective expression of pro-democracy aspirations through mass non-violent demonstrations marked a qualitative and incredible change in the political process in Mali'[14]. The same author quotes estimates of 100,000 participants in the pro-democracy demonstrations: given that the population of Bamako, the capital of Mali, is estimated to be around 400,000 we are talking of around one quarter of the population of the city taking part. This level of mass participation is made all the more remarkable by the fact that earlier pro-democracy demonstrations had been brutally suppressed by the army.

Events in Mali were replicated right across Africa during this period. Pressure for change was predominantly from the bottom up rather than from the top down. Analysing the earlier movement towards multi-partyism in Senegal during the period 1975 to 1985 Robert Fatton[15] has argued that it could be described (borrowing from Antonio Gramsci) as a 'passive revolution', a notion which suggests the dominant role of elite strategy in the process. It may be a little early to speculate on whether recent events constitute a 'revolution' but it does appear that it would be wildly inaccurate to describe them as 'passive' given the mass base of pressure for change. Although subsequent events indicated that political elites frequently made strenuous efforts to manipulate the situation for their own advantage, with very varying degrees of success, the initiation of change came predominantly from below.

The third, and in practical terms probably the most important, new feature of the struggle was the degree of success to be seen in the *outcomes*. Whereas previous struggles for democracy had enjoyed at best limited successes in a limited number of states over a fairly long period the picture changed very considerably this time. In a relatively short period the vast majority of African states moved towards an acceptance of political pluralism and a rejection of the official monolithism of single-party and military rule. In a significant number of these incumbent ruling elites were replaced in government through the mechanism of the ballot box.

In any period of change the balance between old and new is relative: even the most profound transformations inevitably contain within them strong resonances of the past. However, in spite of the elements of continuity noted earlier it is possible to argue with conviction that the features relating to environment, participation, and outcome do mark out recent developments in Africa as constituting something new.

Struggle

There are a number of reasons why the term 'struggle' is appropriate in describing these developments. Perhaps the most obvious is that the simple, everyday meaning of the word, implying using great efforts to bring about a desired end, does accurately describe what has been happening. Across Africa countless individuals and groups have been involved in strenuous efforts to make their political systems more democratic. In many cases this has involved considerable personal cost to those involved both at a mass and elite level. Violent and non-violent elements have been involved although violence has more commonly been used by defenders of the status quo who control the means of state coercion than it has by supporters of change. In the past the term 'struggle' has often appeared to be the monopoly of the Marxist left who have used it endlessly in trying to persuade the rest of us that something called 'the struggle for socialism' was taking place. In relation to Africa that particular 'struggle' was always largely mythical in character and bore little relation to what African people were trying to achieve. The usage suggested here relates much more closely to empirical reality.

To discuss events in terms of a struggle also highlights the extremely contested and conflictual character of the process. In a literal sense we are describing the oppositions of a struggle both for and against democracy. The struggle for democracy has in many cases met with strong resistance from those who benefit from the absence of democracy. Although few would now argue, at least openly, that authoritarian rule provides the best way of providing for the progressive development of Africa (or perhaps just the staving off of disaster) there is no doubt that non-democratic systems have often worked with reasonable efficiency in serving the short-term[16] interests of those who exercise state power. This is not at all surprising because, if stripped of a series of largely spurious ideological justifications, this is exactly what such systems were designed by their architects to do. Elites in control of these systems have interests in resisting change if at all possible because public accountability often appears very threatening. The struggle against democracy has taken many forms which have met with varying degrees of success. These range from the use of high levels of physical coercion to other more subtle methods of undermining the struggle and avoiding its consequences. The tactics and strategies adopted by those struggling against democracy have been at least as varied as those adopted by the would-be democratisers. The fact that the notion of struggle inevitably implies a conflict perspective makes it especially relevant in these circumstances because it forces the observer to focus on the full range of the multitude of participants, both individuals and groups, involved in the process and on the extreme antagonisms which exist.

The focus on struggle and conflict is useful too in that it serves to indicate that there is no predetermined outcome either in relation to individual African states or in relation to African states in general. The study of struggle is not confined to successful struggle, however one may define the latter. In a very real sense the struggle for democracy has not been 'won' in any African state if by that term we meant that a democratic system had been fully consolidated, was in perfect working order, and was immune from collapse or more gradual erosion at some point in the future. On a more optimistic note it could perhaps be observed that nowhere had the struggle been totally 'lost' if that implied that the forces of democracy had been totally eliminated and authoritarianism was completely secure. As the evidence presented in this book will demonstrate it has been very much a mixture of two steps forward one step back/one step forward two steps back. In all cases the result of the struggle for democracy is partial victory or partial defeat, with both conditions being most accurately seen as impermanent.

Democracy

Many writers, immensely more philosophically gifted than myself, have spent their scholarly lifetimes teasing out the subtleties and nuances associated with conceptions of democracy. The result of these endeavours remains the absence

7

of universally accepted definitions and a concept which is still highly contested in analytical and ideological discourse. My interests, on the other hand, lie with the everyday rough and tumble of African politics which presents quite enough of a challenge to my powers of comprehension. Even though the following brief discussion of the meanings of democracy contains nothing to excite any serious interest from democratic theorists it serves as a necessary foundation for later chapters.

To begin with it is necessary to distinguish two aspects of the meaning of democracy as used here: the first relates to the observer and the second to the observed (Africans struggling for democracy) to the extent that this can be known. If the analysis and description of the events is to mean anything there must also be a reasonable correlation between these two. In both cases it is also necessary to distinguish between minimalist and maximalist conceptions of democracy.

To make democracy a usable concept, from an analytical point of view, in understanding events in the real world (in Africa or elsewhere) it is not useful to attach so much to it that it becomes a holdall of all desirable political, economic and social characteristics (eg. economic equality, work-place democracy, gender equality, universal participation in decision-making etc.). More limited but more useful is the notion of procedural democracy of the sort found in Robert Dahl's concept of polyarchy[17]. The latter is distinguished by two broad characteristics which are that 'citizenship is extended to a relatively high proportion of adults, and the rights of citizenship include the opportunity to oppose and vote out the highest officials in the government'. Dahl further argues that the existence of polyarchy in a political order is distinguished by the presence of seven institutions all of which must be present. These are, elected officials, free and fair elections, inclusive suffrage, right to run for office, freedom of expression, alternative information, and associational autonomy. It should be noted that even such minimalist conceptions of democracy go well beyond the mere formal existence of more than one political party.

From the minimalist perspective democratic government is not even necessarily 'good' government. Samuel Huntington, a strong supporter of the procedural definition of democracy, has argued that 'Governments produced by elections may be inefficient, corrupt, shortsighted, irresponsible, dominated by special interests, and incapable of adopting policies demanded by the public good. These qualities may make such governments undesirable but they do not make them undemocratic'[18]. Even if one accepts this argument it should still be pointed out that governments which are accountable to the citizenry through periodic elections and where the possibility exists to 'kick the rascals out' are less likely to behave in this way. Indeed Huntington's description seems to more accurately depict the behaviour of undemocratic governments in Africa.

Maximalist definitions of democracy which would include some or all of the desirable political, social, and economic characteristics listed earlier are in many ways very attractive and contain a far clearer notion of a 'good' society. There are at least three sets of problems associated with them. Firstly it can be argued that characteristics like economic equality, high participation levels, and gender equality should be seen as possible results of democracy (or at least as being more likely to occur in a democracy) rather than as part of its definition. Secondly, maximalist definitions are inherently imprecise on the extent to which these characteristics have to be realised. Is it necessary to have more equality, near equality, total equality? How could these be measured? Thirdly, and probably most importantly, whilst maximalist definitions of democracy may be useful in outlining future goals they are less useful when analysing the political systems of the real world which inevitably fall far short of the ideal. However sympathetic one may be towards some or all of the aspirations expressed within a maximalist conception of democracy it would be unrealistic to insist that all the maximalist characteristics have to be in place before a political system can be described as democratic. Many of my Africanist colleagues take the view that I am overly optimistic about the prospects of a significant number of African states meeting even minimalist conditions for democracy. Whether or not they are correct in this even I would still have to say that there is no prospect whatsoever of any African state fulfilling the total range of aspirations contained within a maximalist conception of democracy in the forseeable future.

This state of affairs has important consequences for any attempt at evaluative analysis of the extent to which particular African states have, or have not, become more democratic over the recent period. When faced with limited improvements in levels of democracy in real world political systems the choice for those who evaluate is either to condemn them for their limitations or to welcome them as improvements: my inclination clearly lies with the latter approach.

What then of the participants in the mass struggle for democracy in Africa? Clearly the participants in the pro-democracy demonstrations in Bamako (Mali) mentioned earlier were unlikely to have been chanting 'we support Robert Dahl's concept of polyarchy' or 'on balance we would prefer a more maximalist definition of democracy' (or the Bambara equivalents). What united pro-democracy demonstrators right across Africa was the rejection of both single-party and military rule and the demand for the introduction of a multi-party political system. The Senegalese scholar Jacques-Mariel Nzouankeu successfully caught the African mood when he wrote that 'Today there is no longer any room for doubt as to the type of democratic government that Africans are demanding. They no longer speak of democracy in general but specifically refer to *pluralistic democracy* and if calls for a *multiparty system* are being voiced... it is because this is the most manifest criterion of a pluralistic democracy' (his emphases)[19]. The ubiquity of the insistence on multi-partyism was very striking and provided a strategically vital area of consensus amongst, what were in other ways, very diverse movements. The Movement for Multi-Party Democracy (MMD) in Zambia, for example, which later constituted itself into a political party and was successful in ousting the incumbent United National Independence Party (UNIP) of President Kaunda in the 1991 elections was formed from an extremely diverse range of groups including trade unions, private business interests, the churches, students, and professional associations[20]. As its very name suggests, what united the MMD was its demand for democracy which was categorically defined as necessitating a multi-party system.

Certainly some of the participants in the pro-democracy movements were seeking political reforms which went beyond the establishment of multi-party systems and free and fair elections. The Kenyan feminist scholar Maria Nzomo, for example describes how various women's groups in Kenya attempted to extend democratisation to include pressure for gender equality[21]. She writes that women 'want gender-based interests to be mainstreamed into the new democratic agenda, and they want to participate on an equal footing with men in the democratisation process' and that women 'need to seize the opportunity presented by multi-party democracy'. However much one may sympathise with these aims it would be unrealistic to assume that all members of the pro-democracy movement in Kenya would do so. Indeed, as Nzomo describes 'the general resistance of the male-dominated Kenyan society to gender-based changes' it would be more realistic to assume that some would actually be opposed.

The goals of the pro-democracy movements in Africa can best be thought of as encompassing a series of *partially overlapping democratic agendas*. There would be a virtually complete overlap in terms of a consensus on the minimalist demand for multi-partyism and free elections but beyond that some groups would have a wider additional agenda not shared by all.

Before concluding this discussion of meanings of democracy there is one further subject that needs to be tackled. Over recent years it has become fashionable amongst some academic observers and international agencies to link political democracy and free market economics in such a way that the latter becomes almost a part of the definition of the former. The nature of the complex empirical relationships between these two in Africa are discussed in detail in later chapters but for the moment they must be de-linked in a definitional sense. Democracy is not synonymous with economic liberalism (whether or not economic liberalism is supportive of democracy is an entirely different question). If, as has been argued above, the key element of democracy is citizen choice, it would be literally absurd to suggest that that choice could not extend to freely electing a government which supported a state-interventionist economic policy.

10

As it happens Africa's first peaceful democratic change of government through the ballot box occurred in Mauritius in 1982 when the Mouvement Militant Mauricien (MMM) defeated the incumbent Mauritius Labour Party (MLP): the MMM was a self-designated Marxist party[22].

This discussion of the terminology and concepts used in examining recent events in Africa has inevitably produced a partial deconstruction of the title of this book. Although it is possible to identify a number of important new elements in the struggle there is also a clear genealogy linking it to earlier periods. The struggle has not been uniformly 'for' democracy because important individuals and groups can clearly be identified as struggling 'against'. The outcomes of this conflict of forces have often been markedly indeterminate. The ultimate goals of pro-democracy activists have not been homogeneous and contain a series of overlapping and non-overlapping elements. Recent political change in Africa cannot be understood as reflecting a single uniform trajectory: analysis and understanding must encompass the uncertainties, complexities, contradictions, ambiguities, and downright enigmas which exist. Temptations to tidy up the developments by simplifying them must be resisted.

Finally one might ask if it is worthwhile to attempt an examination of such recent developments while longer-term outcomes remain so uncertain. Certainly any attempt to come to terms with contemporary political developments anywhere in the world faces inevitable limitations. Events which appear to be very significant at the time may, with hindsight, appear quite trivial: the reverse is also true. Any roughly contemporary evaluation will inevitably need a re-evaluation in the future as outcomes become a little clearer. However, recent changes pose questions which are too important for anyone concerned with the future of Africa and the future of democracy on this planet to simply await the view of history. This book is not the 'last word' on the new struggle for democracy in Africa; it is merely the 'story so far'.

Notes

(1)   In spite of Mugabe's continuing personal support for the introduction of a single-party state the idea was abandoned in September 1990 following its rejection by the politburo and the central committee of the ruling Zimbabwe African National Union – Patriotic Front (ZANU-PF) party. For a discussion of this issue see, William H. Shaw 'Towards the One-Party State in Zimbabwe: A Study in African Political Thought', *The Journal of Modern African Studies*, Vol.24, No.3, 1986, pp. 373-394; Jonathan N. Moyo, *Voting for Democracy: Electoral Politics in Zimbabwe*, Harare, University of Zimbabwe Publications, 1992; Masipula Sithole, 'Is

Zimbabwe Poised on a Liberal Path?: The State and the Prospects of the Parties', *Issue*, Vol.21, No.1-2, 1993, pp. 35-43.

(2)   In addition to the general political transformation two new internationally recognised independent states and one unrecognised 'new state' had come into existence in Africa during this period.

In March 1990 Namibia finally achieved independence from South Africa: see, for example, David Simon, *Independent Namibia One Year On*, London, Research Institute for the Study of Conflict, 1991; and Donald L. Sparks and December Green, *Namibia: The Nation after Independence*, Boulder and Oxford, Westview Press, 1992.

In May 1993 Eritrea achieved its independence from Ethiopia following overwhelming support for the change in a referendum held in April the same year: see, for example, David Pool, 'Eritrean Independence: The Legacy of the Derg and the Politics of Reconstruction', *African Affairs*, Vol.92, No.368, July 1993, pp.389-402; and Okbazghi Yohannes, 'Eritrea: A Country in Transition', *Review of African Political Economy*, No.57, July 1993, pp.7-28: Ruth Iyob, *The Eritrean Struggle for Independence: Domination, Resistance, Nationalism 1941-1993*, Cambridge University Press, 1995.

In May 1991 the political leadership of the northern part of Somalia, which in the past had been British Somaliland, unilaterally declared its independence from the rest of the territory designating itself as the 'Republic of Somaliland'. The existence of chaos and anarchy in Somalia as a whole meant that there was no recognised central government which could either accept or reject this secession and so the status of the 'new state' remained unresolved. See, for example, Abdi Ismail Samatar, 'Social Decay and Public Institutions: The Road to Reconstruction in Somalia' in Martin Doornbos, Lionel Cliffe, Abdel Ghaffar M. Ahmed and John Markakis (eds.) *Beyond Conflict in The Horn*, London, James Currey, 1992, pp.213-216; and Chris Searle, 'Agony and Struggle in Northern Somalia', *Race and Class*, Vol.34, No.2, 1992, pp.23-32. For an interesting comparison of the Somali and Eritrean cases see, Hussein M. Adam, 'Formation and Recognition of New States: Somaliland in Contrast to Eritrea', *Review of African Political Economy*, No.59, 1994, pp. 21-38.

(3)   By a 'fully fledged single-party state' I refer to those where only one political party is allowed, by law, to exist and, where elections take place, participation is confined to members of the party. Election candidates are chosen by, or at least approved by, the party elite. In some such cases in the past (eg. Tanzania, Zambia) a limited amount of electoral competition between members of the same party was permitted. It is extremely important to distinguish between a single-party system and a dominant

party system. In the latter opposition parties and electoral competition are present but, for whatever reason, one party is significantly stronger than the others and tends to dominate the rest as a result of continued success at the polls. In such cases the key question is to establish the reasons for the dominance of one party over the rest. Dominant party systems are not necessarily undemocratic as long as elections are free and fair and other parties are not unreasonably restricted in their activities. Botswana and The Gambia (before July 1994) could be seen as dominant party democracies.

(4) For the background to the situation in Sierra Leone see A. Zack-Williams and Stephen Riley, 'Sierra Leone: The Coup and its Consequences', *Review of African Political Economy*, No.56, March 1993, pp.91-98.

(5) For details of the Nigerian case see, for example, Larry Diamond, 'Nigeria's Third Quest for Democracy', *Current History*, Vol.90, No.555, May 1991, pp.201-204 and 229-231; Anthony A. Akinola, 'Manufacturing the Two-Party System in Nigeria', *The Journal of Commonwealth and Comparative Politics*, Vol.28, No.3, November 1990, pp.309-327; Joseph C. Okorojii, 'The Nigerian Presidential Elections', *Review of African Political Economy*, No.58, November 1993, pp.123-131.

(6) See, for example, Stan Schoeman, 'Swaziland: The Changing Political Climate', *AI Bulletin*, Vol.32, No.8, 1992, pp. 1-2. For a valuable discussion of the context of contemporary Swazi politics see Laurel L. Rose, *The Politics of Harmony: Land Dispute Strategies in Swaziland*, Cambridge, Cambridge University Press, 1992.

(7) For highly critical views of Museveni's 'no-party democracy' see J. Oloka-Onyango, 'The National Resistance Movement, Grassroots Democracy, and Dictatorship in Uganda', in Robin Cohen and Harry Goulbourne, *Democracy and Socialism in Africa*, Boulder and Oxford, Westview Press, 1991, pp.125-141; Amii Omara-Otunnu, 'The Struggle for Democracy in Uganda', *The Journal of Modern African Studies*, Vol.30, No.3, 1992, pp.443-463. Omara-Otunnu argues that 'the no-party democracy currently being advocated by President Museveni boils down to autocratic rule enforced by the military' (p.463). Oloka-Onyango accuses the government of 'human rights abuses that parallel those of previous regimes in extent, if not in publicity' (p.128).

(8) See, for example, Aristide R. Zolberg, 'The Specter of Anarchy: African States Verging on Dissolution', *Dissent*, Vol.39, No.3, 1992, pp.303-311 and I. William Zartman (ed.), *Collapsed States: The Disintegration and Restoration of Legitimate Authority*, Boulder, Lynne Rienner, 1995.

(9) See Inge Tvedten, 'The Angolan Debacle', *Journal of Democracy*, Vol.4, No.2, April 1993, pp.108-118; James Hamill, 'Angola's Road from Under the Rubble', *The World Today*, Vol.50, No.1, January 1994, pp.6-11.

(10) For a discussion of those states where multi-party democracy was retained throughout the post-independence period and those where earlier attempts were made to revive it see John A. Wiseman, *Democracy in Black Africa: Survival and Revival*, New York, Paragon House, 1990.

(11) See Francis Fukuyama, *The End of History and the Last Man*, London, Penguin Books, 1992.

(12) For a useful general discussion with case studies of several of those African regimes which had professed a Marxist-Leninist ideology but which subsequently abandoned it see the special issue (edited by Arnold Hughes) of *The Journal of Communist Studies*, Vol.8, No.2, 1992.

(13) Samuel P. Huntington, *The Third Wave: Democratization in the Late Twentieth Century*, Norman and London, University of Oklahoma Press, 1991. See also the same author's 'How Countries Democratize', *Political Science Quarterly*, Vol.106, No.4, 1991-1992, pp.579-616.

(14) Jane Turrittin, 'Mali: People Topple Traore', *Review of African Political Economy*, No.52, November 1991, pp.98-99.

(15) Robert Fatton Jr., *The Making of a Liberal Democracy: Senegal's Passive Revolution*, 1975-1985, Boulder and London, Lynne Rienner Publishers, 1987.

(16) The high incidence of the violent overthrow of authoritarian leaders in Africa raises serious questions as to whether or not their longer-term interests are served. See John A. Wiseman, 'Leadership and Personal Danger in African Politics', *The Journal of Modern African Studies*, Vol.31, No.4, 1993, pp.657-660.

(17) For a recent restatement of the characteristics of polyarchy see Robert A. Dahl, *Democracy and its Critics*, New Haven and London, Yale University Press, 1989, especially pp.220-224.

(18) Huntington (1991) op. cit. p.10.

(19) Jacques-Mariel Nzouankeu, 'The African Attitude to Democracy', *International Social Science Journal*, No 128, May 1991, p. 373.

(20) See, for example, Michael Bratton, 'Zambia Starts Over', *Journal of Democracy*, Vol.3, No.2, April 1992, and Carolyn Baylies and Morris Szeftel, 'The Fall and Rise of Multi-Party Politics in Zambia', *Review of African Political Economy*, No.54, July 1992, pp.75-91.

(21) Maria Nzomo, 'The Gender Dimension of Democratization in Kenya: Some International Linkages', *Alternatives*, Vol.18, No.1, Winter 1993, pp.61-73.

(22) For a good account of Mauritian politics see Larry W. Bowman, Mauritius: *Democracy and Development in the Indian Ocean*, London, Dartmouth, 1991.

2 The Evidence from 48 States

Any attempt at a broad comparison of the experiences of forty eight different African states over a period of six years or so presents obvious dangers of over-generalisation. We are, after all, dealing with almost one third of the states in the world. Even if one accepts the premise of this book, that one can identify some sort of struggle for democracy which has been occurring in at least most African states, one would not expect that developments in any one state would replicate those in any other. African states are very different from each other, as any study of post-independence politics makes clear. Fundamental differences exist in relation to all the variables which impinge on political life, such as physical size, population, resources, history, foreign influence, religion, culture, and level of economic development. Whilst these factors do not control political life in any completely deterministic fashion they all exercise important influences which help to shape the nature of the political system or any aspect of it. It would also be necessary to add to such factors a series of more specifically 'political' variables such as beliefs, organisation, and leadership.

However, it is precisely because of the existence of a series of concurrent impulses towards democracy in so many different states that the new struggle is of particular interest from a comparative politics perspective. No doubt a significant number of studies of the experiences of individual states will be produced but it is through a broader comparative approach that the dynamics of the process may best be understood. Such an approach precludes the possibility of extended examination of any particular state but, at the same time, it necessitates a summary of the major developments in all states. The major purpose of this chapter is to present a synoptic sketch of the democracy-related changes which have occurred (or, in a handful, not occurred) in all forty eight states since the beginning of 1989.

To choose a single date as a starting point for study in relation to any particular state is inevitably a relatively arbitrary decision: to do so in relation to such a large number of states may seem, at first glance, a decidedly perverse exercise. What is quite remarkable is that the evidence presented very clearly demonstrates that the choice of date is not at all arbitrary and is, in practice, extremely useful as a starting point. Although it was by no means obvious at the time retrospectively it can be seen that 1989 marked the beginning of the period of major change in African politics. At the start of the year there was little observable movement in the direction of democratisation. The military regime in Nigeria had indicated that it was prepared to move towards elected civilian government and a constituent assembly was busy producing a draft constitution in the federal capital, Abuja, (ironically, four and a half years later the same military government refused to accept the results of its own programme when it rejected the winners of the electoral process) but across the rest of Africa movement towards democracy appeared stalled. Certainly there were a number of African pro-democracy activists calling for change but they appeared to be voices crying in the authoritarian wilderness. There seemed to be little prospect that the small number of African democracies was likely to expand.

The evidence presented here in the tables[1] underlines the concentrated nature of change within a limited period of time. At the beginning of 1989 the vast majority of states were ruled by military or single-party regimes: six years later most were operating pluralistic (although not necessarily democratic) systems. However, using the situation at the beginning of 1989 as a bench mark from which to measure change raises certain problems of categorisation. At that time the majority of states were clearly authoritarian and, certainly in a formal sense, non-pluralist[2] but, beyond that, attempts at classification encounter a range of uncertainties and ambiguities. The latter arise from problems relating to (1) distinguishing civilian from military rule, (2) establishing the function of the party in single-party states, (3) assessing the relevance of ideological designation, and (4) recognition of the importance of personal rule.

It might appear to be quite easy to distinguish between military and civilian rule: for the former the regime would be composed of military figures who had probably come to power through a coup d'etat whilst for the latter, regime members would be non-military individuals who had probably come to power through an election (not necessarily a competitive one) or through some process of political ascription (for example a king in a traditional monarchy). The distinction is often nothing like so clearcut. It is relatively common for military regimes to include civilians in the government or to allow civilian bureaucrats to take a dominant role in policy making. For example, one senior civil servant who had served in the Gowon regime in Nigeria in the 1970s expressed the view that apart from specifically army matters 'the military goes along with the civil servants... generally they do not come into policy matters'[3]. Not only do military rulers often civilianise government decision making they also frequently attempt to civilianise themselves or, at least, attempt to make it appear that they have done so. Whereas all Nigeria's military governments have presented themselves as essentially temporary expedients maintaining a goal of returning the country to civilian rule by returning to the barracks there are a number of states where military governments have tried to achieve permanence by reconstituting themselves in civilian guise[4]. To achieve this the military leader will typically create a political party (often rather notional), assume the leadership of the party, and have himself 'elected' president unopposed in a non-competitive election. Examples of military leaders who followed this course include Gnassingbe Eyadema (Togo), Juvenal Habyarimana (Rwanda), Ahmed Kerekou (Benin), Andre Kolingba (Central African Republic), Mengistu Haile Mariam (Ethiopia), Mobutu Sese Seko (Zaire), Teodoro Obiang Nguema Mbasogo (Equatorial Guinea), and Didier Ratsiraka (Madagascar). In the case of such hybrid governmental forms it is not clear whether it is more useful to categorise them as civilian or military. In an extreme case of trying to give a different gloss to what was in fact a particularly crude military regime Jean-Bedel Bokassa had himself crowned as emperor in the renamed Central African Empire in an bizarre coronation ceremony which bankrupted the state.

In single-party states, whether the party is of civilian or military origin, there is no uniformity regarding the function and vitality of the party. In a competitive party system one of the main functions (some would argue the main function) of a political party is to organise itself to compete with other parties in trying to gain the support of the electorate and hence win control of the state. In a single-party state there is no need to do this: even if elections involve some competition between candidates from the same party there is no alternative party with which to compete[5]. Without competition many parties atrophied or became purely ceremonial: as Tordoff notes 'there is no doubt that in the period between independence and the late 1980s party functions in most African states were subject to some decline'[6]. Party atrophy was not ubiquitous: in a few cases, for example in Tanzania the Tanganyika African National Union (TANU – later Chama cha Mapinduzi, Party of the Revolution), and in Mozambique the Front for the Liberation of Mozambique (FRELIMO), the sole parties continued to be relatively lively bodies but they were probably the exception rather than the rule[7]. In most cases there was an enormous gulf between the dominant role that the party was supposed to play and the minimal role that it played in reality. Membership of a party was often meaningless; most especially in those cases, such as Rwanda and Zaire[8], where all citizens were deemed to be party members from birth.

Problems arise in assessing the importance which can be attached to the professed ideological bases of authoritarian regimes. Prior to 1989 a significant number of regimes in Africa described themselves as Marxist-Leninist but it is not easy to decide the extent to which this was a rhetorical claim devoid of real meaning or, alternatively, the extent to which the ideology did guide elite behaviour and the organisation of public life. One way round this problem was that adopted by Crawford Young in a book he wrote over ten years ago when he opted for taking at face value the ideological claims made by regimes. He wrote 'I shall rely primarily upon the ideological self-ascription of a regime's leadership in classifying polities. This means accepting at face value the declaration of a regime that Marxism-Leninism is adopted as a state doctrine'[9]. However, even for Young self-ascription had its limits and he refused to take seriously the totally bogus claims to Marxism-Leninism put forward at various times by Ali Soilih (Comoros), Macias Nguema (Equatorial Guinea) and, most ludicrous of all, 'Emperor' Jean-Bedel Bokassa (Central African 'Empire')[10]. Not all observers, however, would be content with accepting self-ascription and there is no overall agreement on the extent to which self-ascription matched reality. Very often it would appear that perceptions of the importance of the ideology are themselves influenced by ideological positions. It would be widely, but not universally, agreed, that those African regimes which described themselves as Marxist-Leninist were brutal, inefficient, corrupt, and decidedly non-egalitarian[11] (leaving aside the fact that all have now abandoned the ideology). For this reason observers who are reasonably sympathetic to the ideas of Marxism-Leninism are likely to wish to disown such regimes as authentic examples of the ideology in practice: those observers starting from a position hostile to the ideology would be more willing to see such regimes, in part at least, as an inevitable product of the ideology[12].

It is certainly the case that the applicability of the ideological label varies from one self-designated Marxist-Leninist regime to another. Writing on Ethiopia Christopher Clapham concludes that it 'was unique in Africa in constructing a post-revolutionary system of government that could plausibly be described as Marxist-Leninist'[13]. Writing on Benin Chris Allen argues that 'it is inappropriate to conceive of Benin as a Marxist regime at any point in its history'[14]. Both authors may well be correct. Developments since 1989 make it clear that there are no longer any Marxist-Leninist regimes in Africa: what is less clear is whether or not there ever were any.

So far the discussion of the ambiguities surrounding some aspects of the situation at the starting point of 1989 has concentrated on questions of institutions and ideology. In examining ambiguities of military/civilian power relationships in government, the nature of political parties in single-party states, and the rhetorical/substantive characteristics of official state ideologies no mention has yet been made of what many writers[15] would see as the central feature of African

18

political systems, that of the role of the personal ruler. From such a perspective questions of institutional relationships or ideology were entirely secondary in many, some would argue most, cases. They were secondary to the focus on, for example the Banda-state (in Malawi), the Mobutu-state (in Zaire), or the Houphouet-state in (Cote d'Ivoire). Whilst questions of political leadership had often been regarded as important by (most) Africanist political scientists it was the seminal book by Robert Jackson and Carl G. Rosberg, *Personal Rule in Black Africa: Prince, Autocrat, Prophet, Tyrant*, published in 1982 which forced such questions to the centre of the agenda[16]. They wrote that 'politics in most black African states do not conform to a institutionalised system' but 'are most often a personal or factional struggle to control the national government or to influence it: a struggle that is restrained by private and tacit agreements, prudential concerns, and personal ties and dependencies rather than by public rules and institutions'[17]. In their conceptualisation of personal rule Jackson and Rosberg were not resurrecting a 'great man' theory of history, nor even returning to earlier concerns of charismatic leadership which had been influential in studies of African politics in the early post-independence period. For them although the focus is on the personal it is, at the same time, on the system: personal rule is not the absence of a system it is a type of system. Within this type very great emphasis is placed on features relating to patrimonialism[18] (or neo-patrimonialism) and clientelism in conjunction with the political skill of the personal ruler in manipulating networks established on these patrimonialist and clientelist bases. Whilst there may be some danger of overstating the importance of the development of personalist elements in African political systems there is no doubt that Jackson and Rosberg's approach brought to the fore a most important aspect of political life in Africa.

This personalist perspective is important in the study of the new struggle for democracy in two ways. Firstly, it helps to define the situation that existed at the beginning of 1989 and hence to provide an understanding of the context in which struggle occurred. The struggle was not just against authoritarian institutional structures and ideologies but, in many cases, against highly authoritarian leaders who had established very personalised systems of control. Jackson and Rosberg explicitly relate the growth of personal rule to the erosion of party pluralism when they write that 'the public political realm in black Africa, especially the realm of competitive party and electoral activity has been greatly reduced in scope and activity'[19]. Similarly it is necessary to see the recent struggle for constitutional change, and the number of new constitutions that were introduced, in so many of the states examined here in the light of the role that constitutions had played in the growth of personal rule. Referring to this earlier period Jackson and Rosberg observed that 'insofar as constitutions remained important features of rule, they were important less as constraints on the abuse of power and more

19

Table 1 Recent Political Change in Sub-Saharan Africa

State and Date of Independence	Political Status Prior to Recent Change	Democratisation since 1989 (if any)
Angola Independent 1975	Formally a single-party Marxist-Leninist state ruled by the People's Movement for the Liberation of Angola-Workers' Party (MPLA-PT). The country had experienced continuous civil war since independence with considerable involvement by outside powers. Main armed opposition to government from National Union for the Total Independence of Angola (UNITA).	1990 government abandons Marxism-Leninism. 1991 peace agreement including ending of single-party state and acceptance of multi-party elections. 1992 results of September presidential election rejected by UNITA leadership: civil war renewed. Several peace agreements signed in 1993 and 1994 are broken almost immediately.
Benin Independent 1960 (Dahomey before 1975)	Marxist military regime: formally ruled by Benin People's Revolutionary Party (PRPB) but in practice a highly personalised leadership under Matthieu Kerekou backed by the army.	1989 mass opposition to incumbent government. 1990 establishment of national conference and new transitional government (although Kerekou retains presidency). 1991 multi-party elections: Kerekou defeated by Nicephore Soglo in presidential elections: 12 different parties win seats in legislature: 1992 partial army mutiny collapsed when bulk of army remained loyal to new government.
Botswana Independent 1966	Multi-party liberal-democracy governed by the Botswana Democratic Party (BDP) since independence.	No change.
Burkina Faso Independent 1960 (Upper Volta before 1984)	Military regime led by Blaise Compaore and the Popular Front (FP): in power since the assassination of Thomas Sankara in 1987.	1991 referendum endorses new multi-party constitution: Compaore rejects opposition demand for national conference and 'wins' presidential election following opposition boycott and high abstention rate. 1992 legislative elections involving 27 parties: majority of seats won by parties associated with the reconstituted FP but other parties gain minority of seats.

Burundi Independent 1962	Military regime led by Pierre Buyoya. 1992 referendum endorses new multi-party constitution. 1993 opposition leader Melchior Ndadaye of the Front for Democracy in Burundi (FRODEBU) defeats Buyoya in June presidential election; FRODEBU also wins majority of seats in legislative elections; Ndadaye becomes first Burundian president from majority Hutu group; October 1993 Ndadaye assassinated in failed coup attempt by Tutsi soldiers which leads to high levels of communal violence between Tutsi and Hutu. April 1994, new president Cyprien Ntaryamira is killed in a plane crash with Rwandan president, increasing tension in Burundi.
Cameroon Independent 1960	Single-party led by Paul Biya and the Democratic Rally of Cameroonian People (RDPC). 1990 multi-party system established; Biya rejects opposition demand for national conference. 1992 March legislative elections boycotted by some opposition parties; RPDC and its allies win narrow majority; Biya wins October presidential election with under 40% of vote.
Cape Verde Independent 1975	Single-party state led by Aristides Pereira and the African Party for the Independence of Cape Verde (PAICV). 1990 multi-party system established. 1991 opposition Movement for Democracy (MPD) wins January legislative elections and February presidential elections leading to peaceful transfer of power.
Central African Republic Independent 1960	Formally a single-party state with Central African Democratic Rally (RDC) as sole party but dominated by the military under Andre Kolingba who had come to power in a coup in 1981. 1991 restoration of multi-party system. 1993 opposition leader Ange-Felix Patasse of the Central African People's Liberation Movement (MLPC) wins August (first round) and September (second round) presidential election (Kolingba was placed fourth in the first round and eliminated from the contest). Opposition parties win majority of seats in August/September legislative elections. Initial attempts by Kolingba to suppress the results failed.

State and Date of Independence	Political Status Prior to Recent Change	Democratisation since 1989 (if any)
Chad Independent 1960	Military regime under Hissein Habre.	1990 Habre ousted by Idris Deby in further coup. 1992 formation of Political parties (subject to certain restrictions) permitted. 1992 ten political parties formed. 1993 national conference (including opposition representatives) agrees transitional charter to lead to multi-party democracy but the security situation in the country remains unsettled.
Comoros Independent 1975	Single-party state under Ahmed Abdallah and Comoran Union for Progress (UDZIMA) and backed by foreign mercenaries.	1989 Abdallah assassinated in mercenary-backed coup, French forces expel mercenaries. 1990 restrictions on formation of political parties lifted followed by competitive presidential election in March. 1992 new democratic constitution approved in referendum. 1993 repeated delays in holding legislative elections provoke general strike organised by opposition parties. December 1993 elections produce narrow victory for incumbent acting president, Mohamed Djohar.
Congo Independent 1960	Military Marxist regime led by Denis Sassou-Nguesso and Congolese Labour Party (PCT).	1990 opposition parties legalised, PCT abandons Marxist-Leninist ideology. 1991 national conference debates new constitution. 1992 referendum approves new constitution, legislative and presidential elections in June/July/August produce opposition victories, Pascal Lissouba of the Pan-African union for Social Democracy (UPADS) defeats Sassou-Nguesso at the polls to become president. 1993 new legislative elections, following vote of no confidence in government, won by UPADS and its allies; armed clashes between army and PCT supporters following objections to electoral procedures.

Country	Description	Developments
Cote d'Ivoire Independent 1960	Highly personalised single-party state led by Felix Houphouet-Boigny and the Democratic Party of the Ivory Coast (PDCI).	1990 acceptance of multi-party system by government; PDCI win October presidential elections and November/ December legislative elections but opposition claim electoral malpractice. December 1993 death of Houphouet-Boigny.
Djibouti Independent 1977	Single-party state led by Hassan Gouled Aptidon and the Popular Rally for Progress (RPP); opposition conducting guerrilla war.	1992 new multi-party constitution approved in referendum; ruling party wins December legislative elections. 1993 ruling party wins May presidential elections: opposition accuses government of electoral fraud in both elections: armed opposition to government continues.
Equatorial Guinea Independent 1968	Military regime under Teodoro Obiang Nguema Mbasago with notional political party, the Democratic Party of Equatorial Guinea (PDGE).	1991 referendum approves new multi-party constitution but little subsequent progress towards genuine pluralism and continuing poor record on human rights; most opposition groups in exile.
Eritrea Independent 1993	Eritrean People's Liberation Front (EPLF) waging guerrilla war to achieve independence from Ethiopia.	1993 Eritrea becomes independent in May following April referendum on the issue; EPLF government declares four year transition to multi-party democracy.
Ethiopia Never under fully established colonial control	Military Marxist regime led by Mengistu Haile Mariam and the Workers' Party of Ethiopia (WPE) opposed by several guerrilla movements most notably the Ethiopian People's Revolutionary Democratic Front (EPRDF).	1990 regime abandons Marxist-Leninist ideology. 1991 overthrow of Mengistu regime, EPRDF established interim government. 1992 competitive regional elections boycotted by some non-EPRDF movements which claimed electoral fraud. 1994 constituent assembly elections boycotted by most opposition parties.

State and Date of Independence	Political Status Prior to Recent Change	Democratisation since 1989 (if any)
Gabon Independent 1960	Single-party state led by Omar Bongo and the Gabonese Democratic Party (PDG).	1990 multi-party system introduced; legislative elections (1990 and 1991) produce narrow victory for PDG. 1993 opposition claim electoral fraud when Bongo wins December presidential election.
The Gambia Independent 1965	Multi-party liberal-democracy governed by People's Progressive Party (PPP) since independence.	Military coup d'état in July 1994 places country under army rule. Restoration of democracy scheduled for July 1996.
Ghana Independent 1957	Military government led by Jerry Rawlings.	1991 government announces restoration of multi-party system. 1992 Rawlings, as National Democratic Congress (NDC) candidate wins November presidential election; main opposition parties boycott December legislative elections claiming electoral fraud.
Guinea Independent 1958	Military government led by Lansana Conte.	1990 government announces transition to two party system. 1991 government cancels limitations on number of parties. 1992 legalisation of opposition parties. 1993 Conte wins December presidential election and opposition claim electoral fraud.
Guinea-Bissau Independent 1974	Military regime with single-party (the African Party for the Independence of Guinea and Cape Verde – PAIGC) led by Joao Bernardo Vieira.	1990 multi-party system accepted 'in principle' by government. 1991 new multi-party constitution adopted. 1992 first legal opposition rally attracts 30,000 people. 1993 attempted coup leads to postponement of elections. July 1994 elections result in victory for Vieira in presidential election and narrow victory for PAIGC in legislative election.

Kenya Independent 1963	Single-party state led by Daniel arap Moi and the Kenya African National Union (KANU).	1991 large pro-democracy rallies pressure Moi into restoring multi-party system. 1992 splits in opposition allow Moi to win December presidential election with just over one third of the votes; KANU win narrow majority in legislative elections.
Lesotho Independent 1966	Military regime led by Maj-Gen Justin Metsing Lekhanya.	1991 Lekhanya overthrown in further coup; ban on political parties lifted. 1993 long-term opposition party the Basotho Congress Party (BCP) wins March multi-party general election; BCP leader Ntsu Mokhehle becomes prime minister in April. Threats to democracy from military revolt (January 1994) and suspension of constitution by King Letsie (August 1994) defeated, partly through threats of intervention from other South African states.
Liberia – Never under colonial control: Republic founded in 1847	Formally a multi-party system led by Samuel Doe; in practice opposition suppressed by quasi-military government.	1990 Doe killed by rebel forces; country collapses into civil war involving various armed movements; subsequent attempts at peace-making by outside organisations enjoy little success.
Madagascar Independent 1960	Military Marxist government led by Didier Ratsiraka and the Vanguard of the Malagasy Revolution (AREMA).	1990 multi-party system restored. 1991 creation of transitional government involving opposition groups with Ratsiraka retaining the presidency. 1992 referendum approves new constitution; opposition leader Albert Zafy comes top in November first round of presidential elections. 1993 Zafy defeats Ratsiraka in February second round of presidential election and becomes new president; parties supporting Zafy win majority in June legislative elections.

State and Date of Independence	Political Status Prior to Recent Change	Democratisation since 1989 (if any)
Malawi Independent 1964	Highly personalised single-party state led by 'president-for-life' Hastings Kamuzu Banda and the Malawi Congress Party (MCP).	1993 June referendum approves return to multi-party system despite opposition from Banda; November constitutional changes to legalise party pluralism and repeal the institution of life presidency. May 1994, opposition win elections and United Democratic Front (UDF) leader Bakili Muluzi becomes president. January 1995, ex-President Banda charged in court with murder of opponents when in office.
Mali Independent 1960	Military regime under Moussa Traore and notional single-party the Democratic Union of Malian People (UDPM).	1991 Traore ousted in March coup following huge pro-democracy demonstrations; military National Reconciliation Council (CRN) announces return to multi-party democracy; national conference prepares new constitution. 1992 January referendum approves new multi-party constitution; Alliance for Democracy in Mali (ADEMA) wins majority of seats in February/March legislative elections; ADEMA candidate Alpha Oumar Konare wins April presidential election.
Mauritania Independent 1960	Military regime led by Maawiya Ould Sid'Ahmed Taya but with some political pluralism permitted in municipal elections.	1991 July referendum approves new multi-party constitution. 1992 Taya wins January presidential election but violent protest from opposition ensues; main opposition parties boycott March legislative elections.
Mauritius Independent 1968	Multi-party liberal democracy since independence with changes of government through the ballot box in 1982 and 1983.	No change.

Mozambique Independent 1975	Single-party Marxist-Leninist state led by Joaquim Alberto Chissano and the Front for the Liberation of Mozambique (FRELIMO), engaged in civil war with rebel Mozambique National Resistance (RENAMO) guerrillas.	1989 government abandons Marxism-Leninism and agrees to legalise non-violent opposition parties. 1992 peace agreement signed by FRELIMO and RENAMO but violations take place. 1993 agreement on multi-party elections in 1994. FRELIMO win October 1994 elections in which RENAMO is main opposition.
Namibia Independent 1990	Territory in terminal phase of South African control.	1989 South West African People's Organisation (SWAPO) wins majority of seats in November pre-independence elections. 1990 February unanimous adoption of multi-party constitution legislature; March full independence. 1992 multi-party elections for regional councils and local authorities. December 1994, SWAPO again wins general election.
Niger Independent 1960	Quasi-military government under Ali Saibou and National Movement for a Development Society (MNSD).	1990 government announces transition to multi-party system. 1991 ban on political parties lifted and national conference convened. 1992 December referendum approves new multi-party constitution. 1993 alliance of opposition parties wins majority in February legislative elections; opposition leader Mahamane Ousmane wins February/March presidential elections and becomes the country's first Hausa head of state.

State and Date of Independence	Political Status Prior to Recent Change	Democratisation since 1989 (if any)
Nigeria Independent 1960	Military government led by Ibrahim Babangida promising return to civilian rule.	1989 ban on political parties lifted in May but only two would be permitted to contest elections; October bans existing parties and creates two new ones, the Social Democratic Party (SDP) and the National Republican Convention (NRC), to contest elections. 1990 two-party local government elections. 1992 two-party legislative elections produce SDP majorities. 1993 SDP candidate Moshood Abiola wins June presidential election but Babangida annuls result and installs interim government led by Chief Ernest Shonekan; November General Sanni Abacha ousts Shonekan and returns country to military rule. Jule 1994, Abiola arrested and charged with treason, leading to mass pro-democracy strikes.
Rwanda Independent 1962	Quasi-military government led by Juvenal Habyarimana and the Revolutionary National Movement for Development (MRND).	1991 new multi-party constitution established. 1992 coalition government including opposition party leaders established. 1993 peace accord signed with Tutsi-dominated guerrilla movement the Rwandan Patriotic Front (FPR); elections scheduled for 1995. April 1994, assassination of Habyarimana plunges country into genocidal civil war. July 1994, FPR government sworn in Kigali but millions of Hutu become refugees in neighbouring states.

Sao Tome and Principe Independent 1975	Single-party state led by Manuel Pinto da Costa and the Movement for the liberation of Sao Tome and Principe (MLSTP).	1990 new multi-party constitution approved in referendum. 1991 opposition Democratic Convergence Party-Reflection Group (PCD-GR) win January legislative elections and March presidential elections. 1992 PCD-GR performs poorly against MLSTP in local government elections. October 1994, MLSTP becomes major party in legislature following general election victory. August 1995 coup d'état collapses after a few days: elected government restored.
Senegal Independent 1960	Multi-party system which had been restored between 1974 and 1981 following period of single-party rule.	No change.
Seychelles Independent 1976	Single-party Marxist-Leninist state led by Albert Rene and the Seychelles People's Progressive Front (SPPF).	1991 multi-party system restored. 1992 multi-party elections to commission set up to draft new constitution; November referendum on new constitution fails to provide required level of support. 1993 revised constitution endorsed in June referendum; July presidential and legislative elections result in victories for Rene and the SPPF.
Sierra Leone Independent 1961	Single-party system led by Joseph Saidu Momoh and the All People's Congress (APC).	1991 new multi-party constitution approved by August referendum; opposition parties begin forming. 1992 April coup led by Valentine Strasser; new military government suspends democratisation process but pledges commitment to multi-party system. 1993 government announces return to multi-party civilian rule by 1996. 1994 Interim National Electoral Commission established. January 1995, country appears to be on the verge of collapse into anarchy.

State and Date of Independence	Political Status Prior to Recent Change	Democratisation since 1989 (if any)
Somalia Independent 1960	Highly personalised single-party (nominally Marxist-Leninist) state led by Mohammed Siad Barre and the Somali Revolutionary Socialist Party (SRSP).	1991 Siad Barre regime overthrown by military revolt, country fragments into anarchy. 1992 UN intervenes to try to restore order, but achieves little. 1995 UN withdraw.
South Africa Independent 1910 (government control confined to white racial minority)	Although some aspects of the apartheid system had been modified during the 1980s white majority rule was still firmly in place, the franchise did not extend to the majority of the population and the major anti-apartheid groups were banned. A limited multi-party system existed for the minority.	1989 September general election confirms F W de Klerk as president. 1990 February release from detention of Nelson Mandela and simultaneous unbanning of African National Congress (ANC) and other anti-apartheid groups; repeal of most apartheid legislation; government and ANC begin talks. 1991 remaining apartheid legislation repealed; December first meeting of multi-party Convention for a Democratic South Africa (CODESA) to discuss future constitution. 1992 March referendum for whites approves continued reform. 1993 November agreement on interim constitution. April 1994 first ever non-racial national elections lead to ANC victory and Nelson Mandela becoming president of a government of national unity.
Sudan Independent 1956	Fragile multi-party system in the context of civil war.	1989 June coup led by Omar Hassan al-Bashir returns country to military rule. Civil war intensifies with no progress towards democratisation.
Swaziland Independent 1968	Constitutional monarchy; political parties banned.	Pressure for multi-party system but no real change.

Tanzania Independent 1961	Single-party state: Ali Hassan Mwinyi president but Julius Nyerere leader of sole party Chama cha Mapinduzi (CCM-Party of the Revolution).	1990 Nyerere retires from party leadership. 1991 Mwinyi establishes presidential commission to examine possible transition to multi-party system. 1992 multi-party system legalised; elections scheduled for October 1995.
Togo Independent 1960	Highly militarised single-party state led by Gnassingbe Eyadema and the Rally of the Togolese People (RPT).	1991 legalisation of opposition parties; national conference appoints Joseph Kokou Koffigoh as prime minister of provisional government. 1992 September referendum approves new constitution. 1993 Eyadema is credited with overwhelming majority in August presidential election; continual violent harassment of opposition by the army, abysmal human rights deteriorates even further.
Uganda Independent 1962	No-party system led by Yoweri Museveni and the National Resistance Council (NRC).	Continued rejection by Museveni of demands for multi-party system.
Zaire Independent 1960	Highly militarised single-party dominated by the person of Mobutu Sese Seko and his Popular Movement of the Revolution (MPR).	1990 multi-party system restored. 1991 national conference established. 1992 opposition leader Etienne Tshisekedi appointed transitional prime minister but subsequently dismissed by Mobutu. 1993 Zaire moves towards anarchy.
Zambia Independent 1964	Single-party state led by Kenneth Kaunda and the United National Independence Party (UNIP).	1990 multi-party system restored. 1991 opposition Movement for Multi-Party Democracy (MMD) wins October legislative and presidential elections; peaceful transfer of power.
Zimbabwe Independent 1980	Multi-party state dominated by Robert Mugabe and the Zimbabwe African National Union-Patriotic Front (ZANU-PF); widely expected to change to single-party Marxist-Leninist system in 1990.	1990 multi-party system retained as move to single party state is abandoned; no significant change.

as legal instruments that a personal ruler could amend or rewrite to suit his power needs'[20]. Recent change represents, in part, an attempt to fundamentally alter the real purpose of the constitution; to make it a barrier to authoritarianism rather than a tool of authoritarianism.

Even on the basis of a synopsis the preceding tables clearly illustrate an immense diversity of of experience across African states. Whilst it is possible to talk of a struggle for democracy since 1989 in virtually all of them the nature of the process and the unfolding of events is far from uniform. Although subsequent chapters will seek to highlight commonalities where this seems appropriate an equally important task will be to reflect the heterogeneity of the process.

Notes

(1)   The information contained in these tables has been compiled from a wide range of sources. In addition to those books and articles which are either footnoted elsewhere or are included in the general bibliography information has been taken from: *West Africa, New African, Focus on Africa, Africa Demos, African Business, Africa Forum, Africa South of the Sahara, Africa Events, Keesings Archives*, and various British and African newspapers. For an earlier attempt at producing a similar table see Gerald J. Schmitz and Eboe Hutchful, *Democratization and Popular Participation in Africa*, Ottawa, The North-South Institute, 1992, pp.50-53.

(2)   For a discussion of the changing nature of political pluralism see, John A. Wiseman, 'Democracy and the New Political Pluralism in Africa: Causes, Consequences and Significance', *Third World Quarterly*, Vol.14, No.3, 1993, pp.439-449.

(3)   Quoted in Henry Bienen and Martin Fitton, 'Soldiers, Politics and Civil Servants' in Keith Panter-Brick (ed.) *Soldiers and Oil: The Political Transformation of Nigeria*, London, Frank Cass, 1978, p.47. Writing of the same period the Nigerian scholar Ladipo Adamolekun, who also participated on several advisory councils, concluded that 'civil servants dominated the policy process': see Ladipo Adamolekun, *Politics and Administration in Nigeria*, London, Hutchinson, 1986, p.131.

(4)   The fundamental ideal of the moral correctness of civilan supremacy in government has remained a remarkably powerful notion in post-independence Africa. The resilience of the ideal has created severe problems of legitimacy engineering for the large numbers of military governments. The evidence strongly suggests that even the military themselves are influenced by the notion of civilian supremacy. The two major ways in which military regimes have dealt with this problem of

legitimacy deficit have been either to present their rule as a temporary interlude made necessary by particular problems within the civilian political system, or to attempt to civilianise themselves.

(5)   A similar version of this phenomenon can often be found in particular localities in multi-party states. Where one party (whether ruling or opposition at a national level) is, for whatever reason, locally dominant it will often tend to be much less active than it is in areas where party competition is a more significant factor.

(6)   William Tordoff, *Government and Politics in Africa* (second edition), London, Macmillan, 1993, p.118. Fred W. Riggs categorises such systems as 'pseudo single-party regimes' in which 'a government-sponsored official party is created by the rulers, authentic opposition parties are prohibited, and both the elected assembly and the government are, nominally, dominated by the official party...such parties merely front for the ruling circle' See Riggs, 'Fragility of the Third World's Regimes', *International Social Science Journal*, No. 136, May 1993, p.211.

(7)   For a discussion of TANU see Bismark U. Mwansasu, 'The Changing Role of the Tanganyika African National Union', in Bismark U. Mwansasu and Cranford Pratt (eds), *Towards Socialism in Tanzania*, Dar es Salaam, Tanzania Publishing House, 1979, pp.169-192. For FRELIMO see Bertil Egero, *Mozambique: A Dream Undone*, Uppsala, Scandinavian Institute of African Studies, 1987.

(8)   For excellent studies of the Zairian case see; Thomas M. Callaghy, *The State-Society Struggle: Zaire in Comparative Perspective*, New York, Columbia University Press, 1984: Crawford Young and Thomas Turner, *The Rise and Decline of the Zairian State*, Madison, University of Wisconsin Press, 1985: Michael G. Schatzberg, *The Dialectics of Oppression in Zaire*, Bloomington, Indiana University Press, 1988.

(9)   Crawford Young, *Ideology and Development in Africa*, New Haven, Yale University Press, 1982, pp.11-12.

(10)   Ibid. p.330.

(11)   Of course self-styled Marxist-Leninist regimes had no monopoly of these characteristics.

(12)   For examples of discussions of this question see; Tom Young, 'The Politics of Development in Angola and Mozambique', *African Affairs*, vol.87, No.347, 1988, pp.165-184: L. Adele Jinadu, 'The Concept of the Party in the Afro-Marxist State', in Peter Meyns and Dani Wadada Nabudere (eds.) *Democracy and the One-Party-State in Africa*, Hamburg, Institute for African Studies, pp.79-90.

It is noticeable that in recent years many left wing scholarly observers have become more favourably disposed towards multi-partyism and more critical of the claims of single-party states espousing leftist ideologies. Robin Cohen, for example, describes the Leninist idea of vanguardism as a 'primeval notion': see Robin Cohen 'Introduction: Socialism or Democracy, Socialism and Democracy' in Robin Cohen and Harry Goulbourne, *Democracy and Socialism in Africa*, Boulder, Westview Press, 1991, p.6.. More recently Richard Sandbrook has argued that 'the tactical embrace of political liberalization seems the best socialist option': see Richard Sandbrook, *The Politics of Africa's Economic Recovery*, Cambridge, Cambridge University Press, 1993, p.133.

(13) Christopher Clapham, 'The Socialist Experience in Ethiopia and its Demise' in Hughes (ed.) op. cit. p.124.
(14) Chris Allen, Michael S. Radu and Keith Somerville, Benin, *The Congo, and Burkina Faso: Politics, Economics and Society* (Marxist Regimes Series), London, Pinter Publishers, 1988, p.14.
(15) Excluded from this near consensus would be those writing from a heavily structuralist perspective such as that of dependency theory.
(16) Robert H. Jackson and Carl G. Rosberg, *Personal Rule in Black Africa: Prince, Autocrat, Prophet, Tyrant,* Berkeley, University of California Press, 1982.
(17) Ibid. p.1.
(18) For a recent discussion of the patrimonial state in Africa see Adrian Leftwich, 'States of Underdevelopment: The Third World State in Theoretical Perspective', *Journal of Theoretical Politics*, Vol.6, No.1, 1994, p.55-74.
(19) Jackson and Rosberg, op. cit. p.2.
(20) Ibid. p.16.

3 Pressures for Change

Change in the nature of African political systems since 1989 has not come about because authoritarian leaders suddenly decided to mend their ways and introduce measures producing accountability. Change has been forced upon those leaders by their being subjected to a wide range of pressures. The aim of this chapter is to examine the sources and operation of these pressures.

Among observers of African politics there would be universal agreement that these pressures have been a combination of those originating from internal domestic sources and those originating from external foreign sources. This recognition of the operation of a pincer movement of internal and external pressure for democratisation is extremely important in understanding the process but it leaves open the vital question of the relative importance of domestic and foreign pressures. Whilst it is true that the balance between these two will vary from case to case an examination of the literature produced so far on African democratisation suggests a clear majority of specialist Africanist scholars supporting the view that the paramount source of pressure has arisen from essentially domestic forces. The leading French Africanist Jean-Francois Bayart makes the point very explicitly when he writes that 'the external dynamics played an essentially secondary role in the collapse of authoritarian regimes, however much a tenacious myth suggests otherwise'[1]. Naomi Chazan writes that 'domestic explanations lie at the root of the new political climate on the continent'[2] whilst Christopher Clapham argues that 'the most important elements in this process are in my view domestic rather than international'[3]. Adopting a similar approach Claude Welch wrote that 'the fall of single-party systems is more accurately a result of internal pressures'[4], whilst Michael Bratton and Nicolas van der Walle stress that reform was 'primarily in response to indigenous political demands'[5]. Although such views have tended to predominate in the

35

literature they are not ubiquitous: Tom Young, for example, clearly states the contrary view that 'the recent wave of democratisation is largely externally engineered'[6].

My own position is to side very strongly with the view that internal pressures have been the most important in explaining the unfolding of events in Africa since 1989. Whilst accepting that external factors have had a role to play they should not be exaggerated. I cannot, for example, think of a single case in Africa where external pressure for political reform preceded domestic pressure. External pressure should be viewed as providing an extra support for already powerful internal pressure. Even in cases where external pressure contributed a fairly important ingredient in the process, as argueably it did for example in Kenya and Malawi, it is vital to recognise the pre-existence of a determined internal pro-democracy movement struggling to pressurise recalcitrant authoritarian leaderships into accepting reform. Without such movements pressure from external forces would have little to build upon: as Bratton and van der Walle comment, 'in the absence of strong domestic forces pushing for reform state leader are unlikely to succumb to international pressures'[7].

There are at least four sets of reasons why the internal/external debate is of fundamental importance. Firstly it has an analytical importance in understanding the process of democratisation. Although explanations of major political developments will almost inevitably require a multi-causal framework rather than a simplistic mono-causal one if they are to comprehend the complexity of the empirical situation this does not mean that all causes should be assigned the same explanatory weight. Unlike natural scientists, social scientists and historians do not have the opportunity to conduct laboratory experiments where different factors can be added or subtracted by the experimentor to test causal relationships but this does not preclude the possibility of deciding that some factors are more important than others. The above quotations of Africanist scholars represent an attempt at doing precisely that.

Secondly, the emphasis on internal forces represents an important corrective to perspectives which present an overly passive view of African peoples. Such perspectives suggest a virtual incapacity for independent action by Africans who can, at most, respond to external stimuli, or, more often, simply be acted upon. Certainly external factors frequently impose limits on the range of possibilities in Africa but this does not deny the reality of African-initiated action (of a positive or negative type). It is offensively patronising to suggest that anything that happens in Africa is primarily the result of actions undertaken by non-African outsiders. A recognition of the predominant role played by African democrats in the struggle for reform offers an active rather than a passive view of African peoples. I would concur with Richard Joseph when he writes that 'it is the African people who are determining the contours of the transition process and the structures of the newly democratised systems'[8]. External forces play a subordinate role in helping or hindering the struggle of African peoples.

The third reason why this question is important is that the internal/external balance is not just a part of the academic debate about Africa, but a part of the political debate within Africa. In their attempt to deflect the multiple pressures for democratisation many of Africa's authoritarian rulers have tried to prop up their vestigial claims to legitimacy by portraying their existing style of rule as authentically African, and demands for democracy as inspired by interfering foreigners who seek to impose alien ideologies on contented Africans. The Kenyan scholar Peter Anyang' Nyong'o captured the quintessence of the dispute when he observed that 'the struggle for democracy is thus *homegrown* from the point of view of its advocates, though *foreign-imposed* from the perspective of those who defend the single-party regime' (his emphases)[9]. Thus, it is very much in the interests of African autocrats for them to downgrade the importance of domestic pressure and to depict the, in fact rather meagre, foreign support as unwarranted interference. The Ghanaian scholar Gilbert Bluwey observes that 'at the onset of political conditionality the intellectual apologists of authoritarian monolithism invoked the familiar stunt of cultural imperialism and neo-colonialism to scare off the protagonist of conditionality'[10]. It would indeed be unfortunate if an erroneous downgrading of the key role played by indigenous African pro-democracy movements lent credence to the threadbare claims of authoritarian rulers.

Finally, assessments of the relative importance of internal and external factors are important concerns the potential for the development of more consolidated democratic systems in Africa. Although the consolidation process will be influenced by a range of factors the level of internal African support for more democratic political systems will be crucial. Foreign pressure may play a part in persuading reluctant leaders to permit a more open public contestation for power in the short term but it is a weak and unpredictable basis for the longer term development of more secure democracies. Whilst a high level of internal support for democracy does not guarantee successful consolidation, given the many serious problems faced by African states, an absence of such support guarantees failure.

Although I have been stressing the prime importance of internal pressures for democratisation this should not be seen as denying the role of external factors. The latter have certainly played a part; in my view a secondary one, but by no means a negligible one. In explaining the extraordinary momentum of democratisation in so many African states in the period since 1989 it is vital to recognise the conjunction of pressures which occurred at this time. The simultaneous occurrence of a variety of pressures produced results which would have been unlikely if they had occurred in isolation.

Internal Pressures

Internal pressure for democratisation came from a wide range of different groups within society. For convenience the contributions of these groups will be examined individually but it must be stressed that they did not work in isolation: they frequently interacted with each other, supported each other, and often had overlapping personnel.

The Churches

Church leaders from all Christian denominations have played a crucial role in providing support for pro-democracy movements in many African states. Prior to 1989 the churches had frequently provided a critical voice in relation to the denial of human rights and other negative aspects of life under authoritarian[11] rule and were thus well placed to play a significant part when a diverse range of opposition groups coalesced into coherent pro-democracy movements at the end of the 1980s. In authoritarian states where all opposition to the government was banned, and where the state sought either to abolish or strictly control the existence of autonomous groups in society, the churches had a number of advantages which other potentially critical groups usually lacked. Although church leaders were by no means immune to government harassment and coercion their vulnerability was mitigated by several factors.

The exceptional level of public respect for church leaders in highly religious African societies gives them an influence and status which political leaders cannot easily ignore. The church has a number of organisational advantages over other groups. Most church groupings have a long historical pedigree which predates the existence of the contemporary independent African state: indeed many churches played an important role in the nationalist movements and assisted in the independence struggle several decades ago. This combination of popular legitimacy and organisational strength makes it difficult for authoritarian governments to ban the existence of churches in the way that other organisations have been banned. Although individual church leaders have been banned (or worse) the institutional structures have remained largely intact. Church services provide the possibility of bringing together significant numbers of people in the congregation even where other types of mass meeting have been declared illegal by the government. At the services sermons can take an explicitly political tone which is difficult to control: as Widner comments 'sermons constitute priveleged speech and are less subject to bans than newspapers and leaflets'[12]. Many churches also have the advantage of belonging to international communities which can bring pressure to bear on governments which oppress the local church. Although church leaders have often been reluctant to engage directly in 'politics' they certainly possess a significant range of political assets which enhances their participation when they do become involved.

The crucial role of church leaders in contributing to pressure for democratisation is nowhere more clearly illustrated than in the case of Malawi. In the post-independence period Malawi developed one of the most authoritarian political systems in Africa. It provides perhaps the clearest example of the autocratic system of 'personal rule' discussed in the preceding chapter. Since independence in 1964 Malawi had been completely dominated by Hastings Kamuzu Banda. The latter was president for life, the leader of the only legal political party the Malawi Congress Party (MCP), held most portfolios in the government, and ruled in the manner of a traditional absolutist monarch[13]. When he boasted to a group of visiting business men 'Anything I say is law. Literally law. It is a fact in this country'[14] he was accurately describing the reality of political life in Malawi. This position of dominance had been achieved through a ruthless application of coercion. His political opponents were jailed or murdered. Even those who went into exile were not safe: the opposition leader Attati Mpakati, for example, had his hands blown off by a letter bomb in Mozambique in 1979 and was assassinated in Zimbabwe in 1983. Even more than the crushing of opposition the totality of Banda's dominance was illustrated by his control of political debate which was unmatched in Africa. He managed to go beyond media censorship, itself fairly common in Africa until recently, to a situation where even informal discussion of political issues in private came close to disappearing[15]. When conducting historical research in Malawi one scholar discovered that 'political discussion is taboo in Dr. Banda's Malawi...anything bearing on current politics was immediately suspect...when a question caused silence and a chill, followed by protestations of loyalty to Banda...I knew I had trespassed on a topic to be avoided'[16]. An appreciation of this situation, in which public criticism of Banda and his autocratic style of rule had become almost unimaginable in Malawi, is crucial to an understanding of the mould-breaking role played by the churches.

In March 1992, on the first Sunday in Lent, a pastoral letter[17] from Archbishop James Chiona and all the Catholic bishops of Malawi was read out in every Catholic church in the country: it was noted that all the bishops would be in their respective cathedrals on that day. The message contained in the letter represented a political bombshell in the context of Malawi. Using a mixture of biblical exegesis and traditional African proverbs it provided a savage critique of all aspects of public life within the single-party state. The letter attacked inequality, corruption, poverty, illiteracy, censorship, the inadequacy of welfare facilities in the country, and political repression. It called for the removal of all impediments to freedom of political expression and political association. Government reaction was predictably hostile: the bishops were taken to police headquarters in Blantyre for questioning and the confined by force to the house of the Archbishop for several days. There is no doubt that their treatment would have been incomparably harsher were it not for their religious status. The pastoral letter was declared to be a seditious document possession of which would be a criminal offence. A senior official of the MCP Women's League, Mai Manjankosi, called for the bishops to be killed whilst Banda accused them of treachery and warned that his political opponents would be 'meat for crocodiles'. One of Banda's initial responses was to try to divide the Christian churches along denominational lines. The official party newspaper the *Malawi News* accused the 'satanic Catholics' of trying to 'import IRA terrorism into this country to spread here the chaotic situation now existing in Northern Ireland' and of 'trying to discredit the good name of this country and instigate Malawians into open rebellion against their leadership'[18]. The tactic of denominational division failed miserably. A few weeks later the leading figures in the Presbyterian and Reformed churches in Malawi issued an open letter[19] to Banda which supported the stand taken by the Catholics and called for the establishment of a broadly based commission for democratic reform. The Church of Scotland, of which Banda himself is an elder, called on its members to 'pray for this profoundly lonely man who is locked in the prison house of power'[20]. The actions of the churches transformed the situation in Malawi from one where any sort of public political statement other than fulsome support for Banda was virtually unthinkable (and indeed very dangerous) to one where the very basis of the system was open to criticism. In so doing it opened up a new political space for other participants in the rapidly expanding democracy movement.

An equally crucial role in the pro-democracy movement has been occupied by the church in Kenya with the development of what one writer describes as 'Kenya's liberation theology'[21]. Church opposition to many aspects of single-party rule began in August 1986 when 1,200 clergy attending a conference of the National Council of Churches of Kenya (NCCK) condemned the government decision to abolish secret voting in elections and replace it with the queueing system. Although the initial reactions of President Daniel arap Moi's government to the critical clergy were extremely hostile leading churchmen continued to press for the establishment of democracy in Kenya. Leading figures in the early stages were the Anglican bishops Alexander Kipsang Muge and Henry Okullo and the Presbyterian leader Reverend Timothy Njoya. Because Bishop Muge's diocese included Moi's home area he came under particularly heavy pressure. Following especially vitriolic attacks on him at a conference of the ruling Kenyan African National Union (KANU) in 1987 Muge responded by saying that 'I shall not protest against the violation of human rights in South Africa if I am not allowed to protest the violation of human rights in my own country'[22]. Equating Moi's regime with apartheid South Africa was regarded as a particularly stinging critique. In 1990 one government minister, Peter Okondo, warned Muge that if he set foot in his home district he would 'see fire and may not leave alive'[23]. At an open-air sermon in Luhyia district in August 1990 Muge proclaimed 'let Okondo know that my innocent blood will haunt him forever'[24]. On his way home from the sermon Muge was killed in a mysterious 'traffic accident'. The widespread belief that the accident was less than accidental damaged the legitimacy of the regime not least because it followed on the murder of the popular Luo dissident politician Robert Ouko in February of the same year.

As in many other parts of Africa the collapse of single-party regimes in Eastern Europe in 1989 added fresh impetus to the pro-democracy campaigns in Kenya. In a New Year's day sermon at the beginning of 1990 in St. Andrews Church, 'Nairobi's most prestigious pulpit'[25], Reverend Njoya drew clear links between the events of Eastern Europe and the growing demands for multi-party democracy in Kenya. This was followed by a sermon preaching a similar message from Bishop Okullo. In June of the same year the country's eighteen Roman Catholic bishops issued a pastoral letter supporting political liberalisation and Archbishop Manasse Kuria of the Anglican Church of the Province of Kenya (CPK) added his name to calls for an end to single-party authoritarianism. In Kenya, as in Malawi, the church was able to use its relatively privileged position in society to launch a moral crusade against undemocratic rule and open up a critical political space which could be utilised by other pro-democracy groups to bring about changes in the political system.

In South Africa circumstances have dictated that the pro-democracy movement has been largely inseparable from the anti-apartheid movement. The South African political system exhibited some of the features of pluralist democracy but in denying the right of the majority of the population to participate in the electoral process the apartheid system was clearly an undemocratic one which flouted the basic principles of democracy. An end to apartheid was thus a necessary (though not a sufficient) precondition for the establishment of democracy. Events in recent years have clearly demonstrated that the bulk of what constituted the anti-apartheid movement, most especially Nelson Mandela and the African National Congress (ANC), have a clear commitment to the establishment of multi-party democracy in South Africa. In a minority of cases this commitment is rather tenuous: there are certainly a number of unreconstructed Stalinists in the South African Communist Party (SACP) like, Harry Gwala and Govan Mbeki, who have grave doubts concerning the desirability of what they would regard as 'bourgeois democracy'[26]. Amongst the majority of groups which could be identified as being both opposed to apartheid and in support of pluralist democracy the churches played an important role. In examining the role played by the churches in South Africa it is important to note that this was subject to change over time and that different churches worked in very different ways.

For a long time the churches more closely associated with English-speaking South Africa followed a more politically and socially progressive line than did the main church of the Afrikaners, the Dutch Reformed Church (the Nederduitse Gereformeerde Kerk). The ecumenical South African Council of Churches (SACC), which was founded in 1968, brought together the Anglican and Methodist churches (with the Roman Catholics enjoying observer status) and included a very substantial black African membership. Most of the leading clergy most closely associated with the anti-apartheid struggle were prominent within the SACC. They included Archbishop Desmond Mpilo Tutu, Reverend Allan Boesak, and Reverend Frank Chikane. With the major anti-apartheid groups unable to operate in South Africa until after their legal unbanning in February 1989 the churches within the SACC provided a voice for the anti-apartheid movement within South Africa which the government found difficult to handle. As Gann and Duignan observe the churches 'acted as particularly effective spokesmen for the outlawed opposition'[27]. In 1985 the SACC produced the Kairos Document[28] which provided a coherent theological critique of the apartheid state.

Until recently the Dutch Reformed Church in South Africa played a role which was far more supportive of the apartheid system, often supplying biblical justifications for racial segregation. From 1863 until 1986 church services were segregated. However, during the 1980s significant splits began to appear within the white section of the Church which reflected those appearing within the wider Afrikaner community in its attitudes to racial questions. Radical Church ministers like Beyers Naude led the way in abandoning previously held positions and in linking in with the anti-apartheid movement. From 1984 to 1987 Naude was secretary-general of the SACC.

As in Malawi and Kenya, the church in South Africa enjoyed a semi-protected status which could be used in defying an undemocratic government. Whilst churchmen did not entirely escape government harassment and detention they were in a less vulnerable position than the secular opponents of the system who were often dealt with quite ruthlessly by the state security apparatus. Especially when church leaders had achieved an international status, as for example Archbishop Tutu clearly did, the government became too embarrassed to take them off to jail and torture or kill them as happened not infrequently to other opponents. Particularly in the last ten years the churches in South Africa have been an important part of the pressure for democratisation.

In many other African states the church has played a prominent role in undermining the legitimacy of authoritarian regimes and contributing to the pressure for democratic change. In Rwanda in 1989 the Roman Catholic newspaper *Kinyamateka* openly attacked the Habyarimana regime for its corruption and oppression. The following year the Rwandan Roman Catholic bishops published an open letter to all Christians calling for social justice, human rights, and freedom of the press[29]. In Zaire the Roman Catholic church, for long the only effective opposition to Mobutu, at the bishop's conference in March 1990 released a report attacking the single-party state and calling for democratic reforms and freedom of speech[30]. In Madagascar the umbrella group the Christian Council of Churches of Madagascar (Fiombonan'ny Fiangonana Kristiana eto Madagasikara-FFKM) was an important part of the pressure for democratisation of the political system[31]. In 1991, following the killing of pro-democracy demonstrators the Roman Catholic Archbishop of Antananarivo Victor Razafimahatratra called for President Ratsiraka to stand down (he did not do so but was later ousted in competitive elections). The FFKM accused Ratsiraka of being 'non-Christian' and of using *rampy* (traditional charms). In Ghana the Christian Council of Churches was a strong supporter of opposition demands for the restoration of multi-party democracy[32]. In Benin at Easter 1989 the Catholic Church issued a pastoral letter calling for fundamental political change[33].

The role of the churches in the pressure for democratic change in Africa can best be seen as the exercise of influence rather than of power. Lacking any coercive power they provided a moral dimension to the struggle which resonated keenly in societies where religious beliefs are strong and widespread. Paradoxically their lack of coercive power often meant that it was more difficult, although certainly not impossible, for governments to use coercive power against them. Their influence was enhanced by the fact that the churches were not seen as competitors for government power but as more disinterested participants. In the struggle for democracy the churches were able to contribute to the creation of an environment that was more propitious for the other pro-democracy groups.

The perception of church leaders as politically disinterested was reflected in the role they played in several of the National Conferences (discussed in chapter 4) in the Francophone states. Leading prelates acted as chairmen of the conferences in Benin (Archbishop of Cotonou, Isadore da Souza), Congo (Bishop of Owando, Ernest N'Kombo), Congo (Bishop of Atakpame, Philippe Kossi Kpodzro), and Zaire (Archbishop of Kisangani, Laurent Monsengwo Pasinya). The clergy were viewed by both government and opposition figures as having fewer vested interests in the outcomes of the conferences and therefore more neutral in their handling of the proceedings.

The available evidence suggests that Christian clerics played a far more prominent role than did Muslim clerics in the democratisation process. Although individual Muslims often contributed significantly Islamic organisations tended not to[34]. I think it would be unwise to read too much into this fact: I am not implying that somehow African Muslims are less concerned with democracy than are African Christians. Certainly there are interpretations of Islam which could be regarded as antagonistic to democracy but the same could be said of

43

some interpretations of Christianity. Across Africa there is little to suggest that states with Muslim majorities have been less involved in the struggle for democracy than those with Christian majorities. In the three longest surviving African democracies Botswana has a Christian majority, The Gambia has a Muslim majority, and Mauritius has a Hindu majority. Freedom of worship and religious tolerance are practised in all three.

Trade Unions

During the late colonial period African trade union leaders were often prominent in the nationalist struggle for independence. In several cases (eg. Sekou Toure in Guinea, Siaka Stevens in Sierra Leone) the early post-independence government leaders were men who had worked their way up through the union movement. However, with the development of more authoritarian regimes the activities of trade unions were often restricted by government legislation or action. In many cases the autonomy of the unions was severely curtailed and in a number of cases they were banned. Apart from outright banning, tactics used to curtail union power included the creation of 'official' government-friendly unions (in spite of, or perhaps because of, the fact that the government was frequently the main employer), making strikes illegal, bringing unions under the control of the single party, and harassing or bribing union leaders.

However, in spite of this hostile environment trade unions in many African states did manage to retain some degree of autonomy which gave them a capacity for independent action denied to other groups. Their, predominantly urban based, organisational structure and the possession of the strike weapon put them in a position to pressurise governments. Some observers would argue that it was the workers and their unions who were the most important participants in the struggle for democracy: A. S. Wamala, for example, suggests that 'the leaders, at the forefront of the struggle toward democratic pluralism were almost always trade union activists'[35]. Certainly it is true that the trade unions often played an important part especially in those states where a degree of autonomy had been retained during the more authoritarian period.

A good example of the latter situation can be seen by examining the case of Zambia. In spite of various attempts over a long period by the ruling United National Independence Party (UNIP) to exercise control over the trade unions the latter were able to retain a fair degree of autonomy[36]. The main trade union body in Zambia has been the Zambia Congress of Trade Unions (ZCTU) which has eighteen affiliated unions with a total membership of over 400,000, or more than 80% of those in formal sector employment. Its longtime leader was Frederick Chiluba who was imprisoned in 1981 for resisting government attempts to control the unions. Subsequently he repeatedly rejected offers of a place on UNIP's central committee as President Kaunda attempted to neutralise him by co-optation. From the 1970s Chiluba emerged as a major critic of the incumbent government. His opposition was based on a combination of specifically union matters, for example the refusal of the government as the main employer of labour to engage in free collective bargaining, and more general political matters. In relation to the latter this developed from criticisms of the way the single-party state operated in Zambia to criticisms of the whole notion of single-partyism. Continuing economic decline during the 1980s led to an increase in opposition to the government from the unions because their members were particularly hard hit by the decline in the real value of wages and sharp increases in the cost of living in the urban areas. By the end of the decade the focus of union demands was on democratisation of the political system and in late 1989 the ZCTU General Council decided to to campaign for the restoration of a multi-party system. July 1990 saw the formation of the National Interim Committee for Multi-Party Democracy, a body which was soon to transform itself into the Movement for Multi-Party Democracy (MMD). From the start the trade unions provided the main popular base for the movement and its main organisational structure. At the initial meeting Chiluba was placed in charge of organisation and operations. Later in the year Jonathan Simakuni, the national chairman of the Mineworkers' Union of Zambia (MUZ), pledged his union's full support for the movement and urged its members to work for it. In January 1991, after President Kaunda had given in to pressure for political pluralism, the MMD transformed itself into a political party and at its inaugural convention Chiluba was elected party president. Subsequently Chiluba was chosen as the MMD presidential candidate for the October 1991 general elections. He led the MMD to a very substantial victory in the elections and was himself elected as the new President of Zambia when he gained 75% of the votes in his presidential election contest with Kenneth Kaunda. Following his election to the presidency Chiluba resigned from his position in the ZCTU.

It would not be accurate to portray the MMD as solely a trade union based movement. The MMD represented a very diverse range of Zambian groupings which also included business interests, the churches, students, professional associations and many others. Other than the restoration of a democratic system the agendas of these groupings did not fully overlap. However, it is clear that in the struggle for democracy in Zambia it was the trade union movement and its leadership which played a pre-eminent role.

In spite of the leading role of the trade unions in the struggle for democracy in Zambia there was no usage of political strikes to bring pressure to bear on the government. In many other states in Africa, however, strikes were widely and effectively used as an important weapon in the struggle. Initially most of the strikes were related to industrial grievances against the government in its role as the main employer of labour. Late payment, or non-payment of, wages and salaries provided a common source of resentment. Rapidly strikes took on a more overtly political dimension as demands for political pluralism were added to demands for the resolution of industrial grievances. Following the escalation of political demands strikes were frequently called in support of solely political goals. Trade unionists increasingly argued that the interests of workers could only be protected by creating the institutions which could subject the government to a far greater level of democratic accountability than existed at the time. It was widely perceived that this accountability could only come about through a competitive party system.

In Niger the major trade union federation, the Union des Syndicats des Travailleurs du Niger (USTN), had for most of the period since its inception been fairly strictly controlled by the government[37] and had demonstrated little capacity for independent action. Beginning in 1990 the USTN adopted a very different stance. In May it called for the introduction of multi-partyism and the following month organised a strike to protest against the brutal treatment handed out by the security forces to student demonstrators, and to stress its opposition to a wage freeze. In November the USTN called a general strike to support its demands for political pluralism and organised a march of an estimated 100,000 people in the capital Niamey[38]. The general strike lasted for five days during which time it virtually closed down the formal sector in Niger. Shortly afterwards President Ali Saibou announced that a multi-party system would be introduced. In February and March 1992 an army mutiny appeared to threaten the democratisation process, which was by that time relatively far advanced. The mutineers detained Andre Salifou, a university academic who had chaired the National Conference which had negotiated the democratisation process and was at the time chairman of the interim legislature, and seized control of the broadcasting media in Niamey. In response to this threat the USTN organised another widely observed general strike to protest against the actions of the mutineers who then backed down and released Salifou. Thus in Niger strikes were important in initiating the democratisation process and in sustaining it when it came under threat from a section of the army.

Although there are obvious similarities in the political roles of trade unions in Zambia and Niger can be seen it is also important to note one particular point of contrast. Whereas in Zambia the ZCTU already had a long history of antagonistic relations with authoritarian government the situation in Niger was quite different. Here the USTN had for most of its history adopted a fairly docile attitude to authoritarian government and it was only in the changed circumstances of the post-1989 period that it became assertively oppositional, particularly in its use of political strikes.

Pressure exerted through strikes played an important role in the democratisation struggle in many African states. In early 1989 in Benin there was a rash of strikes which to begin with were mainly concerned with economic matters, especially the failure of the regime to ensure payment of wages in the public sector which were by then several months in arrears. As the year progressed trade unionists widened their focus from the issue of wage arrears to an overall criticism of the nature of the political system. The officially-recognised trade union organisation, the Union Nationale des Syndicats des Travailleurs du Benin (UNSTB), came under severe criticism for failing to protect the interests of workers and many affiliated unions withdrew from it to campaign against the government and demand the introduction of political pluralism. This demand was met early the following year. In neighbouring Togo strikes have been an equally prominent part of the struggle for democracy although here the stern, and often violent, resistance of President Gnassingbe Eyadema and the bulk of the army to democratisation has meant that the struggle has had only very limited success so far. Before 1991 the main Togolese trade union organisation was the Confederation Nationale des Travailleurs du Togo (CNTT) which enjoyed little autonomy and was largely subservient to the government. In May 1991 many of the affiliated unions broke away to form the Union Nationale des Syndicats Independants du Togo (UNSIT) which, as its name suggests, rejects government control of the trade union movement. Since its inception UNSIT and its close associates have played a central role in the struggle for democracy. Three widely supported general strikes have been organised in support of the struggle. In June 1991 the first attempted, without success, to force the resignation of Eyadema. In May 1992 a second general strike was organised as a protest against the attempted assassination of opposition leader Gilchrist Olympio[39] by Eyadema's agents. In November 1992 a third general strike, which was universally supported except in parts of the north (where Eyadema has his most significant support base), was organised to support demands that Eyadema ceased using the army to support his position and attack his political opponents.

In attempting to pressurise authoritarian governments to democratise many trade union leaders have been willing to risk their own lives. This is nowhere more clearly illustrated than in the case of Chakufwa Chihana of Malawi. Chihana, who is the leader of the Southern Africa Trade Union Coordination Council (SATUCC) spent many years as an exiled critic of the Banda regime. In April 1992, following the launch of the Catholic Bishop's pastoral letter (discussed earlier), Chihana decided to return home to campaign for democracy. He had no illusions over how dangerous this would be: in a telephone call to his son just before he returned he said 'My son, this is the last time I will be speaking to you. I am going to Malawi and I will be killed. But if I am killed, people in the international community will know there is something wrong with this government[40]'. As soon as Chihana stepped off the aeroplane in Malawi he was arrested by security men and charged with sedition (ie. calling for democracy). Subsequently he spent much of his time in jail but during periods of freedom he continued to campaign for democracy. In November 1992 at the burial of Orton Chirwa (another Malawian democracy activist who had recently died in jail following more than a decade in detention) Chihana delivered a funeral oration to the thousands of mourners when he said that 'Orton Chirwa died fighting for freedom...his death will spark afresh the fire of democracy and we must keep that fire burning'[41]. In the 1994 elections Chihana was the leader of the Alliance for Democracy (AFORD).

In South Africa white trade unions were traditionally strong supporters of the apartheid system and were opposed to the extension of the franchise to the majority groups within the population. However, following the legalisation of black (and increasingly non-racial) trade unions as a result of the recommendations of the Wiehahn Commission in 1979, the South African trade union movement played an important part in the struggle against apartheid and for democracy. Although the newly legalised unions were not free from government restrictions they did enjoy a freedom to operate within South Africa which was denied to most of the anti-apartheid groups before the unbanning of the latter in February 1990. In 1985 a major development of trade union organisation in South Africa took place with the founding of the Congress of South African Trade Unions (COSATU) which initially included 34 affiliated unions. As Lemon noted a major aim of was COSATU was that of 'providing a new focus for the wider political aspirations of black workers'[42]. As Lodge argues 'COSATU represented a widespread belief within the labour movement that political linkages were inevitable and necessary, if only to secure an influential position for workers in the struggle to democratise South Africa'[43]. Although COSATU was predominantly black in its leadership and membership it encouraged white workers to join as members and included a number of white union officials. This policy clearly demarcated COSATU from the other major trade union grouping, the Council of Unions of South Africa (CUSA), which was inspired by black consciousness ideas and insisted on exclusively black participation. Although COSATU remained formally independent of any other political grouping it was very clearly sympathetic to the major umbrella anti-apartheid organisation, the United Democratic Front (UDF). In turn the latter was clearly sympathetic towards the still-banned ANC whose colours it sported[44].

The key central figure linking the trade union movement and the struggle for democracy in South Africa has been Cyril Ramaphosa. The latter was a founder member and general secretary of the National Union of Mineworkers (NUM) from its inception in 1982. He was instrumental in the decision of the union to join COSATU in 1985, a move which considerably enhanced the status of the latter. At the watershed congress of the ANC in July 1991 Mkhondo observes that Ramaphosa 'stole the show' and that 'his election as secretary-general was a recognition that trade unions have played a major role in the struggle against apartheid'[45]. Ramaphosa was the principal ANC negotiator at the Convention for a Democratic South Africa (CODESA) whose meetings eventually led to the promulgation of a democratic constitution for the country. The negotiating skills which Ramaphosa had developed whilst leading the NUM were clearly demonstrated during the long and complicated process of constitution-making. Second in importance only to Nelson Mandela, and thirty four years his junior, Cyril Ramaphosa has been a pivotal figure in South Africa's democratisation process. Following the 1994 election he was defeated by Thabo Mbeki in the competition for the vice-presidency and chose to remain as general secretary of the ANC rather than join the cabinet.

Trade union participation in the struggle for democracy extended far beyond the half a dozen states discussed above. In addition to these examples unions played a significant part (with varying degrees of success) in Burkina Faso, Burundi, Cameroon, Chad, Central African Republic, Comoros, Congo, Cote d'Ivoire, Gabon, Ghana, Guinea, Kenya, Lesotho, Madagascar, Mali, Mauritania, Nigeria, Swaziland, and Zaire. Overall there can be little doubt that in the past few years unions have played a more independent and assertive participatory role in political life than at any time since the late colonial period. They have not sought simply to protect the work-place interests of their members but have endeavoured to bring about a restructuring of the political system on more pluralist lines.

Professional Associations and Human Rights Groups

Whilst trade union participation in the struggle for democracy provided the movement with an important mass base the involvement of professional associations provided important support from the educated elite. Amongst the professional associations involved those representing lawyers were especially prominent but those representing academics and medical doctors were also important. In many ways these associations function like elite trade unions. Whilst they lack the mass membership of industrial unions this lack is to a large extent compensated for by the highly educated and articulate nature of their more limited numbers of members. Their high educational levels can enable them to channel their opposition more effectively and also makes it much less likely that they will be taken in by the bogus ideological justifications advanced by African autocrats to justify authoritarian rule.

Partly due to the nature of their training and professional expertise lawyers represent a particularly interesting and important group. Certainly it would be wrong to romantacise African lawyers *en masse*: there are enough examples of individual lawyers cooperating with authoritarian regimes to further their own material interests for this to be convincing. However, one common feature of authoritarian regimes in Africa has been their general downgrading of the operation of due legal procedure and the freedom of the judiciary. This has taken place under civilian personal rulers who have ignored legal statutes, or altered them at will, and military dictators who rule through coercion-backed decrees which are impervious to legal restraint. Whilst in theory an authoritarian regime could act in compliance with the law, in practice this has rarely, if ever, been the case in Africa. It can also be argued that lawyers have a vested financial interest in the rule of law. Jibrin Ibrahim, for example, has argued that 'for lawyers to be able to maintain their elevated place in society the judicial machine must operate in a fairly just and nonarbitrary manner' and that lawyers have 'a corporate interest in the maintenance of due process, the rule of law and civil liberties'[46]. Lawyers have also been very prominent in many of the human rights organisations which have been established in recent years. Whilst the struggle for human rights and the struggle for democracy are not fully synonomous the two have overlapped to such an extent in Africa that they can be examined together. Whilst it may be possible to imagine an authoritarian regime which respected humman rights the fact remains that such regimes in Africa have generally been gross abusers of human rights. Thus, human rights campaigners have accorded a high priority to the establishment of more democratic political systems which they see as an essential ingredient in the protection of human rights. Overlap also occurs in terms of personnel. In most cases participants in human rights groups have also been participants in pro-democracy groups: this is especially true in relation to those coming from legal and academic professional associations.

At a formal international African level concern for human rights preceded the more recent struggle for democracy. In 1981 the African Charter on Human and Peoples' rights was drawn up in the Gambian capital Banjul (it is sometimes referred to as the Banjul Charter). The Charter was formally adopted by the Organisation of African Unity (OAU) at its summit meeting in Nairobi in June 1981, although it did not come into force until 1986[47]. In addition an African Commission for Human and Peoples' Rights was established and located in Banjul. Although this formal recognition of the importance of human rights issues was welcomed the Charter has not had the far-reaching effects that its supporters had hoped for. A major reason for this is that, in common with other OAU initiatives, there is no real enforcement mechanism through which to ensure compliance by individual governments[48]. In most African states it has been left to domestic human rights groups to campaign as best they can.

In Nigeria lawyers and other professionals have been deeply involved with organisations struggling for the twin goals of democracy and human rights. The

Nigerian Bar Association (NBA) played a very active role especially after the formation of the Association of Democratic Lawyers of Nigeria (ADLN) in 1985[49]. Closely linked with the latter has been the Committee for the Defence of Human Rights (CDHR) established by the medical doctor Beko Ransome-Kuti in 1989. The major coordinating body has been the Civil Liberties Organisation (CLO) which was launched in 1987[50]. The CLO was initially established by two lawyers, Clement Nwanko and Olisa Agbakoba, using their own law office as an operational base. Its initial membership was mainly from the legal profession but also included campaigning journalists like Abdul Oroh and Amma Ogan. The initial campaign of the CLO focussed on an investigation of prison conditions in Nigeria and revealed an horrendous catalogue of detention without trial of political dissenters who were being kept in quite appalling conditions. In December 1988 the CLO published a report on 'Violations of Human Rights in Nigeria'. Following the release of the report CLO leaders including Nwanko and Agbakoba were harassed and detained for a time by the state security forces. Subsequently the CLO shifted its focus onto the transition to civilian rule which was underway in Nigeria by combining with other groups to form the Campaign for Democracy. Although, as we now know, that particular transition was aborted by the military government in 1993, at an earlier stage it did appear to offer the chance of a least a partial democratisation of the Nigerian political system. The CLO and CD were generally supportive of the transition in principle but were extremely critical of many aspects of it. Although they regarded the transition as preferable to a continuation of military rule the mechanics of the transition were seen as far from ideal. In its first bulletin, issued in July 1991, the CLO/CD argued that 'many features of the transition to civil rule programme make it doubtful that the dispensation it will usher in will meet the democratic political expectations of Nigerian citizens'[51]. This bulletin was particularly critical of the human rights agendas of the two parties established by the military government. It argued that 'both parties have thus demonstrated neither the political will nor the capacity to successfully shoulder the arduous task of building democracy in post-military Nigeria in an age in which human rights have become the hub around which the democratic transformation of human societies revolves'[52]. Following President Babangida's decision in June 1993 to abandon the transition process it was groups like the CLO and CD which produced the most vocal opposition to the move (opposition to the election annullment is examined in chapter 6).

In Kenya lawyers' organisations and many individual lawyers played a prominent role in the campaign to pressurise President Moi to restore a multiparty system. Prior to the more recent pro-democracy campaigns human rights lawyers had provided one of the few defences against oppression by the government: as the Kenyan lawyer Gibson Kamau Kuria observed 'with the end of multi-partyism and the death of parliamentary independence, Kenya's activist lawyers have become the only recourse for those who run foul of the president and his henchmen'[53]. Although Moi attempted to woo 'patriotic lawyers' (ie. those who would support him) the Law Society of Kenya (LSK) became one of his major opponents. This was especially true after the election of Paul Muite to the position of chairman of the LSK in 1991. In his acceptance speech Muite called for the registration of opposition parties and for the repeal of section 2A of the Constitution which upheld the existence of a single-party state[54]. Another forum for the pro-democracy movement has been the *Nairobi Law Monthly* edited by Gitobu Imanyara[55]. Although Imanyara was arrested and detained without trial on several occasions the journal continued to be a major mouthpiece of the democracy movement. At one stage Imanyara unsuccessfully took the attorney general to court in an attempt to get the constitutional amendment making Kenya a single-party state declared unconstitutional.

In Zimbabwe lawyers have been prominent in attempts to preserve the more democratic features of the political system in the face of more authoritarian tendencies on the part of some members of the government. In 1992 two new non-party groups, the Forum for Democratic Reform and the Zimbabwe Human Rights Association were launched to support a democratic political culture[56]. Prominent in both groups is Enoch Dumbutshena, previously the first black Chief Justice of Zimbabwe, who has frequently made clear his view of the necessary relationship between human rights and a multi-party system[57]. Other professional associations of lawyers which contributed significantly to democratisation movements in their own states included the Cameroonian Bar Association, the Ghana Bar Association, the Tanzania Legal Education Trust, and the Togolese Bar Association.

In recent years the participation of professional associations in the democratisation process has represented a more significant level of political participation by African educated elites than has been seen since the late colonial period. At that time groups like lawyers played a significant role in the nationalist struggle by contesting the legal structures of the colonial state and seeking to dismantle them. It is no coincidence that in states where opposition leaders were elected to power in recent democratic elections a very high proportion of them were from the highly educated elite. Examples include Nicephore Soglo (former Director for Africa in the World Bank) in Benin, Antonio Mascarenhas Monteiro (lawyer and former Supreme Court Judge) in Cape Verde, Melchior Ndadaye (educationalist) in Burundi[58], Ange-Felix Patasse (agronomist) in Central African Republic, Pascal Lissouba (agronomic engineer and academic) in Congo, Albert Zafy (medical professor) in Madagascar, Alpha Oumar Konare (history professor) in Mali, Mahamane Ousmane (economist) in Niger, Miguel Trovoada (lawyer) in Sao Tome and Principe, and of course Nelson Mandela (lawyer) in South Africa.

52

From one perspective students can be seen as part of the educated elite, or at least as aspirant members of that group. As such they can be seen as having shared the dissatisfactions with authoritarian rule of the educted elites in the professional associations. Perhaps even more importantly the widespread participation of students in the struggle for democracy can be seen as representing a generational facet of the struggle. With the exception of a small number of mature students they are characterised by their relative youth: the vast majority would have been born well after the end of the colonial period and would have no personal memory of those earlier days. Because of this they were less likely to be convinced by justifications for authoritarian rule which rested, in part at least, on the claims of autocratic leaders to have led their countries to independence from colonial domination. Leaders who used such claims, such as Kenneth Kaunda in Zambia, Felix Houphouet-Boigny in Cote d'Ivoire, Hastings Banda in Malawi, and even Robert Mugabe in Zimbabwe (although here the time-scale was rather different), were to discover that they were a declining asset in the search for legitimacy. Evidence suggests that Banda and Kaunda in particular did believe in all sincerity that their leadership of the nationalist movement thirty years earlier still gave them incontrovertible authority. It may well be the case that for some older Malawians and Zambians such considerations retain importanc but their numbers are subject to inevitable decline. The generational aspect has been little investigated in the literature on African democratisation although there have been exceptions like Sukhwant Singh Nannan. The latter writes of how a 'new generation of Africans' believe that 'justification of current systems by reference to the past is meaningless or, to many, a total fraud'[59].

Within the younger generation full-time students enjoy a number of advantages over others in the same age group when it comes to engaging in oppositional political activities. Almost by definition those in higher education will tend to be much better educated than others of the same age who have only been educated to lower levels or, in some cases, received no education at all. In many African states the possession of full literacy differentiates them from the bulk of the population. Because of this they are likely to be more politically aware and in a better position to comprehend the nature of the political process. Because higher education is usually conducted through the medium of a single language (generally English, French, or Portuguese depending on the relevant colonial power) students have no difficulty in communicating on a national basis. The fact of living together, either on campus or close by, makes it relatively easy for students to communicate and to organise politically. This explains why a common response of governments which feel threatened is to close the campus and disperse the students. In many cases sympathetic academic staff are willing to provide students with support and organisational assistance. However, although students possess political advantages they are weakened by a number of disadvantages. Apart from government closure of higher education institutions they are also extremely vulnerable to violent attacks by the police or the army. In many cases governments under pressure from student opposition have launched attacks on higher education campuses which have resulted in large numbers of students being killed or injured. Sticks and stones offer little protection against machine guns and tanks. In addition, unlike industrial workers, students lack an effective strike weapon with which to bring pressure to bear on governments. As in other parts of the world student strikes are easy to organise but largely ineffective as they affect only the students and their teachers. At most a student strike is a minor embarrassment to an authoritarian government.

In spite of these weaknesses African students have a long history of opposition to authoritarian governments. In a study I conducted several years ago of urban riots in West Africa over a nine year period[60] it was clear that students were the most common participants in anti-government disturbances. In the more recent period a relatively common pattern of transformation can be seen in the nature of student protest. Initially much of the protest was grounded on specifically student issues and grievances. Typically these included late payment (or non-payment) of student grants, decline in future employment prospects, government interference in academic freedoms, problems with student food and accommodation, and the general physical deterioration which was apparent in most institutions of higher education. Fairly rapidly this type of issue based dissent changed into a more general protest against the nature of authoritarian rule which was seen as being responsible for the difficulties which students faced. In most cases this dissent then became focussed on demands for the legalisation of opposition movements and the introduction of a multi-party system. African students were very much aware of the role played by their conterparts in Eastern Europe in opposing authoritarian regimes. Once protest had gone beyond specifically student-based grievances they were joined by others of a similar age in the wider urban population.

Across Africa students have contributed to the pressure for democratisation in Benin, Burkina Faso, Cameroon, Congo, Cote d'Ivoire, Gabon, Ghana, Guinea, Kenya, Madagascar, Mali, Malawi, Niger, Nigeria, Sierra Leone, South Africa, Tanzania, Togo, Zaire, and Zambia. In Zimbabwe the struggle has focussed on attempting to ensure the retention of an already existing multi-party system, which appeared to be in danger of being abandoned by the government of Robert Mugabe, rather than moving towards a multi-party system. Here students have played an important part in maintaining the core of the system and in providing support for the opposition parties which are themselves rather weak[61].

In a significant number of cases student pro-democracy demonstrations were followed by violent repression by state security forces. Although by no means the only culprit the government of Zaire has been guilty of some of the worst examples of violence towards students. In May 1990 on the Lubumbashi campus of the National University of Zaire over 300 students were mercilessly killed by security forces[62]. Based on discussions with student informants in Zaire the American journalist Lucy Komisar describes one of the attacks in the following way; 'that night the electricity in the university area was cut...we saw three trucks of soldiers enter...many students went down to find out why the current had been cut...the soldiers began to massacre the students with guns and bayonets...we found blood everywhere in the rooms'[63]. The use of such terror tactics may in the longer term be counterproductive and lead to increased opposition to the government and a total evaporation of any remaining legitimacy.

Had the actions of students been an isolated phenomenon it is possible that authoritarian governments might have contained it with the use of violence. However, as part of a much wider struggle for democratic change, student activity contributed significantly.

The Media

In assessing the role of the indigenous media in the struggle for democracy it is necessary to see it as both a dependent and independent variable; as effect and as cause. The proliferation of pro-democracy newspapers free from government control, for example, can be seen as resulting from the new political space created in the struggle for democracy. Once in existence, however, they can be seen as a significant component of the struggle.

In discussing the role of the media the focus is of necessity almost entirely on the print media (newspapers, magazines, pamphlets etc.) rather than on the electronic media (radio and television). For the most part the latter have been owned or strictly controlled by the state and have been used by the holders of state power to protect their position. Oppositional pro-democracy groups have had little or no access to state controlled radio and television and have relied on the print media which is much easier and cheaper to establish[64]. In examining African newspapers, especially those produced by opposition groups, it is important not to be misled by foreign stereotypes of what a newspaper 'ought' to look like. Most are cheaply produced, cyclostyled broadsheets with poor quality printing. It is the content which is important, not whether they look like a 'proper' newspaper. Assuming it is not imported a newspaper with high printing standards, produced on quality paper, and full of photographs is more likely to come from a government source and to be backed by state funding. A good rule of thumb with African newspapers is that the less impressive they appear the more interesting, in a political sense, their contents are likely to be!

Discussion of the impact of newspapers raises a further duo of problems. The first relates to the relatively low levels of literacy in most African states: most people cannot read newspapers. The second relates to the fact that most newspapers are not written in indigenous African languages but use English or French which are spoken by the elites rather than by the masses[65]. In my experience one needs to be careful not to overstate the impact of these two factors. Rather than seeing newspapers as an isolated means of communication one should see them as a part of a chain of communication in which reading is only part of the chain. Most people cannot read newspapers but, equally, most people know somebody who can. Again from my own experience, this holds true even in remote rural villages. Thus, it is necessary to see newspapers as one link in a communication chain for ideas and information which is partly, or perhaps even largely, oral.

The Zambian case provides a good example of how the new political space opened up in the democratisation process enabled a move away from tight press censorship and towards a more pluralistic print media and how this change in turn contributed further to the development of democracy within the system. Until 1990 both of Zambia's major newspapers, the *Times of Zambia* and the *Zambian Daily Mail*, were strictly controlled by the government and reflected the views of the ruling party. The only other regular publication was the *National Mirror*, which was sponsored by church groups and appeared once a fortnight. Even in late 1990 President Kaunda was insisting that the two major newspapers should 'toe the Party line and reflect UNIP policies' and the editors were ordered not to give coverage of the views or activities of the opposition. In January 1991 the MMD challenged these views in the courts[66]. The courts decided that the newspapers were owned by the people rather than by the ruling party and that Kaunda's directives to the editors were 'illegal, unconstitutional and discriminatory'. From then on these newspapers ceased to be a mouthpiece of government a reflected the political debate within the country in a more accurate manner. Even if their pro-UNIP bias did not disappear altogether it certainly became much less pronounced. In terms of coverage of the 1991 election campaigns the Commonwealth Observer Group came to the conclusion that these newspapers had 'made real efforts to report the campaign in a fair manner'[67]. In addition to this weakening of control by UNIP of the state-owned press the period also saw the development of a new independently owned press reflecting a variety of political inclinations. The pro-UNIP *Eagle Express* was balanced by the pro-MMD *Daily Express* and the more party-neutral *Weekly Post*. In relation to these developments one scholar has argued that 'the emergence of an independent press was one of the healthiest signs that plural politics had taken root in Zambian society'[68]. Overall, the changes which took place in the Zambian print media played an important role in democratic change in the country especially in the period leading up to the 1991 elections when the ruling UNIP was voted out of office.

Developments in Nigeria stand in marked contrast to the growth of press freedom in Zambia. In much of the post-idependence period, and indeed in the late colonial period, Nigeria has exhibited a lively and independent free press which has contributed significantly to political debate in the country[69]. Periodically the press was subject to attempts at government control, under both civilian and military regimes, and independent-minded journalists were subject to harassment from time to time but in comparison with most other African states the Nigerian press retained a critical level of autonomy. There is little doubt, however, that over the past decade or so press freedom has diminished in Nigeria and that journalists have been increasingly subjected to oppression by the state. This has been especially so under the successive military regimes of Muhammadu Buhari, Ibrahim Babangida, and, more recently, Sanni Abacha. Because under these regimes much of the political debate has centred on the the question of a return to democratic civilian rule attacks on the press can be seen as an attempt to thwart pressure for democratisation arising from the media. The leading organ of campaigning journalists has been the magazine *Newswatch* which was founded in 1985 by Dele Giwa, Dan Agbese, Yakubu Mohammed and Ray Ekpu all of whom were experienced journalists[70]. Since its inception the magazine has been frequently proscribed and its staff subjected to government intimidation. In October 1986 the then editor-in-chief, Dele Giwa, was assassinated by a parcel bomb which was widely believed to have been sent by forces acting for the government. Since then others associated with the magazine have frequently been arrested, threatened, beaten up, and intimidated in various ways.

Although *Newswatch* is probably the best known example of a campaigning pro-democracy journal in Nigeria there are numerous other magazines and newspapers which have followed a similar course. Given this context it is unsurprising that one of the first actions of the Nigerian military government following its decision to ignore the results of the 1993 elections and to retain power was to enforce a major clampdown on the press in order to head off criticism from pro-democracy campaigners. In announcing the decision the government's Secretary for Information and Culture, Uche Chukwumerije, rather ingenuously announced that 'the government wishes to reaffirm its commitment to have a free and responsible press'[71]. In the circumstances the word 'responsible' takes on very sinister implications.

In the period since 1989 the experience of the Zambian press outlined above can be seen as more representative of events across Africa than can the more negative Nigerian example. In many states there has been a proliferation of new independent newspapers and magazines: Kwame Karikari, for example, cites the cases of forty new newspapers in Benin and fifteen in Mali[72]. The editorial quality of these newspapers varies enormously. It is safe to assume that not all of these new publications will survive in the longer term even if governments do not return to their old restrictive practices. Many are based on a weak financial and organisational footing. The upswing in demand for newspapers was itself partly created by the popular excitement and enthusiasm in the democratisation process, and in the novelty of the new freedoms, which will be difficult to sustain over a longer period. The revenue from advertising which helps to support newspapers in more developed states exists at a much lower level in Africa. In the longer term the survival of an energetic and relatively free press will be crucial for any consolidation of democracy in Africa.

Old Politicians

Although the recent redemocratisation process has introduced significant numbers of new figures to the African political stage it is also true that there have been a good many familiar faces involved both in applying pressure for democracy and participating in the resulting pluralistic competition for government power. In describing this group as 'old' politicians I am not necessarily suggesting that they were all advanced in years (though some certainly were) but that they were individuals who had at some time in the past played a significant role in politics but who had found themselves, for a variety of different reasons, outside of the political mainstream. Robert Bates describes such people as possessing 'human capital' in terms of their knowledge and experience of the domestic political system. This capital is not transferable because as Bates argues 'the human capital of old guard politicians is also geographically specific'[73]: they thus have a personal interest in investing their 'capital' in the democratisation process at home. Such individuals exhibited a wide variety of experiences partly influenced by the type of authoritarianism they were seeking to change.

In the case of single-party states pro-democracy activists included those who had held senior positions in opposition parties during earlier periods before the introduction of single-partyism and the consequent banning of those parties. They also included those who had previously been significant figures in the ruling parties of single-party states but who had withdrawn from, or had been excluded from, the party for a variety of reasons. This latter group would include those whose exit from the ruling party was brought about by disagreements over policy formulation and implementation and who felt that they could no longer justify their position within the party. It would also include those whose exit was caused by clashes, often of a personal nature, with the top elite within the party. In single-party states dominated by a single personal ruler it had been common for that ruler to force out of the party those who were perceived to pose some sort of threat to the position of the leader or those who had, for whatever reason, incurred the displeasure of that leader. Although those excluded from the ruling party in this way were frequently accused of some sort of impropriety by the leader such accusations often lacked any real substance and could be seen as providing public justification for exclusion rather than as the genuine grounds for it. However, whether the reason for exclusion from the ruling party was based on principled policy disagreement or personal spite (or some combination of the two) the result was very much the same. In either case the politician concerned was excluded from participation in legal political life by the existence of the institutional framework of the single-party state. In a pluralistic democracy politicians who find themselves in this position can take their case to the electorate by joining another party or forming a new one. It is then up to the voters in a competitive election to decide on the merits of the case.

Given this context it is hardly surprising that included among those campaigning for the restoration of democracy were these ousted politicians for whom a restoration of multi-partyism represented the best hope of personal political revival. Some observers have reacted to this situation with a degree of cynicism by portraying the support for democracy of such individuals as being based on selfish personal interest rather than an altruistic belief in the intrinsic value of democracy. However as Bratton points out in relation to Zambia, for example, 'most UNIP defectors joined MMD well before the political transition began'[74]. Given the complexities of human motivation it is extremely difficult, if not completely impossible, to disentangle primary, secondary, and non-existent impulses involved is such a situation. Certainly it would not make sense to try to generalise in relation to recent developments in Africa. The old politicians in the pro-democracy movements ranged from dedicated democrats to self-serving opportunists with most falling somewhere in between. In terms of exerting pressure for democracy one could argue that the fact that many old politicians became involved is rather more important than questions relating to their motivation. Opposition to the single-party state was often efficacious even when it came from individuals who had previously served in the system they now had come to oppose.

In those states where military regimes were in power pressure for democratisation was inevitably closely linked with pressure for demilitarisation because the latter was a necessary, but insufficient, prerequisite for the former. Such cases often produced participation from civilian leaders associated with the pre-military period, or periods, of the of the state's political history. The common interest of such leaders in securing a return to civilian rule often resulted in co-operation between politicians who had previously been antagonistic towards each other, in order to secure their common goal of demilitarisation.

Having outlined the general background to the participation of old politicians in the struggle for democracy it would be useful to examine a number of case studies which provide empirical examples of wider trends. The Kenyan case provides examples of both long term opponents of the regime and more recent defectors from the ruling party involving themselves in pressure for democratisation. Oginga Odinga can be seen as belonging to the first category whilst Kenneth Matiba and Charles Rubia belong to the second. A member of the Luo ethnic group Odinga was originally a leading figure in the ruling Kenya African National Union (KANU) in the early post-independence period and was vice president of the party from 1960 to 1966. At independence in 1963 he joined the cabinet as minister of home affairs and in 1964 became Kenya's first vice president. In 1966 he broke from KANU to form a new party, the Kenya People's Union (KPU) which, for a time, was the main opposition grouping in Kenya. In 1969 the KPU was banned and Odinga was imprisoned for two years. For most of the 1970s and 1980s Odinga, often supported by his son Raila, continued as a critic of the government although he was prevented from presenting any form of electoral challenge. Matiba and Rubia belonged to a younger generation of politicians and had served as KANU MPs and as members of the cabinet. Both had previously shown themselves to be critical and independent-minded figures within the ruling group. In 1986 Rubia had spoken out against President Moi's decision to abandon the secret ballot in favour of the queuing system in elections and shortly afterwards used the floor of parliament to attack a government bill which eliminated security of tenure for the attorney general. Matiba had used his government office to attack corruption and inefficiency in the public sector. Both politicians succeeded in making powerful enemies within KANU and in 1988 were ousted in rigged elections.

In May 1990 Rubia and Matiba called a joint press conference to demand an end to the single-party system, an event which marked the beginning of the open public pressure for democracy in Kenya. The following month they applied for a license under the Public Order Act to organise a public meeting to state the case for a multi-party system. Their application was rejected by the government and for a time both men were imprisoned without trial. The detention of Rubia and Matiba provoked large-scale public demonstrations in Nairobi and other Kenyan towns which the Kenyan scholar Githu Muigai suggests 'became the focal point of the nascent pro-democracy movement'[75]. Demonstrators waved green branches to symbolise their nonviolence and gave two fingered salutes to indicate their support for multi-partyism. Attacks on the demonstrators by the police and the General Service Unit lead to mass violence which resulted in at least fifteen deaths. Although the government continued to reject a change to multi-partyism and to harass its supporters the pro-democracy movement gathered momentum from this time on. In February 1991 Odinga moved to challenge the government stance by announcing the formation of the National Democratic Party (NDP) which was immediately declared illegal. In August 1991 Odinga linked up with Rubia and Matiba to form the Forum for the Restoration of Democracy (FORD). Under the chairmanship of Odinga FORD became the major pressure group campaigning for the restoration of democracy in Kenya. Mass support for the aims of FORD was clearly demonstrated at several huge public demonstrations in various parts of Kenya. The pressure exerted by FORD was one of the major factors in forcing President Moi to abandon his opposition to multi-partyism and in December 1991 the government approved legislation to permit the formation of opposition parties, thus paving the way for pluralistic elections in December 1992. Unfortunately for the Kenyan opposition conflict between FORD leaders, particularly between Matiba and Odinga, produced a detrimental fragmentation of the opposition parties before the election took place. In August 1992 FORD split into two, FORD-Asili led by Matiba and FORD-Kenya led by Odinga. Unlike the MMD in Zambia FORD failed to maintain its unity once the goal of the restoration of democracy had been achieved. In January 1994 Oginga Odinga died from natural causes at the age of eighty two.

A comparison between the MMD in Zambia and FORD in Kenya in terms of the role of old politicians illustrates both similarities and differences. As was shown in an earlier section of this chapter trade unionists, particularly Frederick Chiluba and Jonathan Simakuni, played a predominant role in Zambia. There was no real equivelant heavyweight old politician to compare with Odinga. One reason for this was that the most significant figures in this category were already dead. Harry Nkumbula, the leader of the African National Congress (ANC) (which was the main opposition party in the early post-independence period) had died in 1983 from natural causes. The nearest equivelant to an Odinga figure had been Simon Kapwepwe who had been a major force within UNIP and Zambian vice president until he broke away to form the opposition United Progressive Party (UPP) in 1970. The UPP had been banned and Kapwepwe detained with the introduction of the single-party state in 1972. Although he was later released Kapwepwe was subject to further government harassment until he died of a stroke in 1980. One can only speculate as to the role that Nkumbula or Kapwepwe might have played in the more recent period. In spite of this other old politicians played an important role in the MMD. Arthur Wina, a former finance minister, and Vernon Mwaanga, a former foreign minister, were important in the establishment of the movement. The MMD vice-president Levi Mwanawasa had previously been Solicitor General before being sacked by

Kaunda in 1987. In commenting on the MMD Baylies and Szeftel suggest that it is 'tempting to conclude that, in 28 years in office, Kaunda managed to sack, detain, humiliate or otherwise frustrate enough individuals to form an opposition'[76].

A good example of the situation outlined earlier where civilian political leaders from an earlier period unite to pressurise a military government to democratise can be seen in the case of Ghana. Here the main organisation co-ordinating the pressure on the military government of Jerry Rawlings was the Movement for Freedom and Justice (MFJ) which was launched in Accra in August 1990. The description by Jeffries and Thomas of the MFJ as an 'alliance of all the former political groupings of the First, Second and Third Republics'[77] appears justified by the wide range of ideological groupings within the movement. The chairman of the MFJ was the distinguished Ghanaian historian Adu Boahen who was a veteran of struggles against the military authoritarianism of the Acheampong and Akuffo regimes of the 1970s[78]. Boahen can be identified with the moderate liberal tradition in Ghana but the MFJ also included many left-wing politicians including Johnny Hansen, Kwesi Pratt, and Akoto Ampaw. The movement also established itself amongst Ghanaian political leaders in exile in Britain including Boakye Dijan, J. H. Mensah and Joseph de Graft-Johnson[79]. As well as the revival of multi-party democracy the MFJ demanded the release of all political prisoners and an end to press censorship. Subsequently these demands were met by the regime but the extent to which this resulted from MFJ pressure is still argueable. Jeffries and Thomas capture the enigma well when they write that 'once most of the demands were conceded, they (the MFJ) liked to present the transition to constitutional government and multi-party elections as the result of their own pressure on a reluctant PNDC. Rawlings, on the other hand, argued that he was merely implementing his own, long-planned, democratising political agenda'[80].

Leaving aside such formidable questions one can still note the presence within the pressure for democracy of old politicians in most African states even though the importance of the role they played is variable. Apart from those discussed above several further important examples can be mentioned here. In Benin Nicephore Soglo, who participated in the democratisation process and was elected president in 1991, had previously been Minister of Finance between 1965 and 1967. In the Benin election four former presidents, Sorou Migan Apithy, Justin Tometin Ahomadegbe, Emile Derlin Zinsou, and Hubert Maga, could be observed leading political parties. In Tanzania prominent figures in the process included Oscar Kambona, a former secretary-general of the ruling party and Foreign Minister, and Abdullah Fundikira, a former Minister of Justice. In Cape Verde prominent leaders in the Movement for Democracy (MPD) included Antonio Mascarenhas Monteiro, formerly secretary general of the National

Assembly and president of the Supreme Court, and Carlos Veiga, formerly Attorney General. In the other island Lusophone state of Sao Tome and Principe leaders of the Democratic Convergence Party (PCD) included Daniel Dos Santos Daio, a former defence minister, and Miguel Trovoada who had been Prime Minister between 1975 and 1979. In Cameroon a leading figure in the pro-democracy movement was John Ngu Foncha who between 1961 and 1968 had been Vice President. Perhaps the most remarkable case of the re-emergence of an old heavyweight politician in the democratisation process is that of Ntsu Mokhehle in Lesotho. Mokhehle had been the leader of the Basotho Congress Party (BCP) which narrowly lost the pre-independence election of 1965. In the 1970 election Mokhehle and the BCP won but were prevented from coming to power by a coup led by the defeated Prime Minister, Leabua Jonathan. Following a period in detention Mokhehle spent most of his time as an opposition in exile before returning to Lesotho in 1989. He played a significant role in returning Lesotho to democracy and in the March 1993 general election he and his BCP emerged victorious. In April 1993 Mokhehle was sworn in as Prime Minister (Lesotho is a constitutional monarchy), thus coming to power at seventy five years of age and nearly a quarter of a century after first winning a general election.

Mass Protest

Up to this point the discussion of sources of pressure for democratisation has concentrated on the role organisations and elites which, with the partial exception of trade unions, has presented the pro-democracy movement as being predominantly middle class in composition. In order to present a more balanced and complete picture it is necessary to take into account the important role played by mass protest and action in the struggle for democracy[81]. States where mass action has played a significant part include Benin, Burkina Faso, Cameroon, Central African Republic, Comoros, Cote d'Ivoire, Equatorial Guinea, Gabon, Guinea, Guinea-Bissau, Kenya, Lesotho, Madagascar, Malawi, Mauritania, Niger, Nigeria, Sierra Leone, South Africa, Swaziland, Togo, Zaire, and Zambia.

Although mass demonstrations occurred in the above states it is extremely difficlut to clearly identify the social background of those participating. There is a shortage of empirical evidence, other than of an impressionistic and generalised nature, concerning who was actually engaged in these protests. In spite of this difficulty two observations can still be confidently made on the social composition of demonstrators. Firstly, the sheer magnitude of the numbers involved (estimates of some examples run up to 500,000 participants) very clearly shows that these cannot reasonably be portrayed as elite, middle class events. Genuine mass participation was clearly occurring. Secondly, all the evidence suggests that it was urban dwellers who were involved. The mass protests took place in towns and cities and there is no real indication of significant numbers of rural dwellers travelling into the urban areas to participate. However, although all of the mass protest has taken place in the urban areas it would be mistaken to imagine that the goal of democratisation conflicts with rural interests. This point is made by Thandika Mkandawire when he argues that 'although urban in its origin, the agitation calls for political structures which would, in fact, enfranchise a constituency much broader than the urban one'[82]. One could take this point further by noting that a competitive democracy would place a premium on gaining rural electoral support due to the numerical predominance of the peasantry in most African states. Political parties competing for votes in the rural areas would be forced to seek to persuade the peasants that their interests were central to party policy. Whilst it would be naively romantic to see this as necessarily leading to an empowerment of the peasantry there is no reason to believe that it would work against their interests. The urban character of mass protest in the struggle for democracy is probably better explained by organisational factors than it is by suggesting that it reflects a specifically urban set of interests. In passing one might also raise the question as to whether it makes sense to think in terms of identifiable sets of hostile interests which could meaningfully be categorised in a dichotomous fashion as 'urban' and 'rural'.

Before considering specific examples of the phenomenon it is necessary to try to examine two general questions relating to the incidence of mass protest. Why did this mass oppositional base develop? Why was it increasingly focused on the demand for multi-party democracy?

Mass protest is not in itself a particularly recent feature of African political life. Over the past couple of decades or more African people have frequently taken to the streets in forms of action ranging from relatively peaceful and organised demonstrations to violent and often anarchic riots[83] in response to unpopular policies and government malpractice. In authoritarian political systems mass action was often the only way in which the majority of the population could hope to influence government. Although the riots could be seen as expressions of political discontent they were frequently accompanied by outbreaks of criminal or quasi-criminal activity including the looting of bars and shops and random acts of violence against property.

The incidence of mass protest increased during the 1980s. This increase is partly explained by the problems caused by general economic decline in many African states and partly by the means introduced to deal with that decline such as the structural adjustment programmes (SAPS) imposed by the World Bank and the IMF[84]. Both the disease and the supposed medicine created discontent especially in the urban areas. In Zambia, for example, the government in late

1986 removed the subsidy on refined maize meal (which was the staple food in the urban areas) which resulted in an increase of 120% in its price. This produced several days of violent urban riots, especially in the Copperbelt towns of Ndola and Kitwe, which forced the government to reintroduce the subsidy. In June 1990 a further attempt to increase the maize meal price led to large-scale riots in Lusaka in which more than thirty people were killed. Urban discontent was fuelled by popular perceptions that the ruling elites appeared immune to the economic hardships suffered by most of the rest of the population. The very unequal impact of economic crisis produced a crisis of legitimacy for rulers who were increasingly seen as responsible for economic decline. Attempts by governments to crush the protests through coercive means exacerbated the crisis of legitimacy.

Although the precise time-scale varied from state to state it is possible to identify a qualitative change in the character of mass protest beginning around 1989. From then onwards the focus of mass protest moved from general dissatisfaction with the effects of corrupt and authoritarian rule to a much more specific demand for the democratisation of the political system through the introduction of multi-partyism. The latter was increasingly seen as the only viable alternative to the existing discredited systems of single-party and military rule. Closely tied to this was the view that the restoration of multi-party democracy provided the solution to the multiple difficulties facing African states. This perception has itself created a rather unrealistic level of ecpectation concerning the probable benefits of political reform which is likely to engender frustration when multi-partyism fails, as it surely must, in providing a panacea for all of Africa's problems. In focusing mass protest on demands for democracy the role of elite democracy activists in the churches, trade unions, professional groups and so on were clearly influential. Many mass demonstrations were staged specifically in support of such activists or in response to their arrest by government security forces. Examples of the latter include the mass protests following the arrest of leaders of the Forum for the Restoration of Democracy (FORD) in Kenya in November 1991 and the similar reaction in Malawi to the detention of Chakufwa Chihana in May 1992. This clear linkage between educated middle class activists and the masses served to undermine some of the last threadbare justifications for authoritarian rule which were still being advanced by some of Africa's leaders. The latter had frequently argued that support for multi-party democracy was only to be found amongst a few disgruntled elites who were out of touch with the wishes of the mass of the population. The latter, it had been argued, were perfectly happy with existing political arrangements and had no desire to change to what were portrayed as political systems which were alien to Africa. With vast numbers of African people on the streets demanding multi-party democracy this was no longer a tenable argument. This demonstration effect not only influenced critical groups in Africa and observers from abroad but also had a marked effect on some incumbent leaders who had misled themselves into believing their own rhetoric. This produced a loss of confidence in leaders who were accustomed only to carefully orchestrated demonstrations of support.

A further key factor in promoting mass pro-democracy protest was a growing belief amongst protesters that they could win. From 1989 on African people grew in confidence in their own efficacy and the belief that if enough of the population took to the streets to demand an end to single-party and military rule there was at least a reasonable prospect that this could be achieved. This change in perception was clearly influenced by events on a wider stage. The crucial role played by mass protest in overturning authoritarian political systems in Eastern Europe certainly had its impact. Of even greater relevance was the collective African experience. As the momentum of protest developed across Africa it became clear that in a significant number of cases mass protest was effective in bringing about desired change and that what had in the past seemed to be unassailable political monoliths were, in fact, extremely vulnerable to mass pressure. These perceptions encouraged people to risk participation in oppositional activity in spite of the fact that to do so carried with it very real dangers of physical harm. Although incumbent government leaders were vulnerable to pressure this did not prevent many of them from adopting tactics of harsh repression in response to mass protest. As in Eastern Europe the initial response of African leaders to the challenge of mass protest was often to use the police and the army in an attempt to crush public dissent. In so doing they frequently further weakened their already tenuous legitimacy. However, any discussion of mass pro-democracy protest in Africa must incorporate the realisation that those involved often risked being shot, beaten, raped, tear-gassed, or arrested by the security forces of the state.

A good example of the violent suppression of mass protest followed by victory for the pro-democracy movement is that of Mali. During 1990 there had been a steady build up public opposition to the regime of Moussa Traore and the development of several specifically pro-democracy groups, most notably the National Committee for Democratic Revival (CNID) and Alliance for Democracy in Mali (ADEMA). Traore had come to power in a coup as far back as 1968 and the regime was basically military in character in spite of the existence of a rather notional, and inappropriately named, single party, the Democratic Union of Malian People (UDPM). The first mass demonstration took place in early December 1990 when market traders, the majority of whom were women[85], protested against government economic policy especially new legislation relating to trading licences. The following week CNID organised a pro-democracy demonstration in which an estimated 10,000 took to the streets. On

New Year's Eve an estimated 30,000 people, waving a mixture of multi-party banners and copies of the Koran, demonstrated against the government. President Traore reacted by appointing the hard-line General Sekou Ly as minister of the interior. Ly's first action was to ban all anti-government demonstrations. Mass protests against the ban took place in mid-January in Bamako and in the regional centres of Bougouni, Kayes, Segou, and Sikasso. In Bamako troops used tear-gas and hand grenades to suppress the protest. Several people were killed and hundreds were arrested. Following a brief respite during the month of February pro-democracy protests resumed on 3rd and 4th March when around 100,000 demonstrators took to the streets of Bamako. Smaller demonstrations took place in the regional centres listed above and also in Gao, Kati, and Mopti. Following the refusal of the government to contemplate a transition to democracy mass protest continued to escalate and climaxed in three days of massive pro-democracy demonstrations from 22nd to 24th March. Government response to this was to unleash high levels of violence on the protestors which resulted in the deaths of at least 150 of them. In one incident alone in Bamako 65 demonstrators were burned to death when troops herded them into a shopping centre, blocked the exits, and set the centre on fire[86]. These events precipitated the total collapse of what was left of the claims to legitimacy of the corrupt authoritarianism of the Traore regime. Leading figures in the Malian armed forces accepted that the regime was no longer sustainable in either a moral or a practical sense. On March 26th Traore was deposed and detained by a section of the army led by Lt. Colonel Amadou Toumani Toure which announced the formation of the National Reconciliation Council (CNR). The new military leaders understood that the popular pressure for democracy was such that a retention of military rule under different leadership was not a viable option and within a few days of ousting Traore they announced a rapid transition to multi-party democracy. This transition culminated in democratic elections one year later.

Developments in neighbouring Niger exhibited similar patterns of popular protest[87] although ultimately the response of the government was different from that of Mali. In Niger the incumbent regime, a military based single-party state, was similar to that of Mali although rather less repressive. President Ali Saibou had come to power in 1987 following the death of his predecessor (and cousin) Seyni Kountche. In 1988 he instituted a political party, the National Movement for a Development Society (MNSD), with himself as its leader. In 1989 he was the only candidate in a presidential election. Mass public opposition to the regime began with a student protest, largely concerned with student grievances. On February 9th 1990 a student protest march in Niamey was attacked by soldiers and 14 unarmed students were killed: the incident became known as 'Black Friday'. The following Friday a much larger and more socially inclusive demonstration began after prayers in the central mosque in Niamey. This demonstration was held partly to protest at the killing of the students but it also focused on wider political demands for the democratisation of the political system. Over the next few months Saibou promised reform of the political system but refused to accept multi-partyism. In November the same year an estimated 100,000 protestors marched through Niamey in support of a general strike organised to pressure the government into accepting a transition to a multi-party system. Although Saibou remained in power he conceded the demands of the protestors and began organising the transition process which ended with the election of opposition leader Mahamane Ousmane in the presidential election held over two rounds in February and March 1993. In contrast to events in Mali Saibou's recognition of the overwhelming popular demand for democratisation in Niger meant that, with the exception of the killing of the students on 'Black Friday', the transition was very much less violent in Niger than it had been in Mali.

In terms of sheer numbers of participants involved in mass protest nowhere in Africa can match the case of Madagascar[88]. Here opposition was directed at the government of President Didier Ratsiraka who had been in power since 1975. Although the principle of full party pluralism had been accepted, in theory at least, in 1990 a new constitution introduced in May 1991 appeared to undermine reform by consolidating the power of the incumbent president. Opposition groups refused to accept the proposed constitution and organised a series of mass demonstrations mainly in the capital Antananarivo. The first demonstration on 10th June attracted around 100,000 participants and one on 19th June up to three times that number. By 18th July the numbers participating in mass protest numbered around 400,000. By August mass demonstrations had grown even larger but the government decided to resort to force to suppress opposition. On 10th August at least ten demonstrators were killed in the north-eastern port of Mahajanga. The following day a crowd of 500,000 marched on the presidential palace to demand full political reform. Although the organisers of the march had declared that it was to be non-violent the Presidential Security Regiment attacked the marchers using anti-tank rockets, grenades, and automatic weapons. More than 100 pro-democracy protestors were killed and many more were seriously injured. In the light of this slaughter it is all the more remarkable that when the opposition called a further mass demonstration in Antananarivo in September around 500,000 people again joined in. With his support within the army weakening Ratsiraka agreed to the creation of a transitional government which included opposition figures. Ratsiraka retained the presidency for the time being but was stripped of most of his executive powers. Although he stood as a presidential candidate in the two round elections of November 1992 and February 1993 he was defeated by the opposition leader Albert Zafy.

Government response to mass protest was not everywhere as punitive as it was in Mali and Madagascar but in almost all cases some coercion was used, at least in the first instance, against protestors. In some cases harsh coercion persisted as a continuing response to mass protest and resulted in very limited success for pro-democracy groups. A clear example of such a case is that of Togo. Here the highly authoritarian figure of President Gnassingbe Eyadema has frequently used the army to crush opponents. Unlike Mali where the army ultimately rejected this role the Togolese army has continued to act as a tool of authoritarian leadership. This situation is explained to a significant extent by the careful engineering of the composition of the army by Eyadema over a long period. Around three quarters of the Togolese army is from Eyadema's home region and most are from the same Kabre ethnic group. In addition to this most of the significant commanders within the army are individuals with close personal links to the president. In some cases these links are based on kinship as in the case of Eyadema's half-brother Colonel Donou Toyi Gnassingbe, and his son Lieutenant Ernest Gnassingbe[89]. In Togo it would appear that, for the moment, those struggling against democracy have the upper hand over those struggling for democracy.

In conclusion it can be said that mass protest added an important extra dimension to the internal pressures for democratisation in Africa during this period. The conjunction of elite and mass pressure achieved more than pressure arising from a single source would have been capable of. This actor oriented perspective adds support to the analytical position adopted by Larry Diamond when he writes that 'Democracy is not achieved simply by the hidden process of socioeconomic development bringing a country to a point where it has the necessary "prerequisites" for it. It is not delivered by the grace of some deus ex machina. And neither is it simply the result of the divisions, strategies, tactics, negotiations and stttlements of contending elites. Political scientists who conceive of democratic transitions simply in this way miss an important element. That element is struggle, personal risk-taking, mobilization and sustained, imaginative organization on the part of a large number of citizens'[90].

External Pressures

Although I have already argued that internal pressure for change has played a far more important role in the democratisation process in Africa than has external pressure, and also suggested a number of reasons why the recognition of this situation is so crucial, this is not to deny that outside factors have also been influential.

Any account of recent developments must incorporate the role played by events outside of Africa where the social actors involved had no intention of, or interest in, influencing Africa but where their activities did contribute to the momentum for change. In such cases one could talk of 'unintended external influences'. Here I am thinking particularly of the struggles against authoritarianism in other parts of the world, especially those in Eastern Europe, which took place in 1989. The mass-based popular uprisings in Eastern Europe were influential in an inspirational sense and also provided a practical demonstration that such pressures could lead to desired change. However, it was not the intention of those demonstrating on the streets of Czechoslovakia or Rumania that this should be the case. Events in Eastern Europe not only emboldened pro-democracy activists in Africa it also weakened the confidence of authoritarian leaders: in the memorable phrase of President Omar Bongo of Gabon 'the winds from the East are shaking the coconut trees'.

Having noted the unintended external influences it is necessary to turn to a consideration of deliberate attempts by external forces to influence African states, largely through the imposition of economic and political conditionalities. The deliberate attempt to engineer change in Africa has led to the raising of many questions of an ethical nature. It must be said that whatever attempts are made, or not made, by outside powers to influence events in Africa will inevitably lead to dispute and criticism. Vitriolic criticism will follow from whatever decisions are made relating to economic and/or political conditionalities: for outside powers it is very much a question of 'damned if you do: damned if you don't'. Economic conditionalities imposed since the early 1980s have for the most part concentrated on reducing the interventionist economic role of the state, emphasising producer (largely rural peasant) interests at the expense of consumer (largely urban) interests, and restoring some credibility to currency exchange rates. Those applying economic conditionality (World Bank, IMF, foreign governments etc.) have been widely criticised for undermining the sovereignty of African states, imposing a foreign market-based model, and detracting from (or destroying) the welfare capacities of the African state. On the other hand non-application of economic conditionalities has been criticised for supporting the perpetuation of a prebendalised, clientelistic, rent-seeking state structure, of participating in the exploitation of rural peasant producers by government marketing boards, and of colluding in the development of a debt crisis in many African states. Comparable sets of criticisms have been made relating to questions of political conditionality especially those concerning democracy and human rights. Where foreign agencies attach political conditions to aid they are (again) accused of undermining sovereignty, imposing alien and inappropriate systems of rule, and enforcing a neo-colonial structure. On the other side of the coin failure to impose political conditionality will lead to accusations of providing support for dictatorial leaders who are oppressing their own people and acting in a way which is contrary to the efforts of African activists who are seeking to liberalise and democratise their own political systems.

In Africa questions of 'foreign interference' are all the more delicate and productive of emotional responses because of the historical record of European imperialist involvement which only came to an end three decades or so ago. Because political and economic liberalisation will inevitably create winners and losers in African states we are dealing with a highly contested political arena. Whatever role outsiders decide to play in relation to this contestation they are bound to provoke antagonistic reactions from, at least, some of the participants. Any notion that there sets of policies on external influences on Africa waiting to be discovered which will command universal support within and without the continent must be regarded as fanciful in the extreme.

For well over a decade now the economic links between African states and outside donor agencies have frequently been based on the insistence by the latter that funding can only be granted if certain economic conditions are met. In most cases this has involved the implementation of structural adjustment programmes (SAPs) by African governments under the influence and guidance of these outside agencies. Whilst the precise details of SAPs vary considerably from one country to another a pervasive theme has been the reduction of what are seen to be the negative aspects of state intervention in the economy. Since 1987 there has been a complementary social dimensions of adjustment (SDA) programme, the major aim of which is to ameliorate the potential and negative social effects of SAPs. Assessments of the economic effects of SAPS and SDAs have been a matter of great debate within the literature without producing any generally agreed conclusions[91].

Initially at least economic conditionality was aimed at the restructuring of African economies rather than having any particular effect on African political systems. However, this economistic view was always rather blinkered because if and when economic restructuring took place it was almost inevitably going to have a series of knock-on effects on political structures. In trying to re-shape and reduce the economic role of the state (by making it less interventionist) economic conditionalities were bound to have an effect on the political configurations which had developed in association with the interventionist state. Evidence suggests that in many cases a reduction in the role of the state had the effect of weakening the position of governing elites who had used their control over the economy to construct support coalitions of a clientelist type. The ability to 'buy' support through prebendalism, for example, declined as the number and importance of prebends declined. Liberalisation of currency exchange procedures significantly reduced the benefits for those who had been able to use political power to their advantage on the basis of the huge discrepancies between 'official' exchange rates and the 'real' value of those currencies. Liberalistaion of export produce marketing reduced the opportunities of those in control of the hitherto monopolistic state marketing boards (most of which had been established under colonial rule) to manipulate the gaps which existed between world commodity prices and producer prices. In Ghana, for example, producer prices for cocoa rose from 20% of world price to 51% between 1983 and 1992 as a result of structural adjustment.

These developments produced a crisis amongst the state class which was difficult for government leaders to control. At a sub-elite level bureaucratic retrenchment created further hostility towards governments and political patrons who were left with little patronage to dispense to their clients. The paradox was that governments whose position had been weakened by a history of steady, or in some cases spectacular, economic decline now found themselves further weakened politically by the very measures put in place in an attempt to correct that decline. Such regimes found themselves facing a major crisis of legitimacy which made them far more vulnerable to pressures for democratisation which were growing within the domestic political system (and which were examined earlier in this chapter). These effects of economic conditionalities should not be seen as initiating this crisis of legitimacy but rather as exacerbating a crisis which had been growing for some time previously. The origins of this crisis lay in a combination of economic failure, government inefficiency and corruption, and the alienation of large sections of the population brought about by a long term denial of human and civil rights under a heavy-handed authoritarian rule. Economic conditionalities did not have the objective of promoting democratisation but on balance they acted as a pressure for political reform.

Around the end of the 1980s a wide range of external agencies began to turn their attention to the nature of African political systems as a key factor to be considered when making decisions over aid and investment. This marked a change of focus with political considerations becoming more important in the decision making process. This development resulted from three main sets of influences. Firstly, the collapse of the Soviet Union resulted in changed perceptions of the strategic importance of authoritarian but pro-Western political leaders in Africa. Denial of Western assistance no longer carried the danger of such leaders switching their support to the Soviet 'enemy'. Secondly, there was a growing realisation amongst outside agencies that the application of purely economic conditionalities was inadequate to deal with the economic crisis of Africa. Without simultaneous political reform it was unlikely that economic reform could be sustained because existing political arrangements in many states were simply not conducive to economic development. Thirdly, as we have seen, there was a very rapid growth of pro-democracy movements within Africa which were exerting pressure for political change on authoritarian regimes. Africa's indigenous democratic political reformers were well ahead of external agencies:

I cannot, for example, think of a single case in Africa where political conditionalities were imposed before domestic pressure made itself felt. This point has rather more than mere chronological importance because it shows that outside agencies were in the position of having to decide whether to support already existing domestic pressures for political reform or to ignore them.

The evidence from the late 1980s and early 1990s suggests that, far from initiating political change, outside agencies were responding in a somewhat cautious and hesitant manner to a momentum for change which was already well established in Africa. This caution and hesitancy may be explained by a number of factors. The situation in Africa facing outside agencies was unprecedented and was taking place at a time of major change within the global political system produced by the end of the cold war which had shaped the system for over four decades. The very newness of the circumstances initially produced a rather careful and conservative reaction because policy makers were rather unsure as to how they should react. There was also an already established diffidence over not wishing to be seen to be imposing 'alien systems' coupled with genuine, and not unreasonable, concern as to whether competitive democratic systems were sustainable in African states. Finally, many outside agencies, the World Bank in particular, saw their mission as a 'non-political' one which made them hesitant to become involved with what were clearly political matters. An initial result of this was that many agencies pledged their support for 'governance' rather than 'democracy'. I know that I am not alone in finding 'governance' an elusive and slippery concept to deal with[92]. An examination of the literature dealing with 'governance' indicates two major types of definition. One type of definition is extremely vague and offers little scope for anyone hoping to operationalise it in policy making over political conditionality. Goran Hyden, the editor of a recent major book on the topic, argues that 'governance, as defined here, is the conscious management of regime structures with a view to enhancing the legitimacy of the public realm'[93]. The other type of definition tends to consist of a check-list of characteristics such as government accountability, freedom of speech and media, freedom of political association and so on. In such cases it is difficult to see how governance could be institutionalised other than through a freely democratic competitive multi-party system. Certainly it would appear that such definitions would decisively exclude the major alternative institutional forms of the single-party state or military rule.

This attempt to make external support for democracy implicit rather than explicit carried with it the danger of sending somewhat ambiguous signals to ruling elites in Africa. However, growing internal pressure for democratisation (in which the demand for multi-partyism was unambiguous) coupled with a number of relatively successful democratic transitions in the short term (whatever may be the prospects for long term consolidation) in states such as

Benin, Cape Verde, Sao Tome and Principe, and Zambia contributed to the development of a more explicitly pro-democracy emphasis in political conditionality. Many Western governments, for example, became more willing to make financial aid dependent on freedom for opposition parties, competitive elections, and constitutional reform than had hitherto been the case.

Although this chapter has argued that external pressure, of which political conditionality has been the most important element, has played a relatively minor supporting role in promoting change it is true that the contribution has been crucial in affecting change in some cases. Kenya and Malawi are instructive examples of cases where domestic pressures for democratisation were very strong but where the final decision of highly authoritarian leaders to respond to those pressures was crucially influenced by the addition of externally imposed pressure. In both states internal pressure to end the single-party system was exerted on the regime by church groups, trade unions, human rights groups, and, perhaps most importantly, by gigantic pro-democracy demonstrations. For a time the reaction of Presidents Moi and Banda was to reject these calls for change and adopt repressive measures to deal with the Kenyan and Malawian pro-democracy movements. Whilst it cannot be proved that these two leaders would not have eventually capitulated to the demands of their internal opponents without outside pressure it does appear that such pressure did play an important role. In Kenya the pressure had been building for some time. As early as 1990 the Scandinavian countries had threatened to cut off aid if internal demands for democracy continued to be ignored. Subsequent to this foreign diplomats in Kenya, particularly the US ambassador Smith Hempstone, publicle criticised government intransigence on the issue and gave vocal public support to the pro-democracy movement. In November 1991 aid donors attending the Kenya Consultative Group meeting in Paris agreed to withold aid worth $1 billion until significant political reform had taken place. The following month President Moi announced the end of the single-party state and promised competitive elections, which were held one year later. In Malawi the decision of Western donor nations to withold all but some humanitarian aid (mainly aimed at providing assistance for refugees from Mozambique) was instrumental in persuading President Banda to hold a referendum on proposals for a multi-party system in June 1993. The rejection of single-partyism in the referendum led to the competitive elections of May 1994 when Banda, hitherto a 'president for life' was voted out of office. If one were to seek a single event to encapsulate the extent of recent political change in Africa it would be hard to match this peaceful ousting through the ballot box of this most dictatorial of dictators.

It can be argued that Kenya and Malawi mark the high point of the application of externally imposed political conditionality but even here this has to be set against the greater role played by internal pressure. Thus it would be incorrect to talk of outsiders 'imposing democracy on Africa' because this would imply a contradiction which does not exist (that of imposing choice). One cannot talk of democracy being imposed on Kenya and Malawi although one might be able to talk of it being imposed on two particularly authoritarian leaders who were unwilling to respond to the demands of their own people. In Malawi, for example, political conditionality helped to create the conditions in which, through a referendum, Malawians were able to decide whether they wanted a multi-party system and, having decided in the affirmative, to further decide whether they wanted Banda to continue ruling. In circumstances like this outside pressure can be seen as helping to facilitate a democratic transition by supporting the conditions in which African peoples (rather than just ruling elites) decide their own destiny. As the cases of Kenya and Malawi indicate an internal conflict exists between those who wish to democratise the political system (admittedly for a variety of motives) and those who wish to resist democratisation. Providing some support for the former by exerting pressure on the latter would appear a morally defensible form of intervention. Until recently South Africa appeared to be the only case where such a policy was widely deemed to be acceptable[94].

Conclusions

From around the end of the 1980s almost all of Africa's authoritarian state structures have been subjected to a very wide and diverse set of pressures for democratisation. For convenience of exposition this chapter has examined the sources of pressure individually but it was the conjunction and simultaneity of these pressures which created the powerful momentum for political change. Forces which in isolation from each other might have achieved little or nothing in contesting the hegemony of the authoritarian state proved more effective in combination and provided a challenge which was impossible to ignore and difficult to suppress. Whatever the problems which lay ahead there was a new optimism in Africa concerning the possibility of a 'second liberation'[95].

Notes

(1) Jean-Francois Bayart, *The State in Africa: The Politics of the Belly*, London, Longman, 1993, p.x.
(2) Naomi Chazan, 'Africa's Democratic Challenge', *World Policy Journal*, Vol.9, No.2, Spring 1992, p.281.
(3) Christopher Clapham, 'Democratisation in Africa: Obstacles and Prospects', *Third World Quarterly*, Vol.14, No.3, 1993, p.430.

(4) Claude E. Welch Jr., 'The Single Party Phenomenon in Africa', *TransAfrica Forum*, Fall 1991, p.85.

(5) Michael Bratton and Nicolas van der Walle, 'Toward Governance in Africa: Popular Demands and State Responses', in Goran Hyden and Michael Bratton (eds.) *Governance and Politics in Africa*, Boulder and London, Lynne Rienner, 1992, p.29.

(6) Tom Young, 'Elections and Electoral Politics in Africa', Africa, Vol.63, No.3, 1993, p.299. In an exhaustive search through the literature on recent democratisation in Africa the only other Africanist scholar I came across to stress the primacy of external pressure was Barry Munslow who argued that 'the move for democratisation is being driven primarily from outside the African continent'. See Munslow, 'Democratisation in Africa', *Parliamentary Affairs*, Vol.46, No.4, October 1993, p.483.

(7) Bratton and van der Walle, (1992), op. cit., p.48.

(8) Richard Joseph, 'Africa: The Rebirth of Political Freedom', *Journal of Democracy*, Vol.2, No.4, 1991, p.13. Martin A. Klein supports this view when he writes that 'these stirring events have played themselves out within Africa and the prime movers have been Africans, often courageous people defying intimidation, death threats and torture'. See Klein 'Back to Democracy: Presidential Address to the 1991 Annual Meeting of the African Studies Association', *African Studies Review*, Vol.35, No.3, December 1992, p.5. The Ghanaian scholar Adu Boahen is particularly scathing in his attack on those who downplay the role of African people. He argues that such an approach 'reflects both ignorance and a racist belief that Africans are incapable of initiating anything without outside assistance'. See Boahen, 'Military Rule and Multiparty democracy: The Case of Ghana', *Africa Demos*, Vol.1, No.2, January 1991, p.5.

(9) Peter Anyang' Nyong'o, 'Africa: The Failure of One-Party Rule', Journal of Democracy, Vol.3, No.1, January 1992, p.94.

(10) Gilbert Keith Bluwey, 'Democracy at Bay: The Frustrations of African Liberals', in B. Caron, A. Gboyega, and E. Osaghae (eds.) *Democratic Transition in Africa*, Ibadan, Centre For Research, Documentation and University Exchange (CREDU), 1992, p.43.

(11) For a discussion of this earlier critical tradition see Gatian F. Lungu, 'The Church, Labour and the Press in Zambia: The Role of Critical Observers in a One-Party State', *African Affairs*, Vol.85, No.340, July 1986, pp.385-410. However, Christian churches have not always acted as a critical voice under authoritarian regimes and in some cases have actually played a supportive role in relation to authoritarian government. For one example see Paul Gifford, *Christianity and Politics in Doe's Liberia*, Cambridge, Cambridge University Press, 1993. Gifford suggests that 'Liberian Christianity served

essentially (if unconsciously) to divert attention from the social situation and to leave Doe unchallenged in his mismanagement and corruption' (p.7). For a most useful collection of essays on the more recent period see Paul Gifford (ed.) *The Christian Churches and the Democratisation of Africa*, Leiden, E. J. Brill, 1995.

(12) Jennifer A. Widner, 'Kenya's Slow Progress Toward Multiparty Politics', *Current History*, Vol.91, No.565, 1992, p.216.

(13) See, for example, L. H. Gann, 'Malawi, Zambia and Zimbabwe' in Peter Duignan and Robert H. Jackson (eds), *Politics and Government in African States*, 1960-18985, London, Croom Helm, 1986, especially pp.191-194. For a slightly different perspective on Banda's hold on power see, Peter G. Forster, 'Culture, Nationalism and the Invention of Tradition in Malawi', *The Journal of Modern African Studies*, Vol.32, No.3, 1994, pp.477-497.

(14) Cited in Jackson and Rosberg, (1982), op. cit., p.166.

(15) In other African states where authoritarian governments have controlled the official media there has normally remained a vital, and often highly critical, realm of public debate in the uncontrolled informal sector. See, for example, Stephen Ellis, 'Tuning in to Pavement Radio', *African Affairs*, Vol.88, No.352, July 1989, pp.321-330: Achille Mbembe, 'Power and Obscenity in the Post-Colonial Period: The Case of Cameroon', in James Manor (ed.) *Rethinking Third World Politics*, London, Longman, 1991, pp.166-182: Stephen Ellis, 'Rumour and Power in Togo', *Africa*, Vol.63, No.4, 1993, pp.462-476.

(16) Landeg White, *Magamero: Portrait of an African Village*, Cambridge, Cambridge University Press, 1987, p.245.

(17) The full text of the letter was published in *Index on Censorship*, Vol.21, No.5, May 1992, pp.15-17.

(18) *Malawi News*, Blantyre, March 14-20 1992, p.6.

(19) The text of the letter is contained in *The Malawi Democrat*, Blantyre, June5-18, 1992, p.3.

(20) Ibid. p.2.

(21) Patricia Stamp, 'The Politics of Dissent in Kenya' *Current History*, Vol.90, No.555, May 1991, p.208.

(22) Quoted in Jennifer A. Widner, *The Rise of the Party State in Kenya: From Harambee to Nyao*, Berkeley, University of California Press, 1992, p.191.

(23) Quoted in Stamp (1991), op. cit. p.206.

(24) Ibid.

(25) David Throup, 'Elections and Political Legitimacy in Kenya', Africa, Vol.63, No.3, 1993, p.389.

(26) For a discussion of such factions within the SACP see Tom Lodge, 'Post-Modern Bolsheviks: South African Communists in Transition', *South*

Africa International, April 1992, pp.172-179. Govan Mbeki's views are presented in Mbeki, *Learning from Robben Island: The Prison Writings of Gavan Mbeki*, London, James Currey, 1991.

(27) L. H. Gann and Peter Duignan, *Hope for South Africa?*, Stanford, Hoover Institution Press, 1991, p.20.

(28) An abbreviated version of the Kairos document is included as an appendix in Tom Lodge and Bill Nasson, *All Here and Now: Black Politics in South Africa in the 1980s*, London, C. Hurst and Co., 1992, pp.344-349.

(29) See Catharine Newbury, 'Rwanda: Recent Debates over Governance and Development', in Hyden and Bratton (eds.) (1992), op. cit. pp. 215-216.

(30) See Janet MacGaffey, 'Initiatives from Below: Zaire's Other Path to Social and Economic Restructuring', in Hyden and Bratton (eds), op. cit. p.258.

(31) See Eduardo Serpa, 'Madagascar: Change and Continuity', *Africa Insight*, Vol.21, No.4, 1991, pp.233-245.

(32) See Richard Jeffries and Clare Thomas, 'The Ghanaian Elections of 1992', *African Affairs*, Vol.92, No.365, July 1993, p.341.

(33) See Chris Allen, 'Goodbye to all That: The Short and Sad Story of Socialism in Benin', in Hughes ed., (1992), op. cit. pp.63-81.

(34) For a fascinating study of how Islam could be used to support authoritarian rule and to oppose it see C. S. Whitaker, *The Politics of Tradition: Continuity and Change in Northern Nigeria 1946-1966*, Princeton, Princeton University Press, 1970.

(35) A. S. Wamala, 'The Role of Workers in the Struggle towards Multi-Party Democracy: Africa's Colonial and Post-colonial Experience', *Eastern Africa Social Science Research Review*, Vol.8, No.1, January 1992, p.57.

(36) See, for example, Anirudha Gupta, 'Trade Unionism and Politics on the Copperbelt', in William Tordoff (ed.), *Politics in Zambia*, Manchester, Manchester University Press, 1974, pp.288-319. See also Robert H. Bates, *Unions, Parties and Political Development: A Study of the Mineworkers in Zambia*, New Haven, Yale University Press, 1971.

(37) See Robert B. Charlick, Niger: *Personal Rule and Survival in the Sahel*, Boulder, Westview Press, 1991, especially pp.84-88.

(38) See Jibrin Ibrahim, 'From Political Exclusion to Popular Participation in Democratic Transition in Niger Republic', in Caron, Gboyega and Osaghae (eds), op. cit. pp.51-68.

(39) Gilchrist Olympio is the son of former president Sylvanus Epiphanio Olympio who was overthrown in a coup d'etat in 1963 when, it is widely believed, he was personally murdered by Eyadema.

(40) Interview with Enoch Chihana, *Africa Report*, Vol.38, No.1, January-February 1993, p.30.

(41) Quoted in Melinda Ham, 'Malawi: Loosening the Reins', *Africa Report*, ibid., p.29.

(42) Anthony Lemon, *Apartheid in Transition*, Aldershot, Gower Publishing Company, 1987, p.334-335.

(43) Tom Lodge in Lodge and Nasson (1992), op. cit., p.85.

(44) The question of using the colours of the ANC may appear trivial but this is far from true. In pre-1990 South Africa the use of the black, green, and gold carried powerful symbolic resonances.

(45) Rich Mkhondo, *Reporting South Africa*, London, James Currey, 1993, p.128.

(46) Jibrin Ibrahim, 'The State, Accumulation and Domestic Forces in Nigeria', in Lars Rudebeck (ed.), *When Democracy Makes Sense: Studies in the Democratic Potential of Third world Popular Movements*, Uppsala, Working Group for the Study of Development strategies, 1992, p.117.

(47) See, for example, Scott Davidson, *Human Rights*, Buckingham, Open University Press, 1993, especially pp. 152-162.

(48) The point was underlined by (then) President Jawara of The Gambia in a speech he gave to the Commonwealth Trust in October 1991. He observed that 'the Commission has been receiving complaints in respect of several countries. They have mounted investigations on the complaints received, but its impact on governments and the people at large have yet to be felt'. He further argued that 'the Charter which was drafted in an era of single party regimes cannot meet the aspirations of Africans today'. See Alhaji Sir Dawda Kairaba Jawara, 'The Commonwealth and Human Rights', *The Round Table*, No. 321, 1992, p.42.

(49) The position of the NBA was to some extent compromised in 1989 when the military government, through a combination of intimidation and bribery, forced the ousting of its leader Alao Aka-Bashorun, a human rights activist. See *Nigeria on the Eve of Change to What?*, Washington D.C., Africa Watch report, 1991, p.21.

(50) For an important examination of the CLO written by one of its major participants see Clement Nwanko, 'The Civil Liberties Organisation and the Struggle for Democracy in Nigeria' in Larry Diamond (ed.) *The Democratic Revolution: Struggles for Freedom and Pluralism in the Developing World*, New York, Freedom House, 1992, pp.105-123. The title of Nwanko's article indicates the essential linkage he sees between democracy and human rights.

(51) *Campaign for Democracy Bulletin No.I: The Human Rights Agenda of the Two official Parties in Nigeria*, Lagos, 1991, p.1.

(52) Ibid. p.8.

(53) Gibson Kamau Kuria, 'Confronting Dictatorship in Kenya', *Journal of Democracy*, Vol.2, No.4, 1991, p.124.

(54) See Githu Muigai, 'Kenya's Opposition and the Crisis of Governance', *Issue*, Vol.21, No.1-2, 1993, p.28.

(55) See, for example, his own account in Gitobu Imanyara, 'Kenya: Indecent Exposure', *Index on Censorship*, Vol.21, No.4, April 1992, pp.21-22.

(56) Sithole, 1993, op.cit., p.4.

(57) For example he made this linkage when delivering the keynote address at the International Alert seminar on 'Conflict Resolution in Africa' in London in January 1994.

(58) Melchior Ndadaye was subsequently assassinated in an attempted coup d'etat in October 1993. in April 1994 his successor Cyprien Ntaryamira, an agronomist, was also assassinated (for details see chapter 6).

(59) See Sukhwant Singh Nannan, 'Africa: The Move Towards Democracy', *Strategic Analysis*, Vol.14, No.10, 1992, p.1224. Keith Somerville reports an interview he had with Kenneth Kaunda of Zambia in 1991 in which the latter suggested that one of his reasons for agreeing to abandon the single-party system was that seven out of eight million Zambians had been born since independence. Kaunda apparently recognised that younger Zambians 'wanted a greater say in national affairs than their elders who had known the restrictions of colonial rule and had taken part in the struggle for independence'. See Keith Somerville, 'Africa: Is there a Silver Lining?', *The World Today*, November 1994, pp.215-218.

(60) John A. Wiseman, 'Urban Riots in West Africa, 1977-1985', *The Journal of Modern African Studies*, Vol.24, No.3, 1986, pp.509-518.

(61) For an excellent account of the often fraught relations between the government and the University of Zimbabwe see Angela P. Cheater, 'The University of Zimbabwe: University, National University,, State University, or Party University?', *African Affairs*, Vol.90, No. 359, 1991, pp.189-205.

(62) See Goran Hyden, 'The Efforts to Restore Intellectual Freedom In Africa', Issue, Vol.20, No.1, Winter 1991, p.10.

(63) Lucy Komisar, 'The Claws of Dictatorship in Zaire', *Dissent*, Summer 1992, pp.328-329. see also Winsome J. Leslie, *Zaire: Continuity and Political Change in an Oppressive State*, Boulder, Westview Press, 1993, pp.53-54.

(64) An interesting extension of the media contribution in support of democracy has been the circulation of tape cassettes carrying pro-democracy speeches and songs. For a discussion of this phenomenon in Kenya see 'Kenya's Subversive Cassettes', *New African*, September 1990, p.18.

(65) The main exception to this is Tanzania which has a daily and a weekly in KiSwahili. See Kwame Karikari, 'Africa: The Press and Democracy', *Race and Class*, Vol.34, No.3, 1993, pp.55-56.

(66) For details and a more general discussion of the Zambian press see Robert C. Moore, *The Political Reality of Freedom of the Press in Zambia*, Lanham, University Press of America, 1992.

(67) *Presidential and National Assembly Elections in Zambia: Report of the Commonwealth Observer Group*, London, Commonwealth Secretariat, 1992, p.11.

(68) Bratton (1992), op. cit., p.90.

(69) See, for example, Adigun A. B. Agbaje, *The Nigerian Press: Hegemony and the Social Constitution of Legitimacy 1960-1983*, New York, Edwin Mellen Press, 1992.

(70) For an account of the problems of the magazine written by one of its founders see Ray Ekpu, 'Nigeria's Embattled Fourth Estate', in Diamond (ed.) 1992, op. cit., pp.181-200.

(71) Quoted in *West Africa*, London, No.3958, 2-8 August, 1993, p.1353.

(72) Karikari op. cit.

(73) See Robert H. Bates, 'The Impulse to Reform in Africa', in Widner (ed.), 1994, op. cit. p.22.

(74) Michael Bratton, 'Economic Crisis and Political Realignment in Zambia', in Widner (ed.), op. cit., p.103.

(75) Mugai (1993), op. cit. p.27.

(76) Baylies and Szeftel (1992), op. cit., p.80.

(77) Jeffries and Thomas, (1992), op. cit. p.334.

(78) For an account by Boahen of the aims of the MFJ see Boahen, (1991), op. cit., p.5.

(79) See Kevin Shillington, *Ghana and the Rawlings Factor*, London, Macmillan, 1992, p.171.

(80) Jeffries and Thomas (1992), op. cit,, p.335.

(81) Mass demonstrations have been a common part of the pressure for democracy in many parts of the world in recent years. Samuel Huntington writing on democratisation in Latin America and Eastern Europe notes that 'in virtually all countries a central tactic of the opposition was the mass rally, march, or demonstration against the regime. Such demonstrations mobilize and focus discontent, enable the opposition to test the breadth of its support and the effectiveness of its organization, generate publicity that is often international in scope, enhance divisions within the regime on the appropriate response, and, if the regime responds violently, can create martyrs and new causes for outrage'. see Huntington, (1991), op. cit., p.204.. See also Stephen Zunes, 'Unarmed Insurrections Against Authoritarian Governments in the Third World: A New Kind of Revolution', *Third World Quarterly*, Vol.15, No.3, 1994, pp.403-426.

(82) Thandika Mkandawire, 'The Political Economy of Development with a

Democratic Face', in Giovanni Andrea Cornia, Rolph van der Hoeven, Thandika Mkandawire (eds.) *Africa's Recovery in the 1990s: From Stagnation and Adjustment to Human Development*, Basingstoke, Macmillan, 1992, p.306.

(83) Wiseman (1986), op. cit., presents a comparative study of 46 cases. See also, C. O. Lerche, 'Social Strife in Nigeria 1971-78', *Journal of African Studies*, Vol.9, No.1, 1982, pp.2-12.

(84) Some writers would dispute the economic explanation of mass protest. Bratton and van der Walle, for example, argue that 'it is ultimately misleading to interpret political protest in strictly economic terms'. They suggest that 'there is little or no correlation between the intensity of political unrest on the one hand and the severity of economic crisis or austerity measures on the other' and that 'a purely economic argument fails to explain why the unrest happened when it did' See Bratton and van der Walle (1992), op. cit. p.41.

(85) Although the evidence is scattered and uncoordinated it does suggest that in many African states women played a significant role in pro-democracy mass protest. In August 1992 in Conakry, the capital of Guinea, six women demonstrators were killed when the army fired on a women's protest march organised by the National Democratic Forum (*New African*, November 1992, p.19). In Kenya women protestors have been inspired by the feminist critic of government Wangari Maathai who leads Kenya's Greenbelt Movement. In 1989 Maathai led mass protests against the decision by KANU to build a prestigious office block in a Nairobi park and so destroy one of the few amenities available to the urban poor (see Stamp, 1991, op. cit.).

(86) See Jacques Mariel Nzouankeu, 'The Role of the National Conference in the Transition to Democracy in Africa: The Cases of Benin and Mali', *Issue*, Vol.21, No.1-2, 1993, pp.44-50.

(87) See Jibrin Ibrahim 'From Political Exclusion...', 1992, op. cit.

(88) See Serpa, 1991, op. cit.

(89) See Ellis, 1993, op. cit.

(90) Larry Diamond, 'Introduction', in Diamond ed. (1992), p.5.

(91) See, for example, Peter Gibbon and Yusuf Bangura (eds.) *Authoritarianism, Democracy and Adjustment: The Politics of Economic Reform in Africa*, Uppsala, Scandinavian Institute of African Studies, 1992: Aderanti Adepoju, (ed.), *The Impact of Structural Adjustment on the Population of Africa*, London, James Currey, 1993: Mick Moore (ed.), *Good Government?*, special issue of IDS Bulletin, Vol.24, No.1, January 1993: A. B. Chikwanda, 'Zambia: The Challenge Posed Starkly', *International Review of Administrative Sciences*, Vol.59, 1993, pp.579-583: Christine

Jones and Miguel A. Kiguel, 'Africa's Quest for Prosperity: Has Adjustment Helped?', *Finance and Development*. June 1994, pp.2-5: Ishrat Husain, 'Results of Adjustment in Africa: Selected Cases', *Finance and Development*, June 1994, pp.6-9: Gavin Williams 'Why Structural Adjustment is Necessary and Why It Doesn't Work', *Review of African Political Economy*, No.60, 1994, pp.214-225: World Bank, *Adjustment in Africa*, Oxford, Oxford University Press, 1994.

(92) Thomas M. Callaghy, for example, writes of 'the inability of the international financial institutions to come up with a clear and operational definition of governance'. See Callaghy, 'State, Choice, and Context: Comparative Reflections on Reform and Intractability', in David E. Apter and Carl G. Rosberg (eds), *Political development and the New Realism in Sub-Saharan Africa*, Charlottesville and London, University Press of Virginia, 1994, p.187.

(93) Hyden and Bratton (eds) 1992, op. cit. p.7.

(94) Until the early 1990s anti-apartheid groups in many parts of the world had lobbied, with considerable success, for the imposition of a wide range of sanctions on South Africa. The explicit aim of such sanctions was to bring pressure to bear on the South African government to reform its undemocratic, racially structured, political system. It was argued that the oppressive nature of the South African political system made this a morally legitimate activity (a view, by the way, with which I completely agreed). However, this did raise the question of whether double standards were being applied. Was it more morally reprehensible for a white government to oppress the majority of its population than it was for a black government to do so, as was clearly the case in many African states? To argue that South Africa was a 'special case' would seem to suggest that black ruled states should be judged within a framework of lower moral standards and responsibilities than white ruled ones. This seems to me a supremely rascist line of argument.

(95) Although the terms 'second liberation' and 'second independence' have been widely used within the academic literature they are reported to have originated with the people of the Kwilu region of western Zaire. See Schmitz and Hutchful, 1992, op. cit, p. 35.

4 Preparing the Ground for Democratic Transitions: National Conferences and Referendums

As a result of the pressures for democratic change examined in the previous chapter the majority of African governments conceded the necessity for some form of democratisation of the political system. Although in some cases this concession was grudging and superficial, at least to begin with, it did mark the beginning of a new transitional phase in the process. In moving from authoritarian to more democratic political systems many African states proceeded by way of organised national conferences and/or the holding of referendums. The latter were more widely used than the former but both provided institutional mechanisms which were utilised in the progression from the agreement to democratise to its implementation. As with all aspects of the struggle for democracy in Africa there were important differences between different states. Some states did not use either national conferences or referendums. In those states which did, however, there are enough similarities to make a comparative examination worthwhile.

National Conferences

The use of the national conference in the transitional phase is almost exclusively a Francophone phenomenon; so much so that it may be tempting to see it as representing a partial resurrection of the French political tradition of the States-General[1]. National conferences took place in Benin, Burkina Faso, Chad, Comoros, Congo, Gabon, Mali, Niger, Togo, and Zaire. In addition there were unsuccessful opposition demands for them in Cameroon, Central African Republic, Cote d'Ivoire and Guinea. In marked contrast not one Anglophone state has utilised the national conference mechanism (although some opposition groups in Kenya and Nigeria have frequently demanded one). The only exceptions to this Francophone near-monopoly have been Lusophone Guinea-Bissau and Ethiopia, whose unique history places it in a category by itself. Although the Convention for a Democratic South Africa (CODESA), which drew up the new interim South African constitution exhibited some of the features of a national conference the absence of non-party groups from its composition marks an important difference. The use or non-use of the national conference provides a comparatively rare example of a marked divergence between the democratisation experiences of Francophone and Anglophone Africa.

The origins of the national conference mechanism are to be found in the developments in Francophone Benin in early 1990. The Benin experience assumed the status of an ideal model for the operation of a national conference in the transition to democracy even though some of the later conferences failed in practice to replicate it. This provides a more specific and limited case of the wider phenomenon of African states being influenced by developments within other African states in the struggle for (and against) democracy. In the case of the national conference this influence was largely confined within the Francophone bloc.

Although the Benin case can justifiably be regarded as innovative the actual evolution of events there suggests a large element of serendipity rather than the steady unfolding of some preconceived masterplan. By 1989 Benin was in an undeniable state of crisis. The seventeen year old military-based regime of Ahmed (Mathieu) Kerekou was widely perceived as incompetent and corrupt. The economy was in serious decline and public sector employees were faced with frequent delays, or non-payment, of wages and salaries. As the year progressed strikes and anti-government demonstrations multiplied and became a mass movement for 'democratic renewal'[2]. When the tactics of repression failed to curb protest Kerekou decided to make concessions to his opponents. In December 1989 he agreed to abandon Marxism as the official state ideology, to permit the legal formation of opposition parties by ending the single-party status of his own Benin People's Revolutionary Party (PRPB), and to convene a national conference to discuss changes to the constitution. The conference was understood at that point to have no more than advisory powers and was regarded by some of the opposition as a diversionary tactic. Kerekou himself romantically appealed to the memory of King Ghezo of Abomey who had once called upon "all the sons of the country to plug the holes of the punctured calabash with their fingers in order to save the fatherland'[3]. The conference was held in Cotonou between 19th and 28th February 1990 and included not only representatives from the government and opposition parties but also trade union leaders, religious leaders, representatives from voluntary associations and women's groups, several former heads of state, and a variety of other public figures, making a total of just under 500 persons in all. None of the participants at the conference could at that stage claim a popular electoral mandate because there had been no elections to the conference: the varied groups participating individually chose their own delegates. Furthermore in a strict legal sense the conference had no constitutional standing at the outset, a fact which makes the final outcome all the more remarkable. The Archbishop of Cotonou, Isadore da Souza, was elected as chairman of the conference. After several days of general discussion the conference took the extraordinary step of voting by a large majority to declare itself sovereign. Kerekou's immediate response to this decidedly ad hoc decision was to describe it, not entirely inaccurately, as a 'civilian coup d'etat'. Nzouankeu sums up the step when he writes that 'the national conference replaced the government; it became the supreme political institution of the state'[4]. Kerekou's decision to accept the decision of the conference can be explained in several ways. Firstly, he recognised the weakness of his position and the popular support enjoyed by pro-democracy forces represented within the conference. Perhaps crucially, Kerekou realised that he could not rely on the support of the army if he chose to reject the decision of the national conference and face the explosion of popular protest which that would undoubtedly have provoked. Secondly the conference agreed to allow Kerekou to retain the presidency, with greatly reduced powers, pending democratic presidential elections. Thirdly, it was widely understood that if he accepted the conference decision he would not subsequently be prosecuted for any 'crimes' he had committed whilst in office.

Following Kerekou's acceptance of the situation the conference proceeded to choose an interim prime minister and government to rule until democratic elections could be held early the following year. In the event Kerekou decided to contest the presidential election held in March 1991 but was defeated in the polls by his major opponent Nicephore Soglo who had been the conference's choice as interim prime minister. Clearly the national conference in Benin had a transformative effect on the domestic political system. What had begun as an assembly with no very clearly defined agenda and a somewhat arbitrarily composed membership found itself within the space of a few days dismantling a long established (although, by then, rather precarious) authoritarian regime and creating the institutional framework for the democratisation of the political system of Benin. These developments also had a profound influence well beyond the borders of the country as 'the Benin story became an instant media event throughout Francophone Africa'[5]. Reporting of the national conference of Benin in the electronic and print media of other Francophone states created enormous interest everywhere. A two hour video of the highlights of the conference produced by the Benin government news agency circulated widely, often in the form of pirated copies. The result of this extensive publicity was not only to provide encouragement and inspiration for pro-democracy groups in other states but also appeared to offer a model, in the form of the national conference, through a transition to democracy could take place.

A clear case of the adoption of the Benin model can be seen in the Republic of the Congo (designated People's Republic of the Congo until 1991). Before democratisation the Congolese political system exhibited many similarities with that of Benin. The state was ruled by a militarised single party, the Congolese Labour Party (PCT) led by Colonel Denis Sassou-Nguesso. As in Benin adherence to Marxism-Leninism as the official ideology of the state was claimed by the regime although like in Benin many observers disputed the authenticity of the claim[6]. Although the Congolese economy was stronger than that of Benin the decline in world prices for its oil exports which had occurred since the mid-1980s was causing serious problems and salary arrears in the overextended public sector were becoming common.

By 1990 some liberalisation of the political system was already underway. The morale of the regime had been particularly affected by the collapse of its claimed role models in Eastern Europe and domestic pressure, especially from the trade unions and the churches, was increasing. In July 1990 the principle of a transition to multi-partyism was accepted by a congress of the ruling party. In August a number of political prisoners, including the erstwhile head of state Joachim Yhombi-Opango, were released from incarceration. In December Marxism-Leninism was finally abandoned and the formation of opposition parties was legalised. In February 1991 a national conference was convened to make arrangements for a transition to multi-party democracy. Almost immediately the conference was suspended following a dispute between the PCT and the opposition concerning the balance of representation. By the time the conference re-convened in March the dispute had been settled in favour of the various opposition groups who had gained 700 out of the 1,100 delegates and seven of the eleven seats on the conference's governing body. As in Benin a leading Christian cleric, the Roman Catholic bishop of Owando Ernest N'Kombo, was elected as chairman of the conference. The vice-chairman of the conference was Antoine Letembet Ambily, a leader of the opposition Congolese Movement for Democracy and Integral Development. Conference debates were televised live and created great popular interest not only domestically but also across the Congo river in Kinshasa, Zaire. Although Sassou-Nguesso had earlier insisted that the conference should be consultative rather than empowered to take binding decisions[7] he found himself unable to maintain this position and was forced to agree to opposition demands that the conference be declared a sovereign body which did not require government approval for its decisions. Having established its authority the conference then proceeded to dismantle the existing authoritarian political structure before it was dissolved itself in June after completing the task. Sassou-Nguesso was allowed to retain the presidency for the interim period but most of his powers, including control of the army, were transferred to the prime minister who became head of the government. The conference established a new legislature, known as the High Council of the Republic, which included amongst its duties the drawing up of a new constitution, which was to be subjected to a national referendum, and choosing a new prime minister. The latter post was given to Andre Milingo, a non-party-political technocrat and World Bank official.

By December 1991 the interim legislature had produced a draft constitution. The following month the transition process was threatened by a mutiny by sections of the army, who were believed to be supporters of Sassou-Nguesso, who seized control of strategic positions in the capital. This provoked mass demonstrations in the streets of Brazaville by people opposed to any disruption by the army of the democratic transition. In the event Sassou-Nguesso himself refused to support the mutiny and pronounced in favour of the transition process which caused the mutiny to collapse. Having fended off this threat the transition proceeded with an affirmative constitutional referendum in March 1992 and multi-party elections in July. Although Sassou-Nguesso and the PCT contested the presidential and parliamentary elections they were defeated in both by the new opposition parties.

The roles of the national conferences in Benin and Congo exhibit a striking number of parallels. In both cases the conference was of decisive importance. In contrast circumstances in Mali produced a rather more limited role for the national conference there. The previous chapter showed how mass protest, and the violent response to it, led to the ousting of the dictatorial President Moussa Traore and his replacement by more reform minded regime of Lieutenant-Colonel Amadou Toure. Shortly after the coup the latter established a body called the Transition Committee for the Well-Being of the People (CTSP). This body was headed by Toure but included a majority of civilians associated with the pro-democracy opposition and a minority of military personnel. From the outset it was made clear that the CTSP was to act as a transitional ruling group pending the establishment of a democratic institutional framework. As a part of this process it was the CTSP which established the national conference which met from July 29th to August 12th 1991 in Bamako. The conference was attended by around 1,800 delegates including representatives of the newly created political parties, religious groups, trade unions, women's groups, students, and 165 peasant representatives. Amadou Toure chaired the meetings which were essentially concerned with discussing the precise details of the transition to democracy because the transition itself had already been decided upon before the conference opened. Thus, in contrast to the two previous examples, the conference did not feel the need to assert its sovereignty and it was accepted that Toure and the CTSP would remain as the government until democratic elections could be held. Unlike Kerekou and Sassou-Nguesso, Toure made it clear that he had no intention of taking part in the elections and this made it easier for him to act as a neutral in arranging a contest in which he would not be a participant. The national conference in Mali was not in any way an arena for conflict between an incumbent regime and a competing opposition. During the early days of the conference time was spent criticising the ousted Moussa Traore regime for its corruption, human rights abuses, and brutal authoritarianism (Traore and his colleagues Sekou Ly, Mamadou Coulibaly, and Ousmane Coulibaly were subsequently tried and sentenced to death for their crimes although it was not expected that the death sentences would be carried out). The main task of the conference, however, was to draw up a new constitution which could then be put before the population in a referendum. The new constitution for what was designated as the Third Republic confirmed the existence of a multi-party system together with the independence of the judiciary, freedom of association, speech and assembly, and the right to strike[8]. The constitution was approved in a referendum in January 1992 with democratic legislative elections taking place in February and March and the presidential election in April.

In spite of some differences the national conferences in Benin, Congo, and Mali were all relatively successful in providing an institutional mechanism for the transition to more democratic political systems. However, it would be misleading to see the national conference as some sort of institutional magic wand which can be used to produce a democratic transition whatever the local circumstances may be. To restore balance to the discussion the cases of Togo and Zaire can be examined as examples of states where the holding of a national conference failed to produce an outcome which could reasonably be called a democratic transition. In both cases many of the participants at the conferences started out with aspirations that the Benin experience could be replicated in their own countries but in neither case was this achieved. It is no coincidence that these two cases involved two of Africa's most brutally autocratic leaders.

The Togolese political system has been dominated for more than a quarter of a century by the daunting figure of Gnassingbe Eyadema who came to power in a coup in 1967. Since 1969 Togo had officially been a single-party state with the Rally of the Togolese People (RPT) as the only legally permitted political party. In reality the RPT remained little more than a front for the highly personalised rule of Eyadema which was based more on the support of the military than any popular legitimacy. As indicated in the previous chapter the composition of the army strongly reflected the regional (northern) and ethnic (Kabre) background of Eyadema with several of the latter's close kin in important positions in the command structure.

89

Partly encouraged by events elsewhere in West Africa popular pressure for some democratisation of the political system built up from early 1990. This pressure mainly took the form of street demonstrations which were on several occasions brutally repressed by the police and the army. In March 1991 Eyadema agreed under pressure to the establishment of a multi-party system but, at that stage, refused to concede opposition demands for a national conference. It was clear that both the enthusiasm of the opposition for a conference and the reluctance of Eyadema to agree to one were influenced by the way both sides perceived events in Benin. Whilst the opposition was eager to replicate the Benin experience Eyadema was equally determined to avoid it[9]. In June 1991 a new coalition of opposition forces the Democratic Opposition Front (FOD), which included political parties and trade unions, launched an indefinite general strike to put further pressure on Eyadema to agree to a national conference. In the short term this additional pressure paid off and Eyadema agreed to a national conference which opened on July 8th. The conference included nearly 1,000 delegates representing a wide range of Togolese groupings but it was noticeable that a disproportionately large number were from the south of the country and that the north was underrepresented. The bishop of Atakpame, Sanouko Kprodzro, was elected chairman. Although the latter appealed for moderation and reconciliation the mood of the conference was more combative. On July 11th the conference declared itself sovereign but this move was rejected by government representatives who immediately walked out announcing the suspension of their participation in the conference. Although they returned a week later they still refused to accept the conference's self-proclaimed sovereignty: Eyadema disingenuously argued that sovereignty could only be based on universal suffrage which the conference lacked. Thus although government forces were once again represented at the conference they had made it clear that they would not be bound by any decisions taken.

In retrospect it is clear that the Togolese national conference significantly overestimated its own real power and underestimated that of the incumbent regime. This gave a distinct air of unreality to some of its pronouncements. The conference decided to strip Eyadema of most of his official powers, establish a new interim prime minister and legislature, and dissolve the RPT. Joseph Koffigoh, a southern human rights lawyer, was chosen as interim prime minister. Towards the end of the conference one resolution specifically indicted two of Eyadema's sons for involvement in an earlier massacre of opposition activists. On August 26th Eyadema suspended the conference and surrounded the hall where it was meeting with troops. Although he later rescinded the suspension and allowed the conference to proceed to its ceremonial ending on 28th of August it was clear to most people, although not to all the participants of the conference, that real political power remained firmly in Eyadema's hands and that conference decisions he opposed carried little real weight. Since the conference Eyadema has used his control of the army to harass his political opponents and maintain a tight grip on power. Although presidential elections took place in August 1993, resulting in a 'landslide victory' for Eyadema, few observers would give them any credence due to the intense levels of state violence against its opponents and widespread malpractice in the electoral process. In a formal sense Togo has continued to operate a multi-party system. It is possible that if opposition groups survive they could at some time in the future manage to engineer a greater political opening but for the present time the democratic content of Togolese political procedures may be regarded as minimal to non-existent.

In many ways the case of Zaire is even more depressing from a democratic perspective. Here the national conference certainly failed to deliver any transition to democracy. However, not only has the Zairean state not been democratised one must also face up to the question as to whether, in the case of Zaire, there is indeed a state left to democratise10. Under the leadership of Mobutu Sese Seko Kuku Ngbendu Wa Za Banga since 1965, Zaire has become perhaps the most extreme example in Africa of personalised authoritarianism. Mobutu's rule has been massively corrupt, extremely brutal, and highly capricious. Until 1990, when Mobutu under pressure agreed to allow a multi-party system, Zaire was in theory a single-party state with the Popular Movement of the Revolution (MPR) as the only legally permitted party. In practice the MPR, to which all Zairean citizens automatically belonged, was simply a vehicle for the one-man rule of Mobutu. The real basis of the latter's power lay with his control of the army, or at least those sections of the army which really mattered especially his own presidential guard. In 1990 following mass pro-democracy demonstrations and anti-government strikes Mobutu agreed to allow the existence of opposition parties but no coherent programme for democratisation existed. In April 1991 Mobutu announced that a national conference would convene at the end of the month. Following widespread anti-government protest Mobutu suspended the conference before it had met. At this stage the opposition were unsure as to whether or not they wished to participate in a national conference. Since the legalisation of opposition parties around 130 had come into existence which meant that opposition to Mobutu was in a fragmented state. In an attempt to give it some coherence Etienne Tshisekedi, the leader of the largest opposition party the Union for Democracy and Social Progress (UDSP), persuaded most party leaders to unite in a coalition known as the Sacred Union. The latter was always a rather fragile grouping but at the time it represented some progress in comparison with the existing confusion.

The Zairean national conference eventually opened on 7th August 1991. Although it remained in formal existence until 6th December 1992 (far longer than the national conferences in other African states) it would be misleading to see this as a period of continuous constitutional debate. The conference was beset by frequent suspension and walk-outs by various participants and displayed a very irregular and episodic form of existence throughout its existence. More damaging was the fact that during the whole period violent clashes between government and opposition forces continued to take place in Kinshasa and other centres in which the role of the army as the major support base of Mobutu could clearly be seen. For most of the time events taking place outside of the conference hall overshadowed those taking place within. Taking its lead from conferences elsewhere the Zaire participants declared their sovereignty in April 1992 but this brave gesture was plainly at odds with political reality in the country. In August the conference proceeded to elect its own transitional government with Tshisekedi as prime minister and with the presidency downgraded to a largely ceremonial role but again a gap between conference decisions and the real balance of power within Zaire was apparent. By the time the conference closed in December many decisions had been taken but in reality little or nothing had been decided.

Since the conference ended Zaire has remained in a chronically unstable state but to the extent that it is governed at all it is Mobutu who remains pre-eminent. Attempts by foreign governments to curb his power, through for example economic sanctions, have proved ineffective due to the unusual political economy of Zaire. With an inflation rate in 1993 of 8,319%[11] the formal economy had almost ceased to exist. In a recent insightful article Keith Somerville sums up the situation when he writes that 'with the Zairean economy in ruins and commercial life dominated by the black market, smuggling and other informal means of national and international trade, Mobutu had little to fear...his access to the revenue from the sale of Zairean and Angolan diamonds through Kinshasa enabled him to maintain his primacy within the chaotic Zairean political system, to fund his military and other supporters and to resist foreign pressure'[12].

Comparison of the success or failure of the national conference in providing for a transition to a more democratic form of rule in these five states clearly suggests that the outcome was largely determined by the resources of real power, especially economic and military power, which opposing sides in the conflict were able employ against their opponents. In the struggle for and against democracy which was being played out in the conference arenas it was the relative strengths of incumbent regimes and those seeking to democratise which, more than anything, decided the outcomes. The varied domestic power equations counted far more than the procedural similarities and dissimilarities of the conferences. Whilst the outcomes were not completely predetermined, and did leave at least come scope for participants to manoeuvre with greater or lesser degrees of strategic skill, there is no doubt that putative democratisers faced greater obstacles in some states than in others. These obstacles were far more formidable in Togo and Zaire than they were in Benin, Congo, and Mali.

By the time of the national conferences the incumbent leaders in Benin and Congo, Kerekou and Sassou-Nguesso respectively, were already in relatively weak positions. In both cases the national economy was in a state of crisis (more severe in Benin than in Congo) and neither leader could confidently rely on unconditional support from the army. Whilst neither leader could be seen as an enthusiastic supporter of democratisation they both lacked the power to resist the significant pressure they were exposed to. In Mali the situation was even more propitious because the long-term authoritarian leader, Moussa Traore, had already been removed from the scene through a coup before the conference got underway. The incumbent military regime under Amadou Toure had already committed itself to democratic reform before the conference started. Also of importance was the fact that agreement was reached in Benin and Congo not to seek retribution for the past misdeeds of the leaders which meant the removal of one possible reason for their trying to cling to power at all costs. In Mali the question of retribution for past misdeeds did not apply to the incumbent regime at the time of the conference although it certainly did apply to the regime of the already ousted Moussa Traore.

The contrasts between Benin, Congo, and Mali on the one hand and Togo and Zaire on the other are very marked. There is little doubt that the tone of the national conference debate in the latter two was decidedly confrontational and that both Eyadema and Mobutu had good reason to fear retribution for past misdeeds if they lost power. Both regimes had a long record of corruption and violent repression which made their leaders particularly vulnerable to any possibility of retrospective Nemesis. The logic of personal survival pointed in the direction of maintaining power. Not only did Eyadema and Mobutu have more reason to cling to power, they also had the resources which could enable them to do so whatever the wishes of the national conferences might be. The Togolese economy was in considerably better shape than the others[13] which reduced the pressure on Eyadema in comparison with Kerekou or Sassou-Nguesso. Certainly the formal economy of Zaire was in crisis but, for reasons explained earlier, this did not have the effect of seriously weakening Mobutu. In both cases, as a result of ethnic engineering and material reward directed towards the military, the incumbent leaders could be reasonably confident of the support of the army in their struggle with the opposition. This control of the means of coercion, and a demonstrated intention of making use of this control, was the major factor in subverting the democratising intentions of the national conferences in both Togo and Zaire.

In examining the development of the national conference as a transitional mechanism in a significant number of African (mainly Francophone) states the evidence suggests that its spread was contingent in character. The adoption of the conference mechanism appears to have been heavily influenced by the relatively successful experience of Benin which was itself relatively unplanned and ad hoc in character. One might reasonably hypothesise that had the Benin conference broken down in disorder, or been manipulated by Kerekou to maintain his grip on power, then the wider adoption of the national conference prototype would not have occurred. Apart from providing a model the Benin experience also raised exaggerated expectations regarding the efficacy of the conference as a mechanism for democratic transition irrespective of other circumstances. Campaigns by pro-democracy groups for a national conference in Nigeria for example seem to rest on the explicit assumption that such a development would virtually guarantee democratisation. However, given the character of the Abacha regime, this assumption appears wildly optimistic unless such a development was accompanied by a significant weakening of regime support within the army. The evidence from Togo and Zaire clearly suggests that where the local balance of power lies with those hostile to democratisation the possible achievements of national conference are likely to remain extremely limited. As a transitional mechanism the national conference is severely constrained by local circumstances.

Referendums

As a part of the transition to democracy national referendums were used in twice as many states as were national conferences although several states used both devices. This widespread use of the referendum to test public opinion marked a new departure in African politics because before this it had been almost entirely absent from the political scene. Between 1990 and 1993 some twenty African states made use of a referendum to test popular support for political change. In most cases this consisted of testing popular support for new multi-party constitutions but in a few states it was used for different purposes. Unlike the national conference the referendum was used in Anglophone as well as Francophone states.

In assessing the role of the referendums I would suggest that this can best be achieved by dividing them into two different broad categories according to the major purpose of the referendum. I would thus distinguish between what I would term *legitimising* referendums and *decisive* referendums. In the case of legitimizing referendums the outcome appears to have more or less entirely predictable in advance (although, of course, one should always be careful of the dangers of retrospective inevitability). In some ways this type of referendum may perhaps more accurately be regarded as having the purpose of demonstrating

94

public opinion rather than testing it. Typically this involved the approval of new constitutions after they had already been drawn up, sometimes within a national conference. In such cases the role of the referendum was to bolster the internal legitimacy of the new arrangements and to demonstrate to external powers that the population at large had consented to changes which had taken place. The relative importance of each of these aims undoubtedly varied from state to state: some may be regarded as primarily for internal consumption and some primarily for external consumption although such a clearcut distinction may often be difficult to arrive at. In the case of decisive referendums on the other hand, the outcomes were far less predictable and had the results of the referendum been different to what they were political change would in all probability have taken a different course. In these cases the electorate were rather more involved in direct democratic decision-making instead of simply approving decisions which had been taken. Although the level of uncertainty of outcome varied from case to case some degree of uncertainty was a common feature.

In the sixteen states where what I have classified as legitimising referendums were held new constitutions were approved in all cases. The basic details by state, including referendum date and percentage vote in favour, were as follows: Benin (December 1990, 95.8%), Burkina Faso (June 1991, 93%), Burundi (March 1992, 90%), Comoros (May 1992, 74.25%), Congo (March 1992, 96.3%), Djibouti (September 1992, 96.84%), Equatorial Guinea (November 1991, 98.4%), Ghana (April 1992, 92%), Guinea (December 1990, 98.7%), Madagascar (August 1992, 73%), Mali (January 1992, 99.76%), Mauritania (July 1991, 97.9%), Niger (December 1992, 89.8%), Sao Tome and Principe (August 1990, 72%), Sierra Leone (August 1991, 60%), Togo (September 1992, 98%). In the case of Sierra Leone the referendum exercise proved fruitless because in April 1992 a coup led by Captain Valentine Strasser brought an end, for the time being at least, to the country's fragile democratisation process[14].

Clearly the official approval ratings as expressed in the referendum results were, in most cases, extremely high, so much so that there is perhaps a temptation to see them as suspiciously high. Whilst a certain scepticism would often be justified in the case a near unanimous votes it may not be appropriate in these cases. In most of these referendums constitutional arrangements had been agreed by ruling and opposition elites in advance of the vote. This level of elite consensus (on this issue at least) meant that the referendum campaigns were extremely one-sided with no significant groups campaigning for a 'no' vote. In Niger some of the Islamic leaders urged a boycott of the referendum on the grounds that the new constitution was too overtly secular but this would have been more likely to reduce the turn-out (which in the event was a fairly respectable 56%) than to increase the 'no' vote. Whilst natural caution would seem to dictate an automatic distrust of any 'official' figures emerging from a

95

state like Equatorial Guinea (in this case 98.4% approval with a 94.6% participation rate) in the light of its recent political history[15], at a more general level for most states at least the referendum figures may be regarded as reasonably accurate if only on the grounds that hardly anybody had any serious reason for wanting to falsify them. In marked contrast to many of the later elections there was little in the way of contestation over the results of these legitimising referendums.

Decisive referendums were held in only a few states but because they played a significant role in deciding the eventual outcomes they merit much closer scrutiny. This type of referendum can be observed in the cases of South Africa (March 1992), Seychelles (November 1992 and June 1993), and Malawi (June 1993). The precise local circumstances were very different in each of these cases[16].

The March 1992 referendum in South Africa can be seen retrospectively as the final occasion on which only the white electorate directly participated in national decision-making. The result of the referendum ensured that this would be the case. On 17th March white South Africans were asked to answer 'yes' or 'no' to the following question: 'Do you support continuation of the reform process which the State President began on February 2, 1990 and which is aimed at a new constitution through negotiation?'. Although the precise institutional arrangements of transition had not been worked out at this stage it was very clear both to those who supported democratic reform and to those who opposed it that a continuation of the reform process would inevitably lead to a universal franchise and to a government in which black South Africans, and particularly members of the African National Congress (ANC), would predominate.

In the 1989 general election the incumbent National Party (NP) had campaigned on a reformist platform but at the time few observers had any idea of how rapid and far-reaching that reform was to be. Whilst the release from prison of Nelson Mandela in February 1990 was relatively predictable, if only because of the obviously catastrophic consequences if he were to die in detention, the simultaneous unbanning of the ANC and other anti-apartheid groupings such as the Pan Africanist Congress (PAC) and the South African Communist Party (SACP) took most observers by surprise. Groups which had previously been seen as dangerous 'terrorists' by most whites suddenly became legal organisations with an accepted right to participate in the restructuring of a new South Africa.

In the 1989 election the NP had emerged with a clear majority when it gained 93 seats as against 33 for the more liberal Democratic Party (DP) and 39 for the right-wing Conservative Party (CP). Whilst the DP was generally supportive of the reform process which the NP subsequently initiated the CP was bitterly opposed to it. The CP vociferously claimed that, because NP reforms went far beyond their rather vaguer promises in the 1989 election campaign, the government had no electoral mandate to do what it was doing. It is indicative that for the CP an electoral mandate still meant a white electoral mandate. A series of by-election victories by the CP in 1991 and early 1992 appeared to give credence to its claim that the government of President F. W. de Klerk did not have general white support for the CODESA negotiations which had got underway in December 1991. Although the CP claim was based on a dubious premise (that white majorities counted more than overall majorities) they did have a valid point at the time to the extent that nobody really new what proportion of the white population were supportive of the reform process. In understanding the importance of the referendum this uncertainty which existed at the time is very relevant because it would be mistaken to rely on retrospective knowledge to see the result of the referendum as a foregone conclusion when it was not. In deciding to put the issue of reform to a whites only referendum de Klerk was taking a calculated risk. He announced that if the referendum produced a majority of 'no' votes he would resign from the presidency which would almost certainly have produced a general election which the CP might well have won. The referendum was crucial in shaping the future development of the South African political system.

The referendum campaigns were conducted with great passion from both sides[17]. The right-wing opponents of democratic reform claimed that it would lead to the instillation of a communist government under which whites in particular would lose all their rights and would have their property appropriated by blacks. They claimed that such a government would frighten off foreign investment in South Africa and would lead to economic collapse. Although the CP and its allies claimed that they did not wish to reinstate apartheid their policies of group areas, influx control, and even a return to the ban on mixed race marriage, gave a strong impression that the reinstatement of apartheid was exactly what they did want, even if the word itself was not to be used. It was argued that the problem of unrest within the country could be solved by the use of higher levels of coercion by the state security forces. Underlying all of the 'no' campaign was an undiminished belief in white racial superiority.

Supporters of reform argued that a 'no' vote in the referendum would lead to chaos and make the country ungovernable because it would play into the hands of violent black extremists of the 'one settler-one bullet' persuasion. President de Klerk made extensive use of the links between the CP and the far-right extremist para-military Afrikaner Resistance Movement (AWB) and its fanatical leader Eugene Terreblanche. The president asked white South Africans 'are you going to vote for fascists, for Nazis who will bring a civil war upon this country?'[18]. In a mirror-image of their opponents the supporters of a 'yes' vote argued that any other result would produce economic chaos and destroy the prospects for foreign investment in the South African economy. The support of the major private sector companies within South Africa, and of potential foreign investors in the USA, Western Europe, and Japan, for a 'yes' vote undoubtedly strengthened the case of the reformers. A further significant part of the campaign of the latter was the issue of sporting links with the rest of the world which were in the process of being re-established after years of isolation. Although the question of South African rugby, athletics, and cricket teams once again competing freely in world competitions may appear relatively trivial from a macro-political perspective this is very far from being the case and it would be unwise to underestimate the importance attached to sport in South African popular culture and its relevance to the referendum campaign.

Although the ANC had expressed doubts over the idea of a whites only referendum its leadership supported the 'yes' campaign and Mandela continued to allay the fears of those whites who feared that reform would be the equivalent of racial suicide. Mangosutho Buthelezi and the Inkatha Freedom Party (IFP) also gave support to the 'yes' campaign which undermined claims by the CP that, in the event of a rejection of reform in the referendum, they would be able to do a deal with the Zulu leader. Although they could not participate in the voting most black groups supported the 'yes' campaign although Bishop Isaac Mokoena, the leader of the Reformed Independent Churches Association backed the stance of the CP on the grounds of opposition to communism[19].

As is well known the referendum of 17th of March produced a substantial victory for the reformers[20]. The turnout of 86% was one of the highest ever achieved in South Africa. Of those voting 68.7% gave their approval to the programme of democratic reform with the remaining 31.3% rejecting it: a majority of just over two to one for the 'yes' vote. Although some regional variation was apparent in the results there was only one district, Pietersburg in the Northern Transvaal, which produced a majority of 'no' votes. Even here rejection of reform was not ubiquitous with 37,612 voting 'yes' and 49,820 voting 'no'. Districts such as Cape Town (355,527 to 63,325), Durban (204,371 to 35,975) and Johannesburg (324,686 to 89,957) produced overwhelming majorities in favour of reform although in Kimberley (33,504 to 27,993) and Kroonstad (54,531 to 51,279) it was a much closer run contest. It has been estimated that around 79% of English-speaking whites and 62% of Afrikaners voted 'yes'[21].

The referendum result cleared the way for the reform process to continue. This process led to the 1994 democratic election (examined in the next chapter) and to Nelson Mandela becoming the first black President of South Africa. Quite what would have happened if the referendum result had gone the other way must remain a matter for speculation.

Whilst the South African referendum received considerable attention from the international media the same cannot be said of our second example of a decisive referendum. In fact the island state of Seychelles used a referendum on two occasions in the transition to democracy. Seychelles had been a single-party state since 1978 under the control of President Albert Rene and his Seychelles People's Progressive Front (SPPF-previously called the Seychelles People's United Party-SPUP). Rene had come to power a year earlier when he ousted his predecessor James Mancham of the Seychelles Democratic Party (SDP) in a coup d'etat. Following internal and external pressure Rene announced in 1991 that the ban on other parties would be lifted and that a constitutional commission would be elected to draw up a new democratic constitution which would then be put to the electorate for approval in a referendum. Following the lifting of the ban on opposition parties Mancham returned from exile to lead his newly re-established SDP. The elections to the constitutional commission in July 1992 passed of peacefully and were generally regarded as fair[22] although the opposition parties objected to the refusal of the government to allow overseas-based Seychellois to participate in the election[23]: it is thought that most of the exiles would have supported the opposition. The election gave 58.4% of the vote to the SPPF, with 33.7% to the SDP, and the remainder distributed amongst a number of minor parties. This resulted in a constitutional commission composed of 15 SPPF members and 8 SDP members. When the commission sat it became clear that the SPPF was prepared to use its majority to override the wishes of the opposition members. After a number of heated disagreements the SDP members walked out in protest which left the SPPF members to draw up a constitution entirely to their own liking. This constitution raised objections from the opposition and from other sectors of society including the Roman Catholic church. The principal objections related to the extent of power vested in the presidency and the inadequate protection of civil and human rights within the constitution. The opposition feared that if the SPPF were to win a subsequent election the constitution would permit the continuation of dictatorial rule in a democratic camouflage.

The next stage of the proceedings was for the new draft constitution to be put to a national referendum[24]. For the referendum campaign the opposition parties agreed to unite their forces to urge the electorate to vote 'no' to the constitution as it stood. Legally the constitution needed the support of 60% of those voting in the referendum for it to be adopted. When the referendum was held in November 1992 only 53.7% voted yes. As this figure was less than the share of the vote won by the SPPF in the earlier elections to the constitutional commission it could be inferred that even some supporters of the incumbent ruling party had serious reservations over the constitution. President Rene was now obliged to reconvene the constitutional commission. The rejection of the constitution by the electorate had had a sobering effect on the ruling party with the result that this time the SPPF adopted a far more conciliatory attitude towards the wishes of the opposition members of the commission. The SPPF agreed to meet the objections of their opponents and in May 1993 the commission unanimously adopted a new and thoroughly revised version of the constitution. This version was approved by 73.6% of the voters in a second referendum held on 18th June 1993 and came into effect a few days later.

Whilst the second Seychelles referendum may be regarded as closer in character to a legitimising referendum the first can be seen as belonging to the decisive category. The failure of the initial constitution to gain sufficient popular support in the referendum led directly to the subsequent adoption of a new constitution of a more genuinely democratic type.

The third example of a referendum which was clearly in the decisive category was that of Malawi. Here the combination of strong internal and external pressure forced President Banda to announce in October 1992 that a national referendum would be held on the issue of whether the existing single-party system dominated by the Malawi Congress Party (MCP) should be changed to a multi-party system. Although Banda had been extremely reluctant to concede the holding of a referendum evidence suggests that at this stage he still believed that most Malawians were satisfied with existing arrangements and would reject multipartyism. Many observers expressed scepticism as to whether it would be possible to hold anything resembling a free and fair referendum in what had arguably been Africa's most tightly controlled state.

The process began with disagreement over the composition of the National Referendum Commission (which was to organise the referendum) and also over the date of the referendum. Following protests by the opposition they managed to have some of their representatives appointed to the Commission which had initially been composed of Banda's supporters. The President announced that the referendum would take place in March 1993 but the opposition made it clear that they preferred a later date in order to give themselves more time to campaign. Following the intervention of the UN Secretary-General Boutros Boutros-Ghali a date of 14th June 1993 was agreed. These concessions, won by the opposition, increased the level of optimism concerning the prospects for a fair referendum. In keeping with the established pattern of Malawian politics the campaign to retain the single-party system was highly personalised around Banda. The nonagenarian president toured and spoke extensively in favour of maintaining the status quo claiming that his rule was responsible for stability and development in Malawi. Those supporting the move to a multi-party system, principally the Alliance for Democracy (AFORD) and the United Democratic Front (UDF), based their campaign on the need to replace the existing authoritarianism with democracy, freedom, and a respect for human rights. Although the MCP made extensive use of government control over the official media in the campaign this was offset by a rapid growth of independent newspapers supporting the opposition case.

The actual voting was monitored by representatives from the UN, the Commonwealth, and other European and African states and, in the event, passed off very peacefully. The results showed a majority of 67% in favour of multi-partyism with the remaining 33% against, thus giving a significant victory to the supporters of democratic reform[25]. The other significant feature of the results was the level of regional differentiation they indicated. In the northern and southern regions support for multi-partyism was overwhelming but in the central region all districts but one (Ntcheu) produced majorities in favour of the retention of the single-party state. The central region has always been regarded as Banda's main power base. A similar pattern of the distribution of support can be seen in the 1994 election results (see next chapter).

The precise issues to be decided in the three decisive referendums examined were all different. In South Africa the question related to the continuation of a reform process which was already underway and where the key issue was the adoption of a universal, non-racial franchise: in Seychelles the question related to the precise details of the constitution to be adopted: in Malawi the question involved a choice between a single-party system and a multi-party system. However, although the precise issues in the referendums were different the outcomes were broadly similar in that in each case the decision taken by the electorate was the one with the most meaningful democratic content. When presented with a direct choice clear majorities of white South Africans, Seychellois, and Malawians all rejected the less democratic alternative and gave their support to democratisation.

One further referendum which was held within this period was that in Eritrea which took place from 23rd to 25th April 1993. The Eritrean referendum does not fit easily into either of the two categories we have been using and might best be regarded as falling somewhere in between a legitimising referendum and a decisive one. Here the issue at stake was whether Eritrea was to secede from Ethiopia and become an independent state. Following a national liberation struggle of thirty years duration the breakthrough for the Eritreans came with the overthrow of the Mengistu regime in Ethiopia in 1991. The new Ethiopian regime of Meles Zenawi was much more sympathetic to Eritrean aspirations and had no wish to prolong armed rebellion. Because of this the Ethiopians granted the demands of the Eritrean People's Liberation Front (EPLF) for a national referendum on the question of secession. The referendum, which was closely supervised by the UN and others resulted in a massive vote in favour of independence[26]. No area in Eritrea produced a 'yes' vote lower than 99% and the national average was 99.81% in favour. Although it is necessary to take into account the fact that factional opponents of the EPLF, who might have voted against, were mainly in exile at the time of the referendum there still seems little doubt that popular support for independence was quite genuinely overwhelming. The fact that the outcome of the referendum was eminently predictable in advance would suggest that it belongs to the legitimising category. However, as an extremely rare example of part of a peaceful dismantling of an African state the Eritrean referendum can also be seen as a decisive element in the process. One final point to be noted is that this referendum, whilst it may be seen as a democratic event, was concerned with national independence rather than with a transition to a democratic system as such. At the time of writing EPLF promises to introduce multi-party democracy in an independent Eritrea have yet to be fully realised.

A final case in this context is that of Tanzania. Whilst the latter did not have either a national conference or a referendum it did embark on widespread consultation over the issue of political reform. The procedures involved in this consultative exercise exhibited many similarities with the conferences and referendums held elsewhere even though the specific form of the exercise was different.

By 1990 the Tanzanian government was coming under considerable pressure to democratise its single-party political system dominated by Chama Cha Mapinduzi (CCM, Revolutionary Party of Tanzania)27. In addition to internal demands, including those from ex-President Julius Nyerere who was an increasingly vocal critic of single-partyism, the government had been influenced by events in Eastern Europe and was facing pressure from international aid donors, particularly the Norwegians. However, it may be incorrect to put too much stress on very recent developments: the Tanzanian scholar Mwesiga Baregu argues very persuasively that 'the demands for multi-partyism and democracy in Tanzania are the culmination of a long and cumulative (albeit uneven) struggle against authoritarian rule'[28]. In response to these pressures President Ali Hassan Mwinyi began the consultation process by organising a national symposium in Dar es Salaam in March 1990. The symposium shared some of the features of national conferences elsewhere but it was never designed to be a decision-making body and did not attempt to act as one. In 1991 Mwinyi established a 20 member Presidential Commission to investigate popular feeling on the issue as widely as possible, especially in the rural areas. Without in any way wishing to denigrate the integrity of the members of the Commission it has to be recognised that this method of testing popular opinion has certain obvious defects in comparison with a free and fair referendum. In the context of a still-existing authoritarian single-party state it was inevitable that for many people the Commission would be equated with 'government' which would make it likely that some respondents at least would feel intimidated and be unwilling to voice views hostile to the existing arrangements. In its report the Commission said that whilst a majority of Tanzanians favoured the retention of a single-party system the Commission itself recommended the introduction of a multi-party system. This seemingly contradictory conclusion was based on the observation that 'although the majority of Tanzanians wanted the one-party system to continue, they proposed very many modifications, some of which, in the Commission's view, could only be effectively introduced under a multi-party political system'[29]. It might be noted that in addition to this some of those expressing support for the retention of the single-party state did so for reasons which were hardly supportive of CCM rule. Baregu, for example, reports that 'many feared that many political parties could collude to exploit them even more' and that 'the most cynical question repeatedly raised at the commission's hearings was: If one CCM is such a burden in terms of extracting resources (taxes, sundry contributions, chickens, etc.), what will life under many CCMs be like?'[30]. Following further debate a special general congress of CCM took the decision in February 1992 that multi-partyism should be restored and in May the same year the Tanzanian constitution was amended to legalise opposition parties.

Conclusions

The widespread and unprecedented movement away from authoritarian single-party and military rule in Africa in the early 1990s raised a large number of questions regarding the methods to be employed in the transition process to which there were very few ready-made answers. The immediacy of the pressure for democratisation meant that solutions to the problem had to developed fairly quickly in an atmosphere where political trust between participants was often in short supply and where the suggestion of long-term programmes was likely to be interpreted as an attempt to subvert the process. The use of the national conference and/or the referendum in many states was seen as a potential way out of the existing dilemma whereby procedures of transition could be agreed and popular support for these procedures could be tested and/or demonstrated. Given the often highly conflictual nature of the enterprise it is not surprising that in some cases at least some of the actors involved sought to undermine the whole process. The fluidity of the situation gave considerable scope to both pro and anti-democracy groups to manipulate the situation to their advantage in an improvisational fashion. This helps to explain the varied nature of political outcomes across different states.

Notes

(1) The States-General was the traditional representative system of the French monarchy which was based on the inclusion of the First Estate (the clergy), the Second Estate (the nobility) and the Third Estate (the commoners). It began in the thirteenth century, was abandoned in the sixteenth century, and was revived on the eve of the French Revolution in 1789.

(2) For details see Chris Allen, 'Restructuring an Authoritarian State: Democratic Renewal in Benin', *Review of African Political Economy*, No.54, 1992, pp.42-58.

(3) Quoted in Robert Fatton Jr., 'Democracy and Civil Society in Africa', *Mediterranean Quarterly*, Vol.2, No.4, Fall 1991, p.88.

(4) Nzouankeu, (1993), op. cit., p.45.

(5) See Pearl T. Robinson, 'Democratization: Understanding the Relationship between Regime Change and the Culture of Politics', *African Studies Review*, Vol.37, No.1, April 1994, pp.39-67.

(6) For a background discussion of Congolese politics see the section on Congo by Michael S. Radu and Keith Somerville in Chris Allen, Radu, Somerville, and Joan Baxter, *Benin, The Congo, Burkina Faso*, Marxist Regimes Series, London, Pinter, 1989, pp.145-236.

(7) See Chris Simpson, 'Conference Conumdrum', *West Africa*, 25 Feb-3 March 1991, No.3834, p.263.

(8) For a detailed discussion of the electoral arrangements see Richard Vengroff, 'Governance and the Transition to Democracy: Political Parties and the Party System in Mali', *The Journal of Modern African Studies*, Vol.31, No.4, 1993, pp.541-562.

(9) For a useful comparative discussion of the Benin and Togo national conferences see John R. Heilbrunn, 'Social Origins of National Conferences in Benin and Togo', *The Journal of Modern African Studies*, Vol.31, No.2, 1993, pp.277-299.

(10) The question of the breakdown of the Zairian state has been a matter of debate for a number of years now especially since the publication of Crawford Young's magisterial study *The Rise and Decline of the Zairian State*, (Young, 1985, op. cit.). See also his more recent 'Zaire: The Shattered Illusion of the Integral State', *The Journal of Modern African Studies*, Vol.32, No.2, 1994, pp.247-263.

(11) *New African*, April 1994, p.33.

(12) Keith Somerville, 'The Failure of Democratic Reform in Angola and Zaire', *Survival*, Vol.35, No.3, Autumn 1993, p.71.

(13) The point is well made by Kathryn Nwajiaku in her comparative study of Benin and Togo. She writes that 'at a time when Kerekou's system was

crumbling because of the cumulative effects of cuts in military spending and housing allowances, which by 1988 nearly provoked a coup d'etat, Eyadema could afford to announce an interest free salary advance and a 5% increase for the Forces Armees Togolaises (FAT) to mark the twentieth anniversary of the formation of the RPT. See Nwajiaku, 'The National Conferences in Benin and Togo Revisited', *The Journal of Modern African Studies*, Vol.32, No.3, 1994, p.432. Her article is primarily a critique of Heilbrunn's (1993, op. cit.) comparison of these two states which emphasised the greater strength of civil society in Benin. Nwajiaku argues that 'the differing outcomes of the CNs in Benin and Togo did not result from the strength of opposition forces, but rather from the extent to which the political leadership had lost power' (p.442). This appears to me to be a somewhat tautological position because the relative strengths and weaknesses of incumbent rulers and their opponents can be seen as opposite sides of the same coin.

(14) For details see A. Zack-Williams and Stephen Riley, 'Sierra Leone: The Coup and its Consequences', *Review of African Political Economy*, N.56, March 1993, pp.91-98.

(15) See for example, Max Liniger-Goumaz, *Small is not always Beautiful: The Story of Equatorial Guinea, London*, C. Hurst and Co., 1988.

(16) At one stage it looked as though a referendum, which would have been very similar to the one in Malawi, would take place in Zambia. For many years the Zambian President Kenneth Kaunda had denied that there was any popular support for a multi-party system and as late as April 1990 a UNIP conference had rejected the idea. However, as a result of opposition pressure, Kaunda announced in May 1990 that a referendum on the issue would be held in August of that year. In July he backtracked on this and said that he was postponing the referendum until August 1991. Following further opposition pressure the holding of a referendum was abandoned altogether and the government agreed to introduce a multi-party system without one. The evidence suggests that Kaunda was reluctant to hold a referendum which he was extremely likely to lose.

(17) For a full discussion of the referendum campaigns see Annette Strauss, 'The 1992 Referendum in South Africa', *The Journal of Modern African Studies*, Vol.31, No.2, 1993, pp.339-360. See also Mkhondo, op. cit., especially pp.119-126.

(18) Quoted by John Carlin, *The Independent*, London, 19th March 1992.

(19) Strauss, op. cit., p.340.

(20) Voting statistics take from *The Independent*, London, 19th March 1992.

(21) Donald Simpson, cited in Strauss, op. cit., p.351.

(22) See *Elections to the Constitutional Commission in Seychelles: The Report*

of the Commonwealth Observer Group, London, Commonwealth Secretariat, 1992.

(23) For a useful discussion of this and other legal issues related to democratisation in Seychelles see John Hatchard 'Re-Establishing a Multi-Party State: Some Constitutional Lessons from Seychelles', *The Journal of Modern African Studies*, Vol.31, No.4, 1993, pp.601-612.

(24) For details see *Referendum on the Draft Constitution in Seychelles: The Report of the Commonwealth Observer Group*, London, Commonwealth Secretariat, 1992.

(25) For details of the results see Lewis B. Dzimbiri, 'The Malawi Referendum of June 1993', *Electoral Studies*, Vol.13, No.3, 1994, pp.229-234.

(26) For full details of the referendum results see anonymous article 'Eritrea: Birth of a Nation', *Review of African Political Economy*, No.57, 1993, pp.110-114.

(27) More cynical Tanzanians have suggested a variety of different meanings for the CCM acronym. Bayart (1993, op. cit. p.89) cites the Tanzanian suggestion that it means 'Chukua Chake Mapema' which is KiSwahili for 'dig in and help yourself'. The Tanzanian scholar Mwesiga Baregu notes a further suggestion: 'Chama Cha Majangili' ('party of the crooks'). See Baregu, 'The Rise and Fall of the One-Party State in Tanzania' in Widner (ed.) 1994, op. cit., p.169.

(28) Baregu, ibid., p.159.

(29) See Juma Ngasongwa, 'Tanzania Introduces a Multi-Party System', *Review of African Political Economy*, No.54, 1992, pp.112-116.

(30) Baregu, op. cit., p.171. The notion that the role of the party was to exploit the peasantry did not lack empirical justification although it was distinctly at odds with the prevailing ideology of the single-party state.

5   Parties and Elections

The short-term culmination of the democratisation process in Africa can be seen in the creation of newly legalised opposition parties and their participation in competitive elections in a large number of African states. Whilst, from a longer-term perspective, these developments can only be seen as parts of the initial stage of establishing a democratic system rather than marking its consolidation they are nevertheless extremely important. The creation of coherent and viable opposition parties and the holding of a largely free and fair election certainly does not predetermine future successful consolidation but it does go some way towards predisposing it. Equally, whilst the experience of serious problems in these processes does not inevitably invalidate the chance of future democratisation it does make its attainment more difficult. Thus, early party formation and electoral experience in African states can be seen, to some extent, as indicating the plausible trajectories of democratisation at this stage.

Political Parties

The ending of single-party and military rule in recent years in the majority of African states has created the conditions for the colossal growth in the number of political parties in existence. Whilst no attempt has been made to catalogue these parties on a continental basis (an almost impossible task anyway given the bewildering rate of change) it is certainly the case that they number many hundreds, and quite possibly thousands. Many of these parties are of no real political significance, being too small and/or ephemeral to affect the political process. A fair number are what I would describe as 'vanity parties'[1] where the formation of a party appears to serve no purpose beyond that of increasing the personal esteem of the founder/leader. Assessing whether a party is significant or not depends to a considerable extent on an examination of its electoral performance (assuming that the election itself is not entirely spurious due to excessive malpractice). Political parties which fail to demonstrate even a moderate level of popular support are of interest only to the devotee of the minutiae of political life. It is thus difficult to discuss party systems in any depth outside of the context of elections especially where the parties are of very recent creation and where they were very much focussed on participation in electoral competition, as is the case with the bulk of African political parties. Nevertheless there are a number of observations which can be made in advance of the examination of elections.

Few of the states in question had recent experience of elections involving competing political parties and some, for example the Lusophone states, had no experience at all. Although many states had had some form of opposition movement, either in exile or operating in a covert manner at home, there was a general lack of experience in the organisation of parties in a competitive context. The very rapid development of parties following political liberalisation posed further problems for the creation of a viable opposition especially as past authoritarian constraints on the development of the organisations of civil society weakened the possibility of party formation based on that source. This difficult problem for the new opposition could easily be exploited by incumbent leaders for their own advantage although the ways in which they exploited the situation varied according to local circumstances. In Cote d'Ivoire, for example, evidence suggests that President Houphouet-Boigny moved rapidly to the holding of elections in order to deny the somewhat fragmented opposition enough time to organise some form of united front against the ruling PDCI. In Kenya, on the other hand, President Moi appears to have adopted an opposite approach. Here the incumbent leader delayed the election in order to allow time for what was initially a relatively united opposition in FORD to fragment into factions, a process which Moi himself encouraged. Although this is inevitably a retrospective view which may possibly suggest a rather higher level of Machiavellian skill than either Houphouet-Boigny or Moi actually possessed it does illustrate some of the dilemmas facing new oppositions.

A severe problem for opposition in some states has been the proliferation of political parties since liberalisation[2]. In an abstract sense a large increase in the number of political parties might be seen as enhancing democracy by providing an electorate with a greatly expanded choice. In reality it rarely if ever works like that and party proliferation is more likely to lead to confusion and the ability of incumbent authoritarian elites to cling to power. In this respect it is instructive that the largest number of parties have tended to appear in states where the least progress towards democracy can be seen. Extreme examples of this include

Cameroon with over 50 parties, Togo with over 60 parties, and Zaire with over 250 registered parties. In relation to Zaire one writer observes that 'in addition to independently created parties the list has been lengthened by Mobutu-financed splinter parties through which he sought to strengthen his position and weaken the genuine opposition'[3]. In other cases the problem of proliferation is more apparent than real because a seemingly large number of parties may obscure the reality that a much smaller number can be regarded as serious contenders. Although not approaching the Zairean total the 1994 South African elections were contested by 19 parties on the national list and even more on the provincial lists. However, the majority of these parties were insignificant and in real terms the election offered relatively clear-cut choices. In most areas the electoral competition was between the African National Congress (ANC) and the National Party (NP) although in Kwazulu-Natal the Inkatha Freedom Party (IFP) was a major participant. Even though the system of proportional representation used was extremely generous to minor parties only seven parties ended up with seats in the new National Assembly. The extreme generosity of the system to small parties was indicated by the fact that the African Christian Democratic Party (ACDP) was able to win two seats on the basis of less than half of one per cent of the total national vote. Most parties achieved nowhere near this level of support (a fuller account of the South African elections appears later in this chapter). Clearly the extent to which party proliferation presents a problem for democratisation has to be judged in the light of the particular circumstances existing in particular states.

In a number of cases groups formed to promote the struggle for democracy provided the basis for the creation of new opposition parties following liberalisation. Such groups had already developed an organisational structure, an identifiable leadership, and a substantial degree of popular legitimacy and support, all of which were useful attainments for creating a political party to participate in electoral competition. Such groups included the Movement for Multi-Party Democracy (MMD) in Zambia, the Alliance for Democracy in Mali (ADEMA), the Union for Democratic Renewal (URD) in Congo, the Front for Democracy in Burundi (FRODEBU), the Consultative Group of Democratic Forces (GCFD) in Central African Republic, the United Democratic Front (UDF) and the Alliance for Democracy (AFORD) in Malawi, and the Forum for the Restoration of Democracy (FORD) in Kenya. Subsequently the last named split into two sections thus weakening its electoral prospects. The Namibian case exhibits some similarities to the examples of pro-democracy groups developing into political parties although the context was quite different. Following a long and eventually successful struggle to end South African control of the territory the South West African People's Organisation (SWAPO) transformed itself into a political party to contest the independence elections of 1989 which preceded independence the following year[4]. For most of its history the specific goal of SWAPO had been that of national liberation rather than multi-party democracy but in the event the two became linked together in the independence settlement. Namibia adopted a democratic multi-party constitution and SWAPO won a small overall majority of seats in the elections and so went on to form the government.

Of course, an important difference between SWAPO, which was founded in 1960, and the other groups mentioned above was the greater longevity of the former. In a number of African states opposition parties in the recent period exhibited a fairly clear lineal descent from parties of earlier periods. In the Ghanaian elections of 1992 several of the parties could be seen as representing what one observer described as the 'reformation of the traditional political parties, albeit under new names'[5]. The Busia/Danquah tradition was represented by Adu Boahen's New Patriotic Party (NPP) whilst several parties represented the Nkrumahist tradition including the People's Heritage Party (PHP), the National Independence Party (NIP), and the People's National Convention (PNC). Whilst in Ghana the old party leaders, (Kofi Busia, Joseph Danquah, and Kwame Nkrumah) had long since died, in other African states the original party leaders were still around to resurrect political parties which had been dormant for considerable periods. In the March 1993 election in Lesotho, for example, the major competing parties were the same as had contested the last free elections in that country in January 1970[6] prior to the introduction of single-party and subsequently military rule. On both occasions the main parties were the Basutoland Congress Party (BCP), the Basotho National Party (BNP), and the Marematlou Freedom Party. For the BCP the level of continuity was even more marked because in 1993 the party was still led by its original leader, Ntsu Mokhehle, who had been in exile for most of the period since 1970. In the July 1993 elections in Seychelles the main opposition party was the New Democratic Party (NDP) led by James Mancham which was indistinguishable from the Seychelles Democratic Party (SDP) which had been the main opposition party before the 1977 coup d'etat had forced Mancham into exile. In cases like these above a certain sense of *deja vu* was unavoidable for observers and participants alike.

In advance of new party formation following liberalisation many observers, and some participants, had hoped that new multi-party systems would reflect a clearer ideological dimension than had been the case in the past. At the same time others expressed a fear that the new party pluralism would result in the emergence of a rampant 'tribalism' which would undermine the stability, or even the prospects for continued existence, of many states. An examination of the new party systems would suggest that both the hopes and the fears proved to be rather exaggerated. In the past competitive party systems in Africa have rarely, if ever, been structured so as to offer the electorate clear ideological choices which extend beyond populist or quasi-nationalistic rhetoric. Political parties which have exhibited a significant ideological dimension, in practice usually of a far left variety, have tended to be very marginalised in terms of real political influence. Typically they have consisted of small groups of mainly young, urban intellectuals who enjoy arguing with each other over the finer points of the ideology more than they do the arduous business of trying to generate mass support. For the most part the political programmes of the opposition parties consisted of repudiating the record of incumbent regimes and excoriating existing leadership personnel rather than offering a new masterplan for society. Due to obvious similarities between incumbent regimes it is not surprising that there were similarities between opposition programmes in different states. Key elements were support for multi-party democracy, a defence of human rights, criticisms of government corruption, and an attack on statist approaches to economic development. None of these elements are negligible or unworthy but they hardly add up to an ideological masterplan for restructuring society. Given the record of the past the absence of ideological masterplans can hardly be seen as a matter for regret. Nor is there any evidence that recently created parties have been any more influenced by ethnic considerations than were the incumbent regimes they sought to replace. Whilst ethnicity certainly does play a role in many of the new party systems the crude stereotype of 'tribalistic' parties threatening the integrity of the state appears misplaced. The past record of politics in Africa clearly demonstrates that attempts to impose an authoritarian political order pose a much greater threat to state integrity than does free competition between political parties even if some of the latter develop constituencies which are partly ethnic in character.

Before moving on from this outline of the major characteristics of new party systems to an examination of the electoral experience mention can be made of the unique case of Nigeria where an imposed two party structure was involved in the long delayed, and eventually annulled, democratic transition[7]. To put the two party system in context it is necessary to summarise some of the main features of what was a complex, and at times bizarre, process. On coming to power in a counter coup in August 1985 General Ibrahim Babangida, following the example of all previous military regimes in Nigeria, sought to present army rule as a temporary expedient which would prepare the way for a return to democratic civilian rule. Although he was the first of Nigeria's military rulers to adopt the title President, Babangida declared his determination to create a consolidated democracy which would ensure that his government was the last ever military regime in Nigeria. In 1987 he announced that the transition to democracy (originally promised for 1990, then delayed to 1992 and then 1993, and subsequently abandoned) would take the form of an entrenched two party system with the military government itself deciding which two parties would be recognised for the purposes of electoral competition. Given the historically demonstrated danger of Nigerian politics being reduced to a North/South or Christian/Muslim split it might have been thought than an enforced simple dichotomy was the last thing to be desired. In 1989 the National Electoral Commission (NEC) presented the government with the details of six different political associations from which it was supposed to select two for recognition as political parties. Babangida then announced his rejection of all the existing alternatives and declared that the regime itself was to establish two parties, the Social Democratic Party (SDP) and the National Republican Convention (NRC) which would be respectively 'a little to the left and a little to the right'. All the existing associations attempting to secure recognition were declared to be legally dissolved. Although most Nigerian democrats were deeply unhappy with the new arrangements most also recognised that in the short-term there was little alternative. This position was memorably expressed by the Nigerian Nobel prize-winner Wole Soyinka who argued that 'Nigerians made up their minds that even a mouldy loaf of bread was better than nothing and that the immediate target was to get rid of the military'[8]. Although the parties were to some extent artificial they provided a framework for political competition in what appeared at the time to be the run up to civilianisation of the Nigerian political system. In March 1993 each party chose its presidential candidate. The SDP chose Moshood Abiola a prominent Yoruba Muslim businessman based in Lagos whilst the NRC chose Bashir Tofa, a Hausa businessman from Kano. At the time both Abiola and Tofa were viewed as being closely associated with Babangida and indeed for many Nigerians their emergence as presidential candidates was seen as one further example of the manipulation of the democratisation process by Babangida. In the light of this it was all the more surprising when, following a relatively peaceful presidential election won by Abiola, Babangida decided to scrap the whole process and annull the election results. This provoked a considerable reaction from Nigerian civil society which will be examined in the next chapter.

Whilst it is not unknown for military governments embarking on a process of recivilianisation to attempt to influence the succession by tampering with the transition the character on the Nigerian party system in this period is unique. The peculiar nature of party formation was well encapsulated by the Nigerian constitutional lawyer Olu Onagoruwa when he wrote that 'The normal practice in the history of constitutional government is for people to create parties and parties then to create government. But Babangida has reversed historical experience and commonsense by making government to create parties and parties to create people'[9].

Elections

Evaluating Elections

In a representative democracy elections provide a central mechanism at the heart of the democratic process linking the governed to those who govern. It follows from this that any attempt to assess the extent of democracy within a political system, whether it be an established democracy or one of more recent origin, would necessitate an evaluation of the extent to which the electoral process was in practice free and fair. Whilst formal constitutional provisions relating to elections may by themselves invalidate any serious claim to democracy (eg. where all opposition parties are legally banned or where the franchise is unduly restricted) such provisions cannot alone validate such a claim. Clearly it is possible to have a case where the formal constitutional electoral arrangements are fully consistent with democracy but where what actually takes place is not.

Having made the point that evaluation of elections is very important it also has to be stressed that it is also very difficult. Trying to decide whether an election has been free and fair or, where some evidence of malpractice exists, how significant the effects of malpractice were in relation to the results, is inherently problematic. Following the 1992 presidential elections in Ghana, and opposition claims of rigging, I telephoned two colleagues of mine who are both respected academic specialists on Ghanaian politics to find out what they thought. The first told me that the levels of voter intimidation and other malpractices had been so great as to denude the result of any authenticity. The second told me that, although irregularities had certainly occurred, the victory of Jerry Rawlings was fundamentally a result of his genuine support within the Ghanaian electorate. The contrast between these views is clear. Nor is there anything unique about the Ghanaian case. Most recent elections in Africa have been accompanied by accusations of malpractice on the part of incumbent rulers and/or the opposition. It is not, in my view, overly cynical to suggest that a search for an election which is totally free from misconduct, in Africa or indeed elsewhere, is bound to be a fruitless exercise. In the real world it is simply not useful to dichotomise between totally free and fair election and the rest. What is important is to try to estimate the seriousness and extent of electoral malpractice and its probable effects on the final result. Thus evaluation of elections is necessarily a 'more or less' rather than an 'all or nothing' question which relies heavily on individual judgement of the evidence. An example of this sort of approach is the study by Crawford Young and Babacar Kante of the 1988 elections in Senegal. After examining the evidence for misconduct they write that 'although such malpractices clearly existed, their exact magnitude and their impact on the results are difficult to determine' and that 'in our judgement, fraud and other electoral handicaps of the opposition doubtless enlarged the size of the PS majority but did not change the results...the precise balance of forces is difficult to calculate'[10].

There are a number of sound reasons which explain why evaluating elections is such a formidable and imprecise exercise and why glib judgements should be avoided. To begin with it has to be recognised that any election is a long and complex process in which polling day is only one part. Issues which need to be addressed include voter registration, the demarcation of constituency boundaries[11], intimidation of contestants or voters at any stage, candidate nomination, media freedom, the use of public resources for party purposes by contestants (especially incumbent rulers), location of polling stations, organisation of polling, counting of votes, and the announcement of results[12]. Electoral malpractice may occur in relation to any of these components of the electoral process. To arrive at a full and accurate assessment of all components is a momentous task. Furthermore, it may be very difficult to distinguish between malpractice and maladministration in poor African states with inadequate communication systems, little experience in conducting competitive elections, and bureaucracies which are hardly noted for their efficiency. Recent elections offer countless examples of polling stations opening late (or not at all), insufficiency of ballot papers, confusions over voting cards, ballot boxes going missing, votes being miscounted and so on. While suspicions may justifiably be aroused in cases where such incidents appear to systematically advantage or disadvantage particular participants in the electoral competition, rather than occurring in a random manner, it is still remarkably difficult for observers to arrive at any hard and fast conclusions.

A further barrier to be overcome by an observer is the obvious fact that those trying to cheat in an election will normally go to considerable lengths to cover up their actions because it is in their interests to do so. Thus the observer is looking for evidence that some participants are deliberately trying to hide from him or her. Unless one is careful the understanding of this predicament can lead to the production of some rather dubious conspiracy theories such that an absence of evidence of cheating is taken as an indication of how clever those engaged in cheating have been in disguising the fact (logically it is impossible to prove the proposition that any election is free and fair: whilst evidence of malpractice my disprove such a proposition the absence of such evidence cannot prove it). If an observer discovers some evidence of malpractice should this inevitably be taken as constituting the proverbial tip of the iceberg where the logic of the metaphor is such that the bulk is unobserved, or even unobservable. Of course it is in the interests of those participants disadvantaged by cheating to uncover and publicise such behaviour. It is not surprising therefore that accusations of electoral malpractice are more often heard from election losers that they are from election winners. However, the problem here is again one of political interest. It is in the interests of those losing an election to try to discredit their victorious opponents by claiming that victory was unfairly won and thus trying to undermine the legitimacy of the victors domestically or internationally. I once listened to a public speech by an opposition leader in The Gambia in which he castigated the ruling party over a series of incidents which he claimed had occurred at a polling station during a general election and which threw serious doubt on the integrity of the electoral process. However, when I later had a private interview with this leader he gave me a much fuller account of what had taken place and whilst this account did not actually contradict his earlier public account in factual terms it did place the events in a different light which put the ruling party in a less culpable position and the opposition in a less virtuous one. A final difficulty which needs to be mentioned in relation to evaluating an election is the danger of generalising about an entire electoral process on the basis of observation in one area or a limited number of areas. Evidence suggests that frequently there are considerable variations in electoral conduct in different regions or districts. These differences can result from a number of factors including the attitudes of local party bosses, past experiences of competition and conflict, personal relationships between contestants, local cultural factors, the nature of local cleavages and so on, all of which are likely to impinge on an electoral process. The vantage point of the observer is likely to affect the evaluation.

The point of all the above discussion is certainly not to deny that electoral malpractice has occurred in recent elections: the evidence for misconduct is much too convincing for that. Nor is it to suggest that evaluation of elections is a pointless exercise: the importance of evaluation to an understanding of the democratisation process is much too great for such an evasion of responsibility. The discussion of the difficulties associated with evaluation should rather serve as a warning against the adoption of any cut and dried assessment of recent African elections whether that assessment be positive or negative.

In recent years observation and evaluation of African elections has been significantly internationalised. This marks a largely new departure in African politics although it is too early to say if it will become a permanent feature. Outside observers were involved in the independence elections in Zimbabwe in 1980 and in the Ugandan elections of the same year but the practice was never widely adopted until the more recent period. In part this development is related to the imposition of political conditionality (discussed in chapter 3) because the integrity of an electoral process can be seen as a partial guide to whether the political conditions attached to external finance are being adequately met. However, external evaluation does not only result from externally imposed conditionality because in many states it has been indigenous pro-democracy groups which have been the strongest supporters of an external involvement in the electoral process in the hope that this might eliminate, or more likely reduce, attempts by reluctantly democratising incumbents to rig elections, which they did not really want, in their own favour. Although some incumbent leaders expressed opposition to outside monitoring on the grounds that it contradicted principles of national sovereignty (which in a sense it does) they had little choice but to agree to it. In the circumstances the banning of outside observers would have been widely interpreted as an admission of an intention to cheat.

The most important intergovernmental observers of recent African elections have been the Commonwealth, the United Nations (UN), the European Union (EU), and the Organisation of African Unity (OAU). There have also been a number of nongovernmental organisations involved such as the Carter Centre of Emory University in Atlanta with which former US president Jimmy Carter is closely involved. In many cases these international organisations worked alongside indigenous monitoring groups. As an internationally respected multi-national and multi-racial organisation the Commonwealth has played a prominent role in election monitoring and observation. Following the meeting of Commonwealth leaders in Zimbabwe in 1991 the organisation issued the Harare Declaration which committed it to increased activities to be undertaken in the promotion of democracy in its member states including the monitoring of elections[13]. Since then the Commonwealth Secretary-General, Chief Emeka Anyaoku of Nigeria, has dispatched observer missions to cover elections in a number of member states. In Africa this took place for elections in Zambia, Seychelles, Ghana, Kenya, Lesotho, Malawi and South Africa (at the time of the 1994 elections South Africa was not a member of the Commonwealth although it rejoined shortly afterwards). Outside of Africa Commonwealth teams have monitored elections in Malaysia, Bangladesh, and Guyana. In some cases the role of the UN has gone considerably beyond that of monitoring elections to that of organising the democratisation process. The most far-reaching example of this occurred in Namibia. Here the United Nations Transitional Assistance Group (UNTAG) not only supervised the pre-independence elections of November 1989 but also supplied around 5,000 troops, drawn from 21 different nations, to police the whole transition process[14]. More recently the UN played a major role in supervising the 1994 elections in South Africa and in Mozambique. The role of the OAU has been very limited and might most accurately be described, as one writer suggests, as a 'symbolic gesture'[15]. This results partly from the longstanding OAU principle of 'noninterference in the internal affairs of member states' but also from the organisation's perennial shortage of funds. At the nongovernmental level there are a small number of multi-national African organisations which have participated in a small way in election monitoring: the best known is the Benin based Groupe d'Etudes et de Recherches sur la Democratie et le Developpement Economique et Social (GERDDES)[16].

Due to the perceived importance of election monitoring in the democratisation process the performance of monitoring groups has itself received scholarly attention. In this evaluation of the evaluators the assessments have been mixed. Whilst some scholars have reached very positive conclusions concerning the contribution of monitoring teams[17] others have been extremely critical in their verdicts[18]. Part of the problem arises from the enormous practical difficulties involved in evaluating elections discussed earlier which allow plenty of scope for differences of opinion and judgement. Also, no matter how well resourced and organised a team of observers may be there will always be questions over whether they have 'enough' resources and whether they could have been better organised, or worked harder. Beyond this an even more serious question is raised by the possibility that a positive assessment by international observers of a badly flawed election will result in the granting of democratic legitimacy to a regime which has no entitlement to it and thus, in part at least, undermine the democratisation process. This is the crux of Geisler's criticisms of the Commonwealth Observer Group particularly in relation to the 1992 Kenyan elections. The evidence that these elections were badly flawed is fairly extensive so it could well be asked whether, in concluding that these elections constituted 'a giant step on the road to multi-party democracy', the Group did, in fact, enhance the legitimacy of the of President Moi's victory in an unwarrantable manner. However, the overall conclusions of the Group were far from unambivelant. In its 71 page report[19] the Group provides extensive evidence of electoral malpractice. In particular it stresses that the elections were 'not fair' in relation to (1) the registration process in many parts of the country (2) the nominations process particularly in the Rift Valley, resulting in the unopposed return of 16 KANU candidates (3) the lack of transparency on the part of the Electoral Commission (4) the intimidation, administrative obstacles and violence that marked the political campaign (5) the partisanship of the state-owned radio and television (6) the reluctance of the Government to de-link itself from the KANU Party[20]. This hardly amounts to granting the Kenyan elections a clean bill of health or to what Geisler[21] describes as 'their unanimous acceptance of these seriously flawed elections'. Whilst it would be possible to argue that the Commonwealth Observer Group could have been even more critical of the 1992 Kenyan elections than they were it is impossible to argue that they were not critical.

Because outside observers will almost inevitably be perceived as a 'player in the game' in relation to African elections it is equally inevitable that their role will continue to generate a considerable amount of controversy. However, in assessing the role of external observers, the important question is not whether their presence ensures a free and fair election (it certainly does not) but rather whether on balance their presence is likely to make a particular election less unfair than it might otherwise have been. Like all counter-factual hypotheses this will always be open to argument but I would subscribe to the view that external observers are more likely to have a positive effect than a negative one and that any temptation to abandon monitoring on the grounds that is done imperfectly should be resisted. Although the question of how free and fair the conduct of any particular election has been is likely to remain a contested issue it is still an important one.

Classification of Elections

Before examining case studies of recent African elections it is necessary to draw up a taxonomy of elections through which they can be classified as belonging to particular types. This raises the obvious question regarding the main criteria to be adopted for classification. Until very recently a useful primary distinction was that between elections involving competing political parties and those in which only one party was permitted to participate: that is between multi-party and single-party elections. A large majority of elections would have been placed in the latter category with only a few in the former. The redemocratisation process in the period since 1989 has rendered this distinction almost worthless simply because whatever the problems and imperfections of the electoral process African elections have become multi-party. The single-party type of election, which dominated the African election scene in the 1970s and 1980s has, for the moment at least, all but disappeared from view. Beyond that the above discussion of the polemical and imprecise nature of election evaluation in terms of freedom and fairness indicates that it would be extremely difficult to use that aspect as a means of classification. The demise of apartheid in South Africa has marked the final ending of restricted franchise elections in Africa, which were not uncommon historically[22], and so eliminated a further aspect which could be used in classification of elections. Although a few arguments remain over voting age in a few states (usually involving a choice between 21 and 18) this is now largely a dead issue.

Given recent experience in Africa the classification of elections in terms of *outcomes* is far more useful because it highlights the important new phenomenon of opposition victory at the polls. Thus, the basic classificatory distinction which will be adopted is that between *regime changing elections* and *regime confirming elections*. A *regime changing election* is thus defined as one where, as a consequence of the election results, and as a direct reflection of those results, a new regime comes to power following the completion of the electoral process, and the previously incumbent regime loses power. Within this category of regime change election a further distinction needs to be made between those elections in which the incumbent regime, or significant elements within it, were contesting participants in the election and those where they were not. The latter sub-category is most commonly observed in cases of demilitarisation where a military regime reintroduces a democratic system with competitive elections as a mechanism for bringing about the transfer of power to civilians and where constituent elements of the military regime do not themselves participate in the election. The former sub-category is most commonly observed in cases where what was formerly the ruling party in a single-party state is defeated by an opposition party, or parties, in a multi-party election. This sub-category would also include those cases where a leader of a military regime participated in a democratic election but lost power as a consequence of the election.

At first glance the category of regime confirming election appears fairly straightforward. In such an election an incumbent regime, or at least the major elements within it, are returned to power by the election and are not replaced by their opponents. The regime in question may be clearly civilian but could be of a semi-military type. However, in defining an election as regime confirming it is not necessarily suggested that the wider political system remains unchanged. A significant representation of opposition parties in what was previously a legislature dominated by a monolithic single-party my fundamentally alter the balance and tone of the political system even if the regime is unchanged. Also the surviving incumbent national leader may seek generate more of a sense of compromise and consensus my offering ministerial office to some opposition representatives. In the latter case the still incumbent leader would retain the power to expel such people from the government but not from the party.

This distinction between regime changing elections and regime confirming elections is not directly concerned with the extent to which an election may be seen as having been free and fair. However in practice these features are not totally unconnected. Opposition victory in an election might be taken to demonstrate that either the incumbent regime had not tried to rig the election or that if it had tried to do so it had failed. Of course opposition parties cannot be automatically seen as innocent of malpractice although their lack of control of the state machine does reduce their opportunities in this respect. In general the evidence suggests that electoral malpractice has been a more prominent feature of regime confirming elections than it has of regime changing elections even though regime alternation cannot be regarded as a necessary component of democratic elections.

Finally it is necessary to acknowledge that it is not impossible to find cases which do not properly fit into either of the main categories involved in this classification. The 1993 Nigerian presidential election, for example, was neither regime changing nor regime confirming. The winners of the election, Moshood Abiola and the SDP, did not come to power but the election did not confirm the Babangida regime in power, not least because the latter was not a contestant in the election.

Since 1989 fourteen African states have experienced regime changing elections. In eleven of these incumbent regimes contested the elections and in the other three they did not. States where regime changing elections in which incumbents participated since 1989 were Benin (1991), Burundi (1993), Cape Verde (1991), Central African Republic (1993), Congo (1992 with a regime confirming election in 1993), Madagascar (1993), Malawi (1994), Niger (1993), Sao Tome and Principe (1991 and 1994, alternation of parties), South Africa (1994), and Zambia (1991). States where regime changing elections took place but where incumbent regimes did not participate were Lesotho (1993), Mali (1992), and Namibia (1989, with a regime confirming election in 1994). The allocation of South Africa to the first sub-category rather than to the second is less than totally clear cut. The election brought an ANC dominated regime to power in place of the NP regime but in the run-up to the election the ANC had played an increasingly influential role in the affairs of state and the NP continued to play a diminished but still significant role in government after the election. Also, as a pre-independence election, that in Namibia in 1989 was logically bound to lead to a regime change. As befits the sub-categories outlined earlier both Lesotho and Mali were cases of demilitarisation where the incumbent military regimes abstained from participation in the electoral competition. As indicated above Sao Tome and Principe provides the first example in Africa of a case where a ruling party defeated in one election managed to win the next election. In 1991 the incumbent, and hitherto only, party the Movement for the Liberation of Sao Tome and Principe-Social Democratic Party (MLSTP-PSD) was defeated in a general election in the island state. Following a resurgence of support in local government elections the MLSTP-PSD won two thirds of the seats in the next general election held in October 1994[23].

An examination of the list of states experiencing regime changing elections suggests that in most ways they represent a highly varied group marked by an absence of common features. The geographical spread of these states does not suggest any significant regional dimension to this phenomenon: they are widely spread across the African continent. In terms of size the list includes small states and large states both in relation to population size and to physical size. Their colonial histories are equally diverse, encompassing Anglophone, Francophone, and Lusophone cases and also both settler and non-settler states. Some of them have had extensive experience of military rule in the post-colonial period and some have always retained civilian rule. Attempting to establish some commonality in relation to relative levels of poverty or affluence appears equally fruitless. Judged in relation to World Bank estimates of GNP per capita the list includes some of Africa's richest states (eg. Cape Verde, Congo, South Africa) and some of its poorest (eg. Burundi, Malawi, Sao Tome and Principe). This absence of common features points in the direction of attempting to understand them in terms of their particular local circumstances.

In selecting case studies of recent African elections for inclusion the temptation for anyone with a reasonably hopeful perspective on Africa to include the April 1994 elections in South Africa is very strong indeed. It is a temptation which I have no intention of even trying to resist. By almost universal agreement these elections went better than even the wildest optimist would have dared to predict just a couple of years or even months earlier, creating an emotional high for participants and observers alike which came as a welcome change for a continent which has had more than its fair share of emotional lows. However, the importance of these elections is not simply related to a 'feel-good' factor. Given its size, wealth, and potential, South Africa is an important state in its own right but what happens there could well have an important effect on developments in other parts of Africa, particularly in the southern part of the continent. Whilst these elections were only an early step on the difficult road to a consolidated democracy in South Africa they marked an impressive beginning. The contrast between South Africa and Nigeria[24], the only other state in Africa with the potential to rival the importance and influence of South Africa, is abundantly clear.

As is well known the 1994 elections marked the first occasion on which all South Africans of voting age were able to participate together in choosing a government for the country. The constitutional arrangements for the election had been worked out by the Convention for a Democratic South Africa (CODESA) which had begun work in early 1992 and which included representation from almost all significant sections of South African political opinion[25]. Under these arrangements representatives were to be elected to a National Assembly and to nine provincial legislatures (Northern Transvaal, Eastern Transvaal, Pretoria/Witwatersrand/Vereeniging-PWV, North-West, Orange Free State, Kwazulu/Natal, Northern Cape, Western Cape, Eastern Cape). The new nine province structure was created to replace the traditional four province structure to reflect South African regional diversity. The provincial legislatures indirectly elected the national upper house, the Senate. Apart from choosing a government the National Assembly was to have the task of drawing up the final version of the new South African constitution before the next elections due in 1999. Under the CODESA agreement the 1994 election was conducted on a basis of strict proportional representation from a list system. The latter had two components: a national list and nine provincial lists. Half of the National Assembly of 400 members was elected from the national lists and half from the provincial lists. The latter also served as the basis for deciding representation on the provincial legislatures. A further very important part of the agreement was that at the national level the government should be one of 'national unity' which would include representatives of all parties with significant support rather than being drawn solely from a majority party. Overall the interim constitution represents a compromise between unitary and federal principles and is, in the opinion of Arend Lijphart, 'fundamentally a consociational document'[26].

A critical feature of the election, and one which looked rather unlikely in advance, was that virtually all significant political groupings in the country eventually agreed to participate in it. Until shortly before the election it seemed likely that the legitimacy of the outcome would be called into question by a boycott of the process by some groups. At one stage it seemed that the far left, the far right, and the Zulu based IFP would all be missing. On the far left the main possibility of abstention was that from the Pan Africanist Congress (PAC), the traditional rival of the ANC within the liberation movement. It was not until January 1994 that the PAC formally announced the suspension of the 'armed struggle' by its military wing the Azanian People's Liberation Army (APLA) following strong pressure on the movement by the Zimbabwean and Tanzanian governments. It may not be over cynical to suggest that the reluctance of the PAC to join the democratic process until very late on was due in large part to the concern of the leadership that in an open contest for popular support the party would fare very badly in comparison with the ANC: the final results indicate that this concern was entirely justified. Similar questions over participation in the election occurred for the white far right which could roughly be seen to encompass that just under one third of the white population which had voted against reform in the 1992 referendum (see previous chapter). In practical terms this was a very disparate group ranging from the quasi-fascist fringe represented by the AWB which still retained dreams of resurrecting full-blown apartheid to more pragmatic elements who supported some form of white self-determination, within a *volkstaat*, (which was variously conceived of as a separate independent state, or a degree of regional autonomy) or at least strong (white) minority rights. For a time the far right came together in a united front, the Afrikaner Volksfront (AVF), but as the election approached there were irreconcilable tensions between those who wished to pursue their ends by, perhaps reluctantly, participating in the electoral process and those who still rejected the idea. After considerable bitter faction fighting within the AVF the dominant figure on the pragmatic wing, General Constand Viljoen the former commander of the South African Defence Force (SADF), broke away to form the Freedom Front (FF) which was registered for participation in the election just twenty minutes before the midnight deadline on 4th March 1994. The later election results suggest clearly that the large majority of right wing whites voted for the FF rather than abstain. This was important in underpinning the inclusionary aspect of the election because it meant that only a minority of a minority of a minority refused to take

122

part (rejectionists were a minority of the far right which is a minority of whites who are a minority within the population). An even more serious threat of non-participation in the election was that posed by Mangosuthu Buthelezi and the Inkatha Freedom Party (IFP). Since 1990 the most serious violent conflict in South Africa had been between IFP and ANC supporters. At the end of March 1994 the severity of this conflict had forced the government to declare a state of emergency in Kwazulu/Natal. The problem was increased by the development of severe tensions within the IFP between Buthelezi and his nephew the Zulu king, Goodwill Zwelithini. It was widely recognised that without IFP participation the electoral process would be destabilised in many parts of the country and would be virtually impossible in Kwazulu/Natal. Whilst the decision of Buthelezi to take part in the election, just one week before the polls were due to open, created an administrative nightmare for the election organisers it did mark a very positive development for the electoral process. Overall the 1994 South African election was marked by an extremely high level of inclusiveness and although the decision to participate was taken very late in the day by some groups there were, in the end, no significant groups excluded. The importance of this factor would be difficult to overestimate.

The election campaign was a rather unusual hybrid marked by both 'first world' and 'third world' characteristics. A number of its features would be very familiar to those who observe elections in western democracies. Both the ANC and the NP, the two major parties, made extensive use of opinion polls in an attempt to identify their strengths and weaknesses in the eyes of the voters and used the results to modify campaign strategies and messages. The ANC engaged the services of Stanley Greenberg and Frank Greer who had masterminded the successful presidential campaign of Bill Clinton in the USA and who contributed considerable expertise to the campaign strategy of the party. Not to be outdone the NP hired the British firm Saatchi and Saatchi which had considerable experience in working for the Conservative Party in British general elections. Both parties were advised to concentrate on their plans for the future rather than to focus on the past. Although no parties were permitted to buy advertising time on television all parties used the radio and the press extensively to get their message across in paid advertising. The greater financial resources of the NP and the ANC in comparison with the other parties gave them a considerable advantage (it has been estimated that the ANC had between three and four times the campaign funding of the NP[27] but both had far more than the others). Both the ANC and the NP devoted considerable effort to projecting their national leaders, Mandela and de Klerk, because opinion polling revealed that in both cases the leaders were more popular than their respective parties. As Silke and Schrire commented 'South Africa was witness to a 'first world' advertising campaign to attract a majority of 'third world' voters'[28].

In advance of the elections many observers had expressed fears that they would marked by high levels of violence. In the event violence was very restricted. The worst incidents took place on April 23rd, 25th and 27th when bombs planted by right wing terrorists exploded in central Johannesburg, in Germiston, and at Jan Smuts airport outside Johannesburg, killing and injuring dozens of people. The police moved swiftly to arrest 31 members of the neo-Nazi AWB, who were subsequently charged with murder, also seizing large amounts of explosives, and the bombing campaign came to an end. Apart from these bombs incidents of electoral violence were few and scattered: some foreign television crews were heard to complain that they 'were not getting enough bangs for their bucks'. The elections, which ran for four days from 26th to 29th April (an extra day having been added to allow maximum voting), were marked by exceptional good will and patience that almost all observers found deeply moving. The South African election was probably the most 'observed' election ever with around 5,000 official election monitors (from the UN, Commonwealth, OAU etc) and another 3,000 foreign journalists in addition to all those from South Africa itself. The good will and patience exhibited by voters were badly needed because in organisational terms the election was rather less than perfect: in some areas it was simply chaotic. Whilst allowance has to be made for the fact this was the very first time such an election had been held in the country it is clear that substantial improvements in organisation will be required by 1999 when the mood of the elections will inevitably be rather less euphoric. The Independent Electoral Commission declared that the elections had been 'substantially free and fair'. Whilst this judgement appears reasonably accurate in relation to South Africa as a whole it is extremely doubtful if it can be said of large areas of Kwazulu/Natal. Here the evidence is of considerable electoral malpractice, mostly from the IFP but probably also from the ANC, and although the results (which gave the IFP a narrow provincial majority) were 'convenient' from the perspective of national unity and stability there remain serious doubts as to their democratic validity[29].

With the partial exception of Kwazulu/Natal the final official results of the election represent a reasonably accurate picture of the levels of support for the competing parties across the country. At the national level the two major parties were the ANC and the NP which between them won over 80% of the votes[30]. The proportion of votes and number of seats gained in the National Assembly for each party was: ANC 62.65%, 252 seats; NP 20.39%, 82 seats; IFP 10.54%, 43 seats; FF 2.17%, 9 seats; DP 1.73%, 7 seats; PAC 1.25%, 5 seats; ACDP, 0.45%, 2 seats. The twelve remaining parties all won less than 0.2% and gained no seats. Clearly the use of proportional representation and the absence of a threshold benefited the smaller parties (a 5% threshold, for example would have excluded all but the NP, ANC, and IFP) although it could do little to help the very small parties. In advance some observers had feared that if the ANC won more than two thirds of the seats it would be able to draw up the final constitution without reference to the wishes of other parties. Given the overwhelming emphasis on conciliation and compromise adopted by the ANC and Mandela in recent years it is probably unlikely that the ANC would have behaved in this way but the results put an end to this fear: Reynolds is almost certainly correct when he suggests that 'the greatest sigh of relief that the ANC had not won two thirds of the national vote came from the ANC themselves'[31]. The election clearly demonstrated what all previous evidence had suggested, that the ANC was the most popular party in South Africa and that Nelson Mandela was even more clearly the most popular leader: it is perhaps necessary to remind oneself that only a little over four years earlier Mandela was still in jail and the ANC was still a banned organisation.

At the level of provincial legislatures the ANC again did very well but there was some regional variation. In six out of nine provincial legislatures the ANC emerged with an overall majority of seats but in three it did not. In the Northern Cape the ANC won 15 seats which equalled the combined total of the other parties winning seats, creating a situation of no party having 'overall control'. This could have created a deadlock in the election of the regional premier by the legislature but in the event the ANC candidate was elected when the single DP member supported the ANC and the the FF members abstained. In return the DP member was proposed as Speaker and an FF member was included in the provincial cabinet. In Kwazulu/Natal the IFP ended up with the smallest of majorities when it won 41 out of 81 seats. Here it is likely that the IFP will seek to protect its precarious hold on the legislature by reaching some form of accommodation with the opposition. This could take the form of an agreement with the local NP, which has had strong links with Buthelezi in the past, or just possibly with the ANC. The provincial premier is Frank Mdlalose, an IFP moderate who is known to favour some sort of reconciliation with the local ANC. The ANC's biggest regional setback came in the Western Cape where the NP won 23 out of 42 seats in the provincial legislature with the ANC managing to win just 14.

Given the predominant role played by racial identity in South Africa's politics in the past (largely because it was legally enforced) it is important to examine the way in which this identity shaped voting behaviour in 1994. Because this was a non-racial election in which all the electorate voted on a common basis statistics relating to the racial breakdown of the vote are necessarily estimates[32] rather than official figures. These estimates suggest that although racial identity was clearly related to voting behaviour it was modified in a number of ways. Apart from the FF, whose support was virtually all from whites, and the PAC, whose support was virtually all from blacks, all the other significant parties had multi-racial support although in different proportions. The estimates of racial voting patterns have to be understood in the context of the racial structure of the electorate which is approximately 73% black, 15% white, 9% coloured, and 3% Indian. Around 94% of ANC support was from blacks although it was substantially lower amongst the Zulu than other black ethnic groups. In addition to black votes the ANC gained around half a million coloured votes, 150,000 Indian votes, and 50,000 white votes. It should be noted that the ANC leadership is proportionally more multi-racial than its voters and includes significant numbers of non-blacks in important party positions which is a reflection of the ANC's long-term opposition to racism. The NP's vote was approximately 49% white, 30% coloured, 14% black, and 7% Indian. This suggests the the NP was able to attract around two thirds of the votes cast by members of the coloured and Indian communities: its success in the Western Cape was largely due to support from coloured voters. Although only around 4% of black votes went to the NP the numerical predominance of blacks within the electorate makes this a significant component of overall NP support. It is an historical irony that the party which was the architect of apartheid oppression should enjoy the clearest multi-racial support in the first post-apartheid elections. The ability of the NP to transform its racial image over the last few years has been quite remarkable. The contrast with the DP heightens the irony. The Democratic Party is the direct descendant of the Progressive Party which was the only white party in the decades before 1990 to support the idea of a non-racial South Africa but in the election it picked up very little non-white support. This was a major factor in its dismal overall performance. In many ways the NP had adopted most of its policies and was able to articulate them better. The IFP gained around 85% of its overall vote from blacks but these were almost entirely Zulu, mainly in Kwazulu/Natal but including some from migrant workers in the PWV. The party also picked up around 5% of white votes nationally. The IFP vote was the most regionally concentrated of the major parties with 86% coming from Kwazulu/Natal.

On May 10th 1994 Nelson Mandela was sworn in as the first president of a democratic non-racial South Africa having been unanimously elected by the National Assembly the previous day.

Although it is correct to emphasise the importance of the South African elections this should not be allowed to obscure other important regime changing elections which received considerably less attention from the international media. Although it is impossible here to go into great detail in all of them it is useful to consider other examples. Although Zambia cannot be said to have the same international importance as South Africa the elections held in October 1991 were important for Zambian politics and, because they resulted in the peaceful replacement through the ballot box of long-term incumbent, they were influential in the early stages of the democratisation process in Africa in indicating the inherent potential of that process for delivering change in African political systems. Prior to 1991 Zambia had last experienced competitive democratic elections in 1968, just four years after independence. In 1972 President Kenneth Kaunda responded to a growth of new opposition parties by introducing a single-party state in which his own United National Independence Party (UNIP) was the only legally permitted political party. Subsequent elections involved some very limited competition between UNIP candidates for the legislature but the presidential elections only ever had one candidate and it was always Kaunda. Following the pressure for democratic change, discussed earlier, the Zambian constitution was amended in August 1991 so as to legalise opposition parties and to permit the latter to participate in presidential and parliamentary elections.

The 1991 elections essentially represented two-party elections. Although a number of very minor parties put up a handful of candidates in a few parliamentary constituencies there were only two parties which contested on a national basis and which put up presidential candidates. These were the incumbent UNIP and the MMD: the latter is a good example of the phenomenon discussed earlier in this chapter of pro-democracy movements transforming themselves into contesting political parties once the struggle for multi-partyism had been won. Although the most important organisational and support base of the MMD was provided by the trade union movement, as was its presidential candidate Frederick Chiluba of the Zambian Congress of Trade Unions (ZCTU), the party enjoyed strong support from several other sectors of Zambian society including the private business sector, the main churches, students and educationalists, and a number of old UNIP heavyweights including Vernon Mwaanga and Arthur Wina who had previously been, respectively, foreign minister and finance minister. It is a tribute to Chiluba's leadership that he managed to ward off any dangers of significant opposition fragmentation in the run-up to the election.

Although the elections were generally judged to have been free and fair by internal and external monitors and observers, and generally passed of very peacefully, the MMD was engaged in a constant struggle to prevent UNIP using the advantages of incumbency in an attempt to secure victory. Kaunda refused to end the 28-year-old State of Emergency during the election campaign despite the fact that the main justification for it, the threatening security situation in Southern Africa, had largely disappeared following the changes in South Africa. The State of Emergency gave the government wide discretionary powers to restrict political meetings which did not have an official permit and to control the movement of citizens during the hours of darkness[33]. Although the MMD was able to successfully contest the more partisan applications of these measures in the courts it was a time-consuming business which slowed down the opposition campaign. The MMD cause was also harmed by the refusal of the government to update the voter registration lists which had last been compiled in 1988: this effectively disenfranchised large numbers of younger voters who were believed to be predominantly opposition supporters. Attempts by Kaunda to deny the opposition access to the media were largely curtailed when, following an appeal by the MMD, the Zambian High Court ruled the President's actions 'illegal, unconstitutional, and discriminatory'. Under the single-party state little distinction had been made between UNIP and the government. Especially in the early part of the campaign UNIP was prone to use public resources (finance, transport, telephones etc.) for party political purposes. Finally we should point to a generalised fear-factor. Following nearly two decades of authoritarian single-party rule the MMD had to go to great lengths to convince the population that they now had the legal and moral right to oppose Kaunda and UNIP without fear of being severely punished by the state. The election results clearly indicate that none of the above difficulties were insurmountable for the MMD but it was often an uphill struggle.

The organisation of the election on polling day itself appears to have gone very smoothly in spite of some, inevitable, administrative hiccups. The Commonwealth Observer Group report how 'well before sunrise, queues of voters had formed at many polling stations...there was an air of peace and quiet as the mainly silent, or quietly whispering, voters waited to cast their votes'[34]: the Group concluded that the elections 'were conducted in a calm and orderly manner and gave the people of Zambia the opportunity to vote for the Presidential and National Assembly candidates of their choice'[35]. The votes from each of the 3,489 polling stations were transported to designated counting centres in the various parts of the country. In advance the MMD had requested that votes be counted at polling stations to avoid the possibility of ballot boxes 'going missing' on their way to the counting centres but this had been rejected. In the event the actual counting of votes, including the agreement on what constituted invalid (ie. spoilt) ballot papers, did not give rise to any real disagreement.

The results of the election, which may be seen as an accurate reflection voter preference, represented a massive opposition victory and a massive defeat for Kaunda and UNIP. In the presidential election Kaunda gained one quarter of the votes with the remaining three quarters going to Chiluba. In the parliamentary elections the MMD did even better winning over 80% of the votes and 125 out of the 150 seats. The rest of the seats and nearly all of the rest of the votes went to UNIP with minor parties gaining no significant support and winning no seats. Although Kaunda and his party did relatively well in his home area of Eastern Province there was no significant evidence of ethnic or 'tribal' voting patterns. Although the claims of politicians that 'we are all Zambians now' may understate the continuing role of ethnicity in Zambian politics it is also clear that the old stereotype (usually advanced by opponents of African democracy including, in the past at least, Kaunda himself)) that multi-partyism can only produce tribal conflict and instability is not validated by the Zambian experience of genuinely competitive elections.

The orderliness of the transition was enhanced by the grace and dignity with which Kaunda accepted his defeat and his expulsion from office after twenty seven years in power. He escorted the new President Chiluba on a tour of State House and in a farewell speech on Zambian television he was dignified and generous towards his victorious opponent. Such public behaviour probably did not come easily to Kaunda and, as Chan and Chingambo report, 'only when he left the television studio and came to his limousine did he betray his feelings...personally detaching the presidential pennant from his car, he wept as he handed it to his driver, climbed in and moved away'[36]. For some observers the very size of the MMD victory is seen as posing problems for the development of democracy in Zambia because in some ways a single-party state has been replaced by one in which one party, albeit a different one, has become dominant. It could be argued that a more numerous opposition representation in parliament would have been healthier for Zambian democracy. However, at the end of the day, the critical factor is surely that it was the Zambian electorate, voting in a freely democratic fashion, who determined the outcome.

Following the victory for the supporters of multi-party democracy in the 1993 referendum in Malawi (discussed in the previous chapter) the country moved towards its first ever post-independence competitive elections to be held in May 1994. As in Zambia elections for the presidency and for the legislature were held on the same day. Electoral competition in Malawi was largely a three party affair although there were a handful of inconsequential minor parties. The three major parties were the incumbent ruling party, the MCP of President Hastings Kamuzu Banda, and two parties which had emerged from the pro-democracy movement whose pressure had contributed to the recent constitutional changes in Malawi. These two were AFORD led by trade union leader Chakufwa Chihana, and the UDF led by Bakili Muluzi a Muslim businessman who had previously been a senior figure in the MCP and a member of Banda's cabinet. Of the minor parties only the Malawi National Democratic Party (MNDP) of Kampelo Kalua contested the presidential election.

The election campaign was generally conducted in a peaceful manner. A major contribution to the peaceful nature of the campaign was the decision take by the Malawian army in December 1993 to disarm the Malawi Young Pioneers (MYP)[37]. In theory the latter were the youth wing of the MCP but in practice they had for many years been little more than a group of organised thugs used to intimidate opponents of the President: their forceful elimination from the political scene was a major bonus for the electoral process. The Malawi Congress of Churches continued its policy of supporting democracy by launching a nationwide campaign of education to explain to the population how democratic elections were organised. A contribution to this task was also made by the Legal Resources Centre run by Vera Chirwa the widow of Orton Chirwa, a long-term opponent of Banda who had died in political imprisonment in October 1992. On polling day, 17th May, the voting process took place without any major incidents and with remarkably little administrative confusion[38]. The turn out was estimated to be some 80% of potential voters many of whom queued for up to twelve hours to cast their votes.

The results of the election demonstrated an unequal three way split between the parties, which was predominantly structured along regional lines, with the UDF emerging as the most popular party. In the presidential election Bakili Muluzi (UDF) gained 47.3% of the votes with 33.6% going to Hastings Kamuzu Banda (MCP), 18.6% to Chakufwa Chihana (AFORD), and just 0.5% to Kampelo Kalua. Although Muluzi narrowly failed to gain an overall majority of the votes he clearly won the election and was installed as President on May 21st. Muluzi gained the bulk of his support in the Southern Region including 91% of the votes in his home district, Machinga, and falling below 50% in this region only in the Shire Valley, which is the home base of MCP secretary-general Guamba Chakuamba. The support base of Banda and Chihana is equally regionally based with the former polling well in Central Region, and the latter in Northern Region. In the legislative elections the UDF gained 84 seats with 55 going to the MCP, 36 to AFORD, and none to the minor parties. The same regional distribution of support which was evident in the presidential election was also evident in the legislative election although there were a fair number of individual constituencies which went against the trend due to specific local circumstances: the UDF, for example, won 14 seats in Central Region, whilst the MCP won 5 in Southern Region. Only in Northern Region, where AFORD won all the seats, was there almost monolithic support for one particular party: unfortunately for AFORD this is the region with the smallest population and least number of constituencies. The legislative elections left the UDF five seats short of an overall majority in the National Assembly but, following protracted negotiations, AFORD agreed in late September to support the government, in return for which Chakufwa Chihana was appointed Second Vice-President in Bakili Muluzi's administration.

In the light of Malawian political history possibly the most surprising thing about the elections, apart perhaps from the fact that they took place at all, was the grace with which Banda accepted electoral defeat. In a speech made even before the final result of the presidential election was officially announced he acknowledged that Muluzi was the 'clear winner' and promised that in opposition the MCP would contribute to 'building a better democratic Malawi'[39]. For years observers of Malawi had assumed that Banda would remain in office until his death and that when he died Malawi would be plunged into an intractable succession crisis which might tear the country apart because his highly personalised rule precluded a peaceful succession. The possibility that Banda would be voted out of office in a peaceful democratic election, which produced a new president with a high level of popular support and a multi-party parliament, would have been regarded as an absurd flight of fancy. But, that is what happened!

As indicated earlier there were a small number of cases of regime changing elections in which the incumbent regime did not take part as contestants. The Francophone state of Mali in West Africa provides a useful example of this type of election. The discussion in chapter three indicated how the mass struggle for democracy resulted in the overthrow of the authoritarian regime of Moussa Traore, which had been in power since 1968, by a reformist group within the military which then prepared the way for the holding of democratic elections in the country. Malian elections also differed from those in, for example, Zambia and Malawi in other important respects especially in the number of political parties involved and the types of voting systems used[40].

Following the liberalisation of the political system 47 different political parties emerged in Mali. This picture of fairly extreme party proliferation has to be modified by an examination of how many of these parties had any significance for the political system. To some extent this relies on a retrospective judgement based on election performance (see below) but it could be noted that half of these so-called parties did not even reach the stage of putting up candidates in local elections in January 1992 when the voting system used was most favourable towards minor parties and when taking part required minimum effort. In fact only three of the parties can be considered to be major parties of national importance whilst a few more can be seen as minor parties with at least some significance even if this was extremely localised.

The most important party was the Alliance for Democracy in Mali (ADEMA) led by Alpha Oumar Konare which developed from the major pro-democracy grouping in the period of the struggle for democracy. Konare was a major academic who had written extensively on Malian history. From 1978 to 1980 he had been a minister in Traore's government but had resigned in protest when the latter had gone back on an earlier promise to democratise the political system[41]. Subsequent to that he founded a cultural organisation called Jamana in 1983 which served partly as an umbrella for those opposed to the authoritarian government. In his administrative work with Jamana Konare built up a network of contacts on a national basis which were later utilised by ADEMA. The other main pro-democracy group which also transformed itself into a political party was National Committee for Democratic Revival (CNID). The latter was led by Mountaga Tall, an able politician whose national appeal was limited a little by his ethnic identification with the minority Toucouleur group. The third major party was the Soudanese Union-Democratic African Rally (US-RDA) which was the direct descendant of the party which had ruled Mali until it was overthrown by the Moussa Traore coup in 1968: originally founded in 1946 it was one of the oldest parties in Africa. The US-RDA had always been internally factionalised on ideological lines but it was the representative of the more moderate faction, Tieoule Konate, who led the party in the elections. Like ADEMA the US-RDA had a strong national organisational structure.

The first elections to be contested following democratisation were the January 1992 municipal elections. For these elections the voting system was based on an extreme version of proportional representation which, because the councils were large (up to 55 members), meant that parties needed only a small proportion of the vote in any municipal area to gain a seat. Only the three main parties put up candidates in all areas but overall 19 parties won seats. Nearly two thirds of the seats were won by the three main parties, with ADEMA clearly the most successful, and only nine parties could count their seats in double figures. Nevertheless this left all councils without a party with an overall majority and two with more than 10 parties represented.

It was to avoid this sort of situation that a different electoral system was adopted for the National Assembly elections held in February/March 1992. The legislative elections were based on multi-member constituencies in which the winning party in each constituency, either on a first round or a second round of voting, won all the seats for that constituency. Only ADEMA and CNID put up party lists in all constituencies although US-RDA contested a large majority. Although it was ultimately the Malian electorate who determined party representation in the legislature, in what was regarded as a free and fair election, the electoral system was consciously designed to maximise the chances of one party winning an overall majority of seats (and hence provide a stable basis for government) an to minimise the chances of extreme proliferation of party representation in the National Assembly. To a large extent this goal was achieved. ADEMA won a clear overall majority with 73 out of 115 seats with 9 going to CNID and 8 to US-RDA. The remaining 25 seats were divided up amongst eight minor parties. Richard Vengroff has calculated that if the election had been based on the extreme version of proportional representation similar to that which was used in the local elections (and if all voters had voted for the same party as they did) then ADEMA would have won 43 seats and no party would have had an overall majority[42].

In April 1992 the election process was climaxed by the presidential election. This election was organised over two rounds whereby if no candidate won an

132

overall majority in the first round the two best supported candidates proceeded to a second round. In the first round the ADEMA candidate Alpha Konare came fairly close to winning an overall majority with 46% of the vote in spite of there being 9 candidates in all: Tieoule Konate of the US-RDA came second with 14.5% in spite of the fact that the radical faction within the party put up a separate candidate, Baba Haidara, who won 7.5% of the vote. In the second round of the election Konare won convincingly with 69% of the vote, well ahead of Konate with 31%. The following month Konare resigned as leader of ADEMA in, line with the constitutional provision which bars the President from membership of a political party. In June he was installed as the first President of Mali to have been democratically elected in the post-colonial period.

Regime Confirming Elections

Since 1989 twenty one African states have held at least one competitive election which turned out to be regime confirming. By definition all of these involved incumbent regimes. Regime confirming elections took place in Angola (1992), Botswana (1989 and 1994), Burkina Faso (1992), Cameroon (1992), Comoros (1994), Cote d'Ivoire (1990), Djibouti (1993), Ethiopia (1994), Gabon (1990, 1991, and 1993), The Gambia (1992), Ghana (1992), Guinea (1993), Guinea-Bissau (1994), Kenya (1992), Mauritania (1992), Mauritius (1993), Mozambique (1994), Senegal (1993), Seychelles (1993), Togo (1993 and 1994), and Zimbabwe (1990).

Although all of these elections belong to the regime confirming category they represent, in other ways, a less than homogeneous group. In Angola the 1992 elections were[43] only partly completed when the electoral process, and along with it the whole democratisation process, collapsed. The September elections resulted from the peace agreement between the incumbent Popular Movement for the Liberation of Angola (MPLA) and the dissident guerrilla group the National Union for the Total Independence of Angola (UNITA) which ended (temporarily as it turned out) the catastrophic civil war which had been fought between the two since Portuguese decolonisation in 1975. The National Assembly elections gave the MPLA a clear but not overwhelming victory but it was the presidential elections which led to the breakdown of the process. In these elections Jose Eduardo dos Santos (MPLA) won 49.67% of the vote whilst his main opponent Jonas Savimbi (UNITA) won 40.7%, with the rest going to minor candidates. Under the electoral rules this should have resulted in a second round run-off between dos Santos and Savimbi for the presidency but the latter unilaterally abandoned the elections at this point and returned to armed struggle against the MPLA government, thus plunging Angola back into civil war. Although around 800 foreign observers and election monitors had deemed the elections to be free and fair, although not without administrative defects, Savimbi claimed that they had been rigged against UNITA. A more plausible explanation is that the first round of the presidential elections indicated that although Savimbi does have substantial support amongst the Angolan electorate the level of his support is insufficient to produce victory in a democratic election. Rather than accept defeat he denigrated the election and pulled out. The humanitarian cost to the Angolan population of this decision has subsequently been enormous. Although Angola represents an extreme case it does raise a salient general point relating to the democratisation process in Africa in regard to the importance of losers of elections being willing to accept defeat. Whilst any participant has the undeniable right to point out electoral malpractice when it occurs it is very damaging to the process when election losers make allegations of malpractice when it has not taken place or grossly exaggerate it when it has taken place on a small scale. One does not have to be a supporter of the MPLA (which itself has a past record of intolerant authoritarianism) to recognise that Savimbi's rejection of the election result was extremely damaging to the possibility of establishing democracy in Angola.

In several of the states listed above the regime confirming elections cannot be seen as indicating a recent conversion to multi-party competition. The states in question are Botswana, The Gambia, Mauritius and Zimbabwe which had been continuously multi-party since independence, and Senegal which had returned to full multi-partyism in 1981. In these states the holding of competitive elections was already part of established political practice, a fact that made the military coup in The Gambia in July 1994[44], which was followed by the banning of all political parties there, all the more depressing from a democratic perspective.

The Togolese elections also represent something of an anomaly, but for quite different reasons. In the August 1993 presidential elections the incumbent Gnassingbe Eyadema was re-elected in circumstances which made a mockery of the notion of a free and fair election. However, in the elections for the National Assembly held in February 1994, which although far from perfect enjoyed more credibility than the presidential election, parties opposed to President Eyadema emerged with a narrow majority in the legislature. Overall it is more accurate to categorise the Togolese elections as regime confirming rather than as regime changing but it must also be said that Eyadema's continuing ability and willingness to use the military to maintain his position remains more important in determining the location of political power in Togo than does anything which goes on in Togolese polling stations.

One general final point that needs to be made regarding these regime confirming elections is that the category refers only to the national level of the political system. Alongside these presidential and parliamentary elections one frequently finds local elections taking place, often on the same day at the same polling stations. If these local elections are taken into account the overall picture reflects a greater diffusion of power within the political system than does a concentration solely on national level results. It is frequently the case that opposition parties which fail at the national level still succeed in gaining control of local government structures in some parts of the country. In Kenya, for example, although the 1992 election was regime confirming at the national level the opposition took control of many local councils including all the most important towns like Nairobi, Mombasa, Nakuru, Kisumu, Eldoret, and Kitale[45]. Kenya is not at all unusual in this respect and whilst control of local councils is everywhere less important than control of central government it is by no means unimportant.

At the national level in Kenya it was more a case of the opposition losing the elections than it was of the incumbents, President Moi and his KANU party, winning them. Although the opposition parties had clearly been disadvantaged by the range of unfair strategies employed by Moi during the campaign, which were outlined earlier in the chapter, the combined opposition still managed to win nearly two thirds of the votes in the elections held on 29th December 1992. Whilst it is true that a completely free and fair election would almost certainly have resulted in an even higher proportion of the votes being won by the opposition, electoral malpractice cannot, by itself, explain how an incumbent won the election with only a little over one third of the popular vote. Blaming Moi's chicanery goes only a little way to explaining how the opposition managed to snatch defeat from the jaws of victory. Following the legalisation of opposition parties by a very reluctant Moi in December 1991 the opposition FORD appeared almost unbeatable. In January 1992 a party rally in Nairobi drew an ecstatic crowd of more than a hundred thousand supporters. At this stage the FORD leadership reflected a wide ethnic base including Kikuyu, Luo, Luhya, Kamba, and Kisii, and a wide regional base with only Moi's heartland in the Rift Valley excluded. The first major split in the opposition came in February when Mwai Kibaki, a former dissident minister in Moi's government, formed the Democratic Party (DP), a move which effectively undermined a united Kikuyu opposition to the incumbent regime. Although Kibaki had strong support from many northern Kikuyu there were, at that stage enough, Kikuyu remaining in FORD to make the latter a powerful ethnic and regional coalition. However, as the year progressed lines of cleavage within FORD related to personal and ethnic factors became deeper until the party split into two sections[46]. Both insisted on retaining the original name and they became FORD-Asili (meaning 'original') and FORD-Kenya. The former emerged as a predominantly southern Kikuyu party under the leadership of Kenneth Matiba whilst the latter was predominantly Luo and was led by the veteran politician Oginga Odinga. As the results of the election clearly indicate this fracturing of

135

the opposition virtually handed the election victory to Moi and KANU. Although there were four other very minor parties the main contestants were the four named above. In the presidential election Moi won 36.5% of the votes ahead of Matiba (26%), Kibaki (19.45%), and Odinga (17.48%). Because the election was based on the system of simple plurality, with no second round, Moi was re-elected as President on the basis of an underwhelming minority of the total vote. In Central Province he received just 2% of the vote. The legislative elections presented a similar pattern with a divided opposition allowing the incumbent KANU to win an overall majority of seats with just over one third of the total vote: KANU won 100 seats (but this included 16 'uncontested'), the two FORD parties won 31 each, the DP won 23, and 3 went to minor parties with a local base. Although the opposition parties ended up with a substantial minority of seats in the National Assembly with which to challenge the hegemony of the president and his party they still ended up losing an election which a year earlier had appeared very winnable.

Conclusions

This examination of new political party formation and the holding of competitive elections clearly shows an incomparable rise in the level of political participation in black Africa from Tombouctou in the north to Cape Town in the south. This reversed the post-independence trend which for the most part exhibited a decline in participation, which had usually been deliberately engineered by those in power. Although the procedures of increasing participation have often been flawed, in some cases debilitatingly so, far more people in Africa have been taking part in the political process. This increased participation can be seen at both elite and mass levels of the political system. At the elite level it has been marked by a re-entry into the political process of counter-elites, that is those alternative political leaders who had previously been excluded from, or had withdrawn from, the political processes of party formation and electoral competition. Members of this 'opposition-in-waiting' became major participants in the more open arena of public contestation. The weakened control of authoritarian leaders over the mechanisms of domination, for example the hitherto single-party, also created new openings for non-dominant members of existing elites to break free from existing structures and play a more substantial and independent role within the political system. The importance of defecting members of ruling parties in new oppositional structures is an example of this phenomenon. At elite level less restrictive modes of party formation and competition enhanced and expanded the framework of political participation.

Whilst competition between elites is an important characteristic of democracy the outcome of that competition is dependent on mass participation in the electoral process which decides who shall be winners and who shall be losers. The decisive role of the electorate can only exist when they have a choice to make, a feature which in the past has been largely missing from the acclamatory type of elections in Africa. In the more recent competitive elections examined here the electorate have been making choices. Mass participation is symbolised by the by the frequent image of long queues of Africans waiting to cast their votes. The time and effort which large numbers of Africans have been willing to expend in participating in elections puts to shame the half-hearted approach of the electorate in many more established democracies and demolishes the notion that Africans don't 'care about democracy'. Of all the arguments against democracy in Africa that one is the most fatuous.

The discussion of parties and elections in this chapter is inevitably limited by the relative recency of the movement towards democratisation in Africa. Although they sometimes carried strong echoes from the past the new party systems were very hastily constructed in response to the new political openings as they appeared. It is to be expected that the parties and their interrelationships will be subject to considerable evolution and change, not least in response the experience of electoral competition from which both winners and losers will seek to learn lessons. The discussion of elections has been focussed on the 'first' post-redemocratisation elections because, with the sole exception of Sao Tome and Principe, 'second' elections have yet to take place. At present it is impossible in most African states to conduct the sort of longitudinal election surveys which are possible in states like Botswana[47]. Not all states which have had first elections will necessarily progress to second elections but those that do will offer a fascinating basis for comparison.

Notes

(1) In suggesting the notion of the 'vanity party' I am borrowing from the phenomenon of 'vanity publishing': that is where some books are published entirely at the author's expense to feed his or her vanity. Alternative labels for such parties might be 'DIY parties' or 'cottage industry parties. The important factor is the social status attached to being a party leader or even perhaps a 'presidential candidate' irrespective of the lack of real significance of the 'party'. This question of status attached to party leadership is a factor working against the logic of uniting smaller parties into one larger party. Put simply, twenty parties have twenty party leaders, whereas twenty parties uniting to form one party have only one party leader!

(2) This tendency towards factionalism and party proliferation is amusingly

encapsulated by the Senegalese politician quoted by Bayart who suggested that 'in Senegal when there are three of you, you form a party, and when there are five of you, you split into factions'. See Bayart, op. cit., pp.228-229.

(3) See S. N. Sangmpam, *Pseudocapitalism and the Overpoliticized State*, Aldershot, Avebury, 1994, pp.236-237.

(4) For details see Lionel Cliffe (with Ray Bush, Jenny Lindsay, Brian Mokopakgosi, Donna Pankhurst and Balefi Tsie), *The Transition to Independence in Namibia*, Boulder and London, Lynne Rienner, 1994.

(5) Jeff Haynes, 'Sustainable Democracy in Ghana? Problems and Prospects', *Third World Quarterly*, Vol.14, No.3, 1993, p.458.

(6) For a study of the 1970 Lesotho elections see B. M. Khaketla, *Lesotho 1970: An African Coup Under the Microscope*, London, C. Hurst, 1971. For the 1993 elections see Roger Southall, 'The 1993 Lesotho Election', *Review of African Political Economy*, No.59, 1994, pp.110-118.

(7) For discussion of the annullment of the 1993 election see Emeka Nwokedi, 'Nigeria's Democratic Transition: Explaining the Annulled 1993 Presidential Election', *The Round Table*, No.330, April 1994, pp.189-204: Peter M. Lewis, 'Endgame in Nigeria? The Politics of a Failed Democratic Transition', *African Affairs*, Vol.93, No.372, July 1994. pp.323-340: Ajayi Ola Rotimi and Julius O. Ihonvbere, 'Democratic Impasse: Remilitarisation in Nigeria', *Third World Quarterly*, Vol.15, No.4, 1994, pp.669-689. For an analysis which is overtly sympathetic towards Babangida see Tunji Olagunju, Adele Jinadu and Sam Oyovbaire. *Transition to Democracy in Nigeria (1985-1993)*, Ibadan, Spectrum Books Limited, 1993.

(8) Interview with Wole Soyinka by 'Biyi Bandele-Thomas, *Index on Censorship*, No.8-9, 1993, pp.32-33.

(9) Quoted in Akinola, op. cit., p.316.

(10) Crawford Young and Babacar Kante, 'Governance, Democracy and the 1988 Senegalese Elections', in Hyden and Bratton (eds,), op. cit., p.68.

(11) It is instructive that the term 'gerrymandering', which is used to describe any improper and biased designation of constituency boundaries, originates not from Africa but from America. In 1812 Governor Eldridge Gerry of Massachusetts, in an attempt to gain unfair party advantage, constructed one district boundary which had the shape of a salamander (hence 'gerry-mander).

(12) For a useful discussion of these issues see Carl W. Dundas, 'Transparency in Organising Elections', *The Round Table*, No.329, 1994, pp.61-65. Dundas, a former Director of Elections in Jamaica, introduces further issues including political party funding and limits on campaign expenditure which would be very difficult to control in the African context.

(13) See Patsy Robertson, 'Monitoring African Elections', in Douglas Rimmer ed., *Action in Africa*, London, James Currey, 1993, pp.154-157. For a statement of the British Government view see Linda Chalker, 'Development and Democracy: What Should the West be Doing?', *The Round Table*, No.329, 1994, pp.23-26.

(14) For details see Richard Dale, 'The UN and African Decolonization: UNTAG in Namibia', *TransAfrica Forum*, Fall 1991, pp.31-48.

(15) Larry Garber, 'The OAU and Elections', *Journal of Democracy*, Vol.4, No.3, 1993, pp.55-59.

(16) For details see Honore Koffi Guie, 'Organizing Africa's Democrats', *Journal of Democracy*, Vol.4, No.2, 1993, pp.119-129.

(17) See, for example, Eric Bjornland, Michael Bratton and Clark Gibson, 'Observing Multi-Party Elections in Africa: Lessons from Zambia', *African Affairs*, Vol.91, No.364, July 1992, pp.405-431.

(18) See Gisela Geisler, 'Fair? What has Fair got to do with it? Vagaries of Election Observations and Democratic Standards', *The Journal of Modern African Studies*, Vol.31, No.4, 1993, pp.613-637.

(19) *The Presidential, Parliamentary and Civic Elections in Kenya. 29 December 1992, The Report of the Commonwealth Observer Group*, London, Commonwealth Secretariat, 1993.

(20) Ibid. p.39.

(21) Geisler, op. cit. p.624.

(22) For example settler regimes usually operated racially based franchises; until the 1980s Liberia had a property based franchise; and in Nigeria's First Republic (1960-1966) women in the Northern Region were denied the vote.

(23) For details of the 1991 elections see John A. Wiseman, 'Early Post-Redemocratisation Elections in Africa', *Electoral Studies*, Vol11, No.4, 1992, pp.279-291. For the 1994 elections see Gerhart Seibert, 'All Change', *New African*, No.325, December 1994, p.39.

(24) The contrast between South Africa and Nigeria was keenly felt by Nigerian supporters of democracy. Adewale Maja-Pearce commented that 'South Africa is free and Nigeria is in chains'. See Maja-Pearce 'The Press in Nigeria', *Index on Censorship*, No.6, 1994, p.211.

(25) For a very useful summary of the background to the election see Robert Mattes, 'The Road to Democracy: 2 February 1990 to 27 April 1994' in Andrew Reynolds ed., *Election '94 South Africa: The Campaigns, Results and Future Prospects*, London, James Currey, 1994, pp.1-22.

(26) Arend Lijphart, 'Prospects for Power-Sharing in the New South Africa', in ibid. p.224. The notion of consociational democracy which Lijphart developed refers to a type of power-sharing democracy which he argued

was more appropriate to plural societies than was a purely majoritarian form: see Lijphart, *Democracy in Plural Societies*, New Haven, Yale University Press, 1977.

(27) See Hermann Giliomee, 'The National Party's Campaign for a Liberation Election', in Reynolds (ed.), op. cit., p.58.

(28) Daniel Sille and Robert Schrire, 'The Mass Media in the South African Election', in ibid., p.141.

(29) For an interesting first-hand account of the election in Kwazulu see Prunella Scarlett, 'The Ndwedwe Experience', *The Round Table*, No.331, 1994, pp.299-301.

(30) For a detailed analysis of the results see Andrew Reynolds, 'The Results' in Reynolds (ed.) op. cit., pp.182-220. Further discussion of the results can be found in James Hamill and J. E. Spence, 'South Africa's Watershed Election', *The World Today*, July 1994, pp.128-132: Alexander Johnston 'South Africa: The Election and the Emerging Party System', *International Affairs*, Vol.70, No.4, 1994, pp.721-736: J. E. Spence, 'Everybody has Won, So we All Must Have Prizes: Reflections on the South African Election', *Government and Opposition*, Vol.29, No.4, Autumn 1994, pp.431-444.

(31) Reynolds, ibid., p.182.

(32) For the most part the estimates given ar those of Reynolds (ibid,) which were calculated from turnout figures, regional support and opinion poll indicators. The conclusions of other writers do not differ significantly on this matter.

(33) For details see Keith Panter-Brick, 'Prospects for Democracy in Zambia', *Government and Opposition*, Vol.29, No.2, 1994, pp.231-247. See also Commonwealth Secretariat, *Zambian Elections...*', 1992, op. cit.

(34) Ibid. p.16.

(35) Ibid. p.21.

(36) Stephen Chan and Chanda L. J. Chingambo, 'Democracy in Southern Africa: The 1990 Elections in Zimbabwe and 1991 Elections in Zambia', *The Round Table*, No.332, 1992, p.196.

(37) For details see Jan Kees van Donge, 'Kamuzu's Legacy: The Democratisation of Zambia', paper presented to the African Studies Association (UK) conference University of Lancaster, September 1994.

(38) See Rachel Rawlins, 'Gone With the Wind', *Focus on Africa*, Vol.5, No.3, July-September 1994, pp.40-43 for an illustrated account.

(39) Reported in *Keesings Archives*, News Digest for May 1994, p.39993.

(40) Much of the data in this account of the Malian elections is taken from two excellent articles by Richard Vengroff. See Vengroff, 1993, op. cit. and Vengroff, 'The Impact of the Electoral System on the Transition to

Democracy in Africa: The Case of Mali', *Electoral Studies*, Vol.13, No.1, 1994, pp.29-37.

(41) See, for example, the 'Profile' of Konare in *West Africa*, 11-17 May 1992, p.787.

(42) Vengroff, 1994, op. cit.

(43) For accounts of the Angolan elections see Patrick Smith 'Angola: Free and Fair Elections' *Review of African Political Economy*, No.55, November 1992, pp.101-106: Elaine Windrich, 'Media Coverage of the Angolan Elections', *Issue*, Vol.22, No.1, 1994: Tvedten (1993), op. cit.

(44) For details of the coup see John A. Wiseman and Elizabeth Vidler, 'The July 1994 Coup d'Etat in The Gambia: The End of an Era', *The Round Table*, No.333, 1995, pp.53-65.

(45) See Rok Ajulu, 'The 1992 Kenya General Elections: A Preliminary Assessment', Review of African Political Economy, No.56, March 1993, pp.98-102.

(46) For details see Joel D. Barkan, 'Kenya: Lessons from a Flawed Election', *Journal of Democracy*, Vol.4, No.3, July 1993 pp.85-99: D. Pal Ahluwalia 'Democratic Transition in African Politics: The Case of Kenya', *Australian Journal of Political Science*, Vol.28, 1993, pp.499-514: Throup, 1993, op. cit.

(47) See, for example, Roger Charlton, 'The Politics of Elections in Botswana', *Africa*, Vol.63, No.3, 1993, pp.330-370.

6 Post-Election Developments

As indicated in the previous chapter a large majority of African states reached the stage in the democratisation process of holding competitive elections even though in some cases the electoral process was flawed to a greater or lesser extent. The only state not to reach that stage, following an agreement to do so, was the tragic case of Rwanda. In 1991 the quasi-military government of President Juvenal Habyarimana had agreed to permit the formation of parties in opposition to his own Revolutionary National Movement for Development (MRND) and the following year he included some opposition leaders in a coalition government. In August 1993, after many months of negotiation, Habyarimana signed an agreement in Arusha, Tanzania, with Col. Alex Kanyarengwe of the rebel Rwandan Patriotic Front (FPR) which scheduled fully democratic elections in Rwanda for 1995. In April 1994 this fragile commitment to democracy was shattered when Habyarimana was assassinated by unknown[1] assailants who shot down his plane as he was returning from peace talks in Tanzania. This killing sparked off the most dreadful catastrophe of post-independence Africa as Hutu death squads (known as 'interahamwe') launched a campaign of genocide against the Tutsi minority in Rwanda which cost the lives of at least half of the Tutsi population. The Tutsi-dominated FPR guerrillas invaded from their bases in Uganda and seized power in the Rwandan capital Kigali as millions of Hutu fled into exile in neighbouring countries. Although large numbers of Hutus were murdered by the invading Tutsi forces the killings were not on the organised scale of those perpetrated by the *interahamwe*. These utterly tragic events not only curtailed any prospect of democratisation in Rwanda they made it almost impossible to imagine how any form of political order could be restored to the devastated Rwandan state[2].

Appalling as events in Rwanda undoubtedly were they cannot be seen in any way as representative of a wider Africa in spite of the extensive coverage they received in the world media where, true to form, African disaster was perceived as more newsworthy than any positive development: the South African elections were the solitary exception to this general pattern. In those states in which the redemocratisation process progressed as far as completing competitive elections (which excludes Angola) not one has yet seen the restoration of single-party rule. Although there are certainly some states (eg. Kenya, Togo, Burkina Faso, Mauritania) where government treatment of opposition falls well below the standards expected in a democracy opposition parties continue to play an important role within the political system as a countervailing force to regime hegemony. Such states might best be seen as semi-democracies, being neither fully democratic nor fully authoritarian. In those states where democratisation involved simultaneous demilitarisation none has yet witnessed the restoration of military rule (Nigeria, of course, never demilitarised as was supposed to happen after the elections). It would be unduly optimistic to expect this situation to continue indefinitely. Any examination of post-election developments is necessarily limited by the relatively short period of time involved which is at most a few years and in many cases rather less. The examination is also limited by the need to concentrate on those developments most closely associated with democratic politics, including threats to the latter, rather than an overall survey of the post-election period. In several states the democratic process and the prospects for democratic consolidation have been seriously threatened and undermined by a variety of political crises.

Burundi provides a classic case of a state where progress towards democracy, including the holding of a democratic election, was severely damaged by subsequent political crisis. Like neighbouring Rwanda, Burundi has had a wretched history of ethnic conflict between its Tutsi minority and Hutu majority[3]. In Burundi, unlike Rwanda, until relatively recently it was the Tutsi who dominated the political system and controlled the coercive powers of the state apparatus, including the armed forces. Until the 1993 elections the Burundi government was directed by Major Pierre Buyoya who had seized power in a coup in 1987 when he ousted his military predecessor Colonel Jean-Baptiste Bagaza. The regime was dominated by the military although there was a notional ruling single-party, the Union for National Progress (UPRONA). The Buyoya regime was more reform minded than its predecessors and although it remained Tutsi dominated it adopted a more conciliatory attitude to the Hutu and included a few of the latter in the government. In 1992 Burundi changed to a multi-party system with elections promised for the following year. The main opposition party to emerge was the Front for a Democratic Burundi (FRODEBU) led by Melchior Ndadaye. Although there were a few minor parties UPRONA and FRODEBU were the major contestants in the 1993 elections. Although neither party campaigned as an ethnic party, and both contained elements from both ethnic groups, it was virtually inevitable that UPRONA was perceived as Tutsi dominated and FRODEBU as Hutu dominated. The presidential elections were held on June 1st 1993 followed by those to the National Assembly on June 29th4. The elections were regarded by Burundians and outside observers alike as completely free and fair and 97.3% of registered voters cast their ballots in an atmosphere of calm good spirits. The results gave a clear victory to FRODEBU whose candidate Melchior Ndadaye won 64.75% of the vote in the presidential election decisively beating Buyoya, who stood as the UPRONA candidate, gaining 32.9%. In the legislative elections FRODEBU won 71.4%, whilst UPRONA won 21.43% with the rest going to minor parties. Buyoya accepted his defeat with great dignity and an absence of malice. Ndadaye thus became the first Hutu president of Burundi in the freest election the country had ever known. Although he had won by a large majority Ndadaye announced his intention to build on the new mood of national reconciliation by forming a government of national unity (referred to in Kirundi as '*intwaro rusangi*' meaning shared power) in which FRODEBU held only 13 out of 23 ministerial portfolios. Nine of the cabinet ministers were Tutsi including Sylvie Kinigi of UPRONA who was appointed as prime minister, the first woman to hold such an important governmental office. Ndadaye promised that in future the president and prime minister would always be from different ethnic groups. Given the history of ethnic conflict and authoritarianism in Burundi the 1993 elections and their immediate aftermath appeared nothing short of a political miracle.

On 21st October tragedy struck the newly democratised political system of Burundi. Renegade elements within the army launched a coup attempt. Although the coup collapsed two days later, Ndadaye and several members of his government were assassinated by the rebels. The coup attempt provoked widespread popular resistance and as Filip Reyntjens observed 'the events also show the profound change that the country has undergone: the people refused to be robbed of their newly acquired democracy, and their resistance has been a major reason for the failure of the coup'5. On a more negative and sombre note it must be observed that the botched coup attempt provoked a considerable amount of inter-ethnic killing more reminiscent of Burundi's past. Whilst the coup had failed in its major aims it succeeded in seriously destabilising the political system. Against a background of crisis Prime Minister Sylvie Kinigi attempted to restore political order and in January 1994, following an emergency change to the constitution, Cyprien Ntaryamira was elected President by a vote of 78 to one by the National Assembly. Ntaryamira announced that he would continue the policy of his murdered predecessor in establishing a government of national unity. He appointed Anatole Kanyenkiko, a Tutsi UPRONA member who also happened to have a Hutu wife, as prime minister and announced a cabinet in which 40% of the ministers were Tutsi. On April 6th 1994 the ill-fated democratisation process in Burundi was subjected to a further calamity when President Ntaryamira was killed in the shooting down of Rwandan President Habyarimana's plane in which he just happened to be travelling at the time. In September 1994 Sylvestre Ntibantunganya, the former Speaker of the National Assembly and a Hutu, was unanimously chosen as Burundi's third President in a twelve month period. Like his predecessors Ntibantunganya formed a coalition government with considerable Tutsi UPRONA representation. Against a background of continuing ethnic clashes in the country the new government began yet another attempt to establish political order.

A less propitious sequence of events would be difficult to imagine. Although the 1993 elections provided a most promising start to democratisation in Burundi the process was always likely to be fragile and the country needed a period of peace and stability in which the conciliatory figure of Nadadaye might begin the consolidation of the process. The limited evidence from his short time in power suggests that this might have been a real possibility. Although the army Chief of Staff Lt. Col. Bikomagu may well have understated support for the coup within the army when he claimed that '99.9% of the army had been opposed to the coup'[6] it remains true that a relatively small group of soldiers was able to inflict enormous damage on the democratisation process. In the context of the political history of Burundi the coup attempt was inevitably going to be interpreted in ethnic terms (given its collapse it may never be possible to establish its true motivation) and lead to communal violence. This situation was exacerbated by the death of President Ntarymira, which almost certainly resulted simply from the misfortune of being in the wrong place at the wrong time, which was also perceived in ethnic terms. It remains to be seen if the democratisation process in Burundi can be reconstructed but the disaster of neighbouring Rwanda provides a terrifying alternative scenario if the reconstruction of democracy fails.

The small mountainous kingdom of Lesotho in southern Africa has survived two major threats to its democratisation process in the period since the elections of March 1993. The first threat came from the military and the second from the king. In both cases assistance from other countries in the region was important in keeping the democratically elected government in power. The 1993 election was the first democratic election in Lesotho since 1970[7]. In the intervening period the country had experienced single-party rule from 1970 to 1986, under the Basotho National Party (BNP) who had seized power after losing the 1970 election to the Basutoland Congress Party (BCP), and fairly unstable military rule from 1986 until the 1993 elections. The elections thus represented a dual process of demilitarisation and democratisation. Although there were a few minor parties the election was essentially a two party contest between the BCP, still led by its original leader Ntsu Mokhehle, and the BNP, now led by

Rets'elisitsoe Sekhonyana[8]. Although fears had been expressed in advance of the election that the well known sympathy of many in the army for the BNP might interfere with the electoral process this did not occur and the election was widely judged to have been free and fair: the Commonwealth Observer Group, for example, concluded that 'the outcome of the election reflects a free expression of the will of the people of Lesotho'. The results gave the BCP just on three quarters of the popular vote with almost all the rest going to the BNP. Because the election had been conducted under a rigid first-past-the-post system this resulted in all 65 seats in the National Assembly going to the BCP. Whilst this result was 'democratic' in terms of the electoral system used, in that it accurately reflected the way the Basotho people had voted, it can be regarded as unfortunate for democracy in at least two ways. Firstly, it meant that the National Assembly was in practice completely dominated by one party and that the possibility of critical inter-party debate within the legislature between government and opposition was denied. Secondly, it was hardly likely to encourage any commitment to the democratic process on the part of the BCP who had gained no parliamentary representation in spite of gaining nearly one quarter of the vote. It seems reasonable to argue that some form of proportional representation which would have allowed for the, far from insignificant, minority of the votes received by the BNP to be translated into minor representation in the legislature would have been more conducive to the prospects for democratic politics in Lesotho especially at such an early stage in the democratisation process. This propensity for the first-past-the-post electoral system to distort the outcomes of elections is not unique to Lesotho. Nevertheless when Ntsu Mokhehle was sworn in as Prime Minister (the Basotho king remains the constitutional Head of State) at the beginning of April 1993 it was clearly with the support of a large majority of the Basotho electorate.

The first major crisis for Mokhehle's government came in January 1994 when the military revolted following government rejection of an unsigned demand for a doubling of soldiers' pay. Fighting broke out in Maseru between different factions within the army some of which were believed to support the BNP and some the BCP. It was widely believed that the BNP leader Sekhonyana had been involved in some incitement of the soldiers[9]. At this point the disturbances did not represent a full blown attempt at a coup but, with the government appearing powerless to intervene in the conflict, there was a distinct possibility that it would develop into a coup with one or more factions attempting to seize control of the state. Had this happened it might have resulted in a return to military rule or, quite possibly, a descent into civil war. Neither prospect was attractive to Lesotho's neighbours who then decided to become involved. A combination of South Africa's foreign minister, Pik Botha, together with Mandela and de Klerk and Presidents Masire of Botswana and Mugabe of Zimbabwe met and made it clear that they would not accept a military government in Lesotho. The possibility of these three states sending troops to Lesotho was raised but of more immediate influence was the threat to seal the country's borders: because of its landlocked position surrounded on all sides by South African territory Lesotho has always been extremely vulnerable to this sort of action. Following this threat, and the involvement of negotiators from the Commonwealth, The UN, and the OAU, peace was restored and Mokhehle's government regained its rather tenuous hold on power.

The settlement of this conflict proved to be no more than a brief respite for the Mokhehle government because in August 1994 King Letsi[10] announced that he had dissolved parliament, suspended the constitution and dismissed the government. In taking this action the king had the support of some factions within the army and within the BNP. This monarchist coup provoked widespread popular opposition. As soon as the king broadcast his announcement thousands of demonstrators spontaneously marched on the royal palace to denounce the king's action and pledge their support for the elected government[11]. Five demonstrators were shot dead by police and troops defending the palace. A few days later the country was brought to a halt by a general strike organised in opposition to the coup. Once again the leaders of neighbouring states involved themselves in the affairs of Lesotho. President Mandela condemned the royal coup and insisted on the immediate reinstatement of the democratically elected government. At first the king refused but when South African paratroops began 'manoeuvres' on the Lesotho border and South African warplanes flew low over the military barracks in Maseru he backed down and agreed to the restoration of the Mokhehle government.

The events of 1994 indicate that, in spite of its strong claims to democratic legitimacy, the elected government of Lesotho is far from secure. Powerful anti-democratic factions remain within the army, the monarchy has a tarnished reputation, and the main opposition party appears to have no interest in anything approximating to the role of 'loyal opposition'. On the other hand there have already been two occasions on which powerful neighbours have intervened to support democracy. Even internally the situation is not entirely bleak: as Southall notes 'the substantial growth of the trade union movement, the withdrawal of the Catholic Church from the political arena[12], the networking of various non-government organisations with a small, activist, Basotho intelligentsia, and not least, the development of an independent press, all indicate the emergence of a civil society, with links throughout the region'[13]. Also, the reaction to the August coup made it clear that thousands of ordinary Basotho were willing to risk their lives to protect democracy. Overall the situation is less unpromising than that of Burundi, partly due to the absence of ethnic cleavage in Lesotho, but it is clear that Basotho democracy is far from consolidated. As in Burundi it does not

147

appear that there is any stable authoritarian alternative to democracy: in both the choice appears to lie between democracy and chaos.

In a few of the recently redemocratised states governments have faced serious security problems in the post-election period which whilst not actually threatening the survival of the regime have nevertheless hindered the progress of democracy. In both Mali and Niger, for example, the governments have been involved in low intensity civil wars with Tuareg rebel groups[14]. These governments were elected in regime changing elections in 1992 (Mali) and 1993 (Niger) and inherited the rebellions from their predecessors. The Tuaregs, a largely nomadic Berber people, inhabit the desert northern areas of both states and have been hostile to successive central governments for the whole post-independence period. Military aid from Libya, which has its own Tuareg population, has enabled the rebels in both states to continue insurgency campaigns attacking government installations and personnel. In return the armies of both Mali and Niger have often been accused of the brutal treatment of the Tuaregs[15]. A major problem for the governments attempting to negotiate with Tuareg rebels has been that the latter are highly factionalised and divided into a large, and constantly changing, number of groups making different demands on the centre. These demands range from complete secession to some form of regional autonomy, recognition of Tamashek (the Tuareg language), and a greater share of resources. In June 1994 the Niger government met with Tuareg representatives and agreed 'in principle' to the establishment of semi-autonomous regions for the Tuareg with their own elected assemblies but, on past experience, it would be over-optimistic to view this as marking a final end to conflict. In an independence anniversary speech in late 1994 President Konare of Mali advocated a policy of dialogue but admitted that the Tuareg rebellion was 'the most urgent and worrying problem facing the government'[16]. Because in both Mali and Niger fighting is confined to the remote northern areas it has little direct effect on the majority of the population in the more populous southern areas but for democratic governments to be virtually in a state of undeclared war with sections of their own populations can hardly be considered as conducive to democratic consolidation. Whilst in neither state can the problems be regarded as having been caused by democratisation the latter development has yet to provide a solution.

In terms of post-election developments Nigeria would probably have to be regarded as representing the nadir of democratic aspirations. As was noted earlier the twin process of democratisation and demilitarisation in Nigeria actually ended up producing a government which was neither democratic nor civilian. In fact the annulment of the results[17] of the relatively well conducted elections in Nigeria which gave victory to Moshood Abiola and the SDP paved the way for the military government of Sanni Abacha which is generally regarded as the most oppressively authoritarian regime ever experienced by the Nigerian people. The catalogue of oppressive measures adopted by the regime is very extensive. All political activity and organisation has been banned in Nigeria. Vast numbers of political opponents, real or imagined, have been imprisoned and often subjected to serious ill-treatment[18]. Amongst those particularly in danger of imprisonment have been the leaders of human rights groups (discussed in chapter 3) and the leaders of Nigeria's trade unions. In June 1994 Abiola himself was arrested and charged with treason following his assertion at a mass meeting in Lagos that he was the rightful President of Nigeria. The free press in the country has been all but obliterated with the closing down of all publishing houses known to be in any way critical of the government. The regime has even taken to publishing fake copies of newspapers containing pro-government propaganda[19] designed to confuse the population. In August and September 1994 Abacha sacked the remaining civilian members of his government along with some senior military members, such as Rear Admiral Allison Madueke and Major-General Mohammed Chris Ali (respectively the navy and army chiefs of staff) , whom he suspected of not fully sharing his hardline approach. On 6th September any final attempt at judicial checks on government was ended with a decree which forbade any legal challenge to any actions of the government. In addition to all of these 'official' measures of oppression it is necessary to take into account the brutal suppression by the army of pro-democracy demonstrations which has cost hundreds of innocent lives.

Whilst the above actions of the Abacha regime inevitably point towards a thoroughly pessimistic assessment of the prospects for democracy in Nigeria other post-election developments in the country give at least some grounds for hope. The other side of the picture to government oppression is the resistance which the latter has provoked amongst many Nigerians who have not been willing to acquiesce in the suppression of democracy by the army and have continued to struggle for what they regard as their right to democratic government. This continuing struggle for democracy in Nigeria is all the more remarkable in the light of the terror tactics used by the Abacha regime to brutally crush it. The personal price in terms of imprisonment, torture, and death already paid by Nigeria's pro-democracy activists is very high. In April 1994 the numerous human rights and pro-democracy groups came together to form the National Democratic Coalition (NADECO)[20] to serve as a co-ordinating body for their activities. In October 1994 the human rights lawyer Gani Fawehimini founded a, strictly illegal, political 'party', the National Conscience, to campaign for democracy but was almost immediately detained. As might be expected such groups have been mainly middle class in terms of their leadership with lawyers, academics, students, writers, and journalists playing a prominent role. However, the pro-democracy movement has also involved mass participation from the organised working class through anti-government demonstrations and strikes. Probably the most important strike was that of the oil workers from July to September 1994 which posed serious financial difficulties for the regime. On July 4th the blue-collar National Union of Petroleum and Natural Gas Workers (NUPENG) began a strike in protest against the election annulment and were joined a week later by the white-collar Petroleum and Natural Gas Senior Staff Association of Nigeria (PENGASSAN). The strike paralysed the economy but was eventually broken after two months following the arrest of many of the union leaders including the NUPENG secretary-general Frank Kokori, the army takeover of the unions' headquarters buildings, the dissolution of the Nigerian Labour Congress (NLC), and the killing of a number of striking workers. In June 1994 over 1,000 market women marched in Lagos to demand the release of Abiola and the restoration of democracy only to be beaten and tear-gassed by the police.

The strength of mass-based opposition to the continuation of military rule in Nigeria has been made very clear since the abandonment of redemocratisation in 1993. Whilst this commitment to democracy, under very difficult and dangerous circumstances, from Nigerian civil society[21] can be seen as indicative of an underlying hostility to authoritarian rule, which could prove to be an important element in the construction of some future Nigerian democracy, the immediate future appears bleak. Although Abacha has established a new constitutional conference few Nigerians have any remaining faith in the willingness of the regime to hand over power to a democratically elected government at some future date. Without some significant move towards genuine democratisation in the near future the future existence of the Nigerian state appears uncertain. Following an election which was encouragingly free from serious north-south tensions the cancellation of the redemocratisation process has had the effect of promoting the development of such tensions. The Nigerian journalist Pini Jason reflects a widespread view when he writes that 'the Nigerian military, despite all pretences, is no longer a national institution...it is essentially part and parcel of the northern political establishment[22]. Wole Soyinka has highlighted the dangers to Nigerian national unity arising from this latest round of military authoritarianism when he writes that 'it may prove terminal to the existence of the nation' and that 'in Sani Abacha's self-manifesting destiny as the last Nigerian despot, we may be witnessing, alas, the end of Nigerian history'[23]. Nigeria provides a classic example of the struggle for and against democracy in Africa. As in a significant number of African states the choices appear to be between some form of democracy and political disintegration.

During the same period another setback for democracy in Africa emerged from an unexpected source when, in July 1994, a military coup in The Gambia brought to an end Africa's longest surviving multi-party democracy[24].

Simultaneously the coup ended the period in office of the man who was, at the time, the longest serving national leader in Africa, Sir Dawda Kairaba Jawara. The latter, who had ruled The Gambia since independence in 1965, first as Prime Minister and then as President following the establishment of a Republic in 1970, was the very last of the generation of African leaders who had led their countries into independence in the 1960s and had remained in power ever since. Although Jawara's People's Progressive Party (PPP) had won every election in the post-independence period it had always faced competition from a range of opposition parties which had, ironically, had their best ever result in the 1992 election when they won 11 out of 36 seats in the legislature. Although the government had been marred by some corruption and bureaucratic inefficiency The Gambia had remained an open, tolerant, and vigorous democracy for nearly thirty years and it was somewhat ironic that just as the majority of African states were moving in that direction the country should be subjected to its first ever period of authoritarian rule[25].

The coup was undertaken by a group of very young (none were over thirty years of age) junior army officers led by Lt. Yahya Jammeh and appears, rhetoric to the contrary, to have been motivated largely by the grievances and ambitions of the military in general and the coup leaders in particular. Following the coup large numbers of political leaders, including some from what had hitherto been the opposition, were arrested, all political organisations were banned, and the democratic constitution was annulled. This was followed by a clamp-down on The Gambia's lively independent press during which journalists were arrested, deported, and beaten up by soldiers. A failed attempt at a counter-coup in November 1994 led to several deaths and increased repression. In January 1995 two of the most important figures in the military government were arrested for trying to assassinate Jammeh. Although the military regime announced that democratic civilian rule would be re-introduced in 1996 the record of other military governments in the region in keeping to such promises gave little basis for optimism.

The Gambian coup when seen alongside developments in Burundi, Lesotho, and Nigeria, clearly indicates a continuing vulnerability of democracy in Africa, whether it be recently re-established or of a more longstanding variety, to military intervention. Although African armies are not necessarily or ubiquitously anti-democratic in orientation they continue to pose the greatest threat to the establishment and consolidation of democratic political systems. To some extent the establishment of democratic government may be seen to threaten the corporate interests of the military because, as the Nigerian economist John Mukum Mbaku has recently demonstrated, democratic regimes in Africa tend to allocate far smaller proportions of budgetary allocation to military expenditure[26]. The dilemma for democratically elected governments is apparent: a high defence budget might reduce the chance of military overthrow but it would, at the same time, necessitate a lower level of expenditure on other government functions such as health and education which may prejudice the prospects of future electoral support in a democratic system. Any attempt to 'buy off' the military runs the risk of undermining government legitimacy amongst the voters for failing to provide welfare benefits. Whilst authoritarian governments, whether they be military or civilian, can escape the electoral consequences of high, largely unproductive, military expenditure, the situation is more difficult for governments which rely on maintaining popular support in a competitive political system. In addition to this, overall expenditure on the military offers no guarantee of immunity against a coup in situations where important factions within the army have other grievances against the government. Such grievances are often of a particularistic nature based on ethnicity as was the case in the Burundi coup which although it failed was extremely destabilising and damaging to the democratisation process. The refusal of the Nigerian military to hand over power to the democratically elected government has also been interpreted by many Nigerians as resulting from ethnic and regional considerations. Earlier evidence from states such as Togo and Zaire also indicated the ways in which particularistic linkages between the military and incumbent authoritarian leaders can be used by the latter to debilitate the democratisation process without involving a full blown seizure of power by the army.

The brevity of the post-election period makes it impossible to construct definitive conclusions based on an examination of developments within that period. However, the limited evidence available does enable one to make at least a tentative hypothesis that it is the African military which poses the greatest threat to the democratisation process. Although a number of governments have contrived to limit the effects of democratization none has yet resorted to an attempt at re-establishing the single-party state. In a number of states where opposition parties failed for one reason or another to win control of government in the elections they have faced considerable difficulties but they have remained in existence as important participants in the political process. In those cases where previously incumbent parties in what had been single-party states were transformed into opposition parties by electoral defeat they have not been subjected to the sort of proscription which they had themselves inflicted on opposition parties in the past. In Zambia, for example, ex-President Kenneth Kaunda, once he had reversed his earlier decision to retire from politics, was permitted to operate as a vocal critic of the MMD government in a manner which he had denied to his opponents in the past, although there was increasing opposition to him from younger elements within UNIP who felt that the party needed new leadership to mount a challenge on the government[27]. The generous terminal gratuity and pension package which the new government awarded Kaunda contrasted vividly with the latter's past treatment of political opponents.

Whilst few, if any, of Africa's new democracies can be considered to be fully consolidated the post-election period has not, for the most part, been one of reversion to the monopolistic authoritarianism which dominated much of the political history of the post-independence period.

Notes

(1) For speculation on who was responsible for the assassination of Habyarimana see 'Who Killed the Presidents', *New African*, June 1994, p.14. Although some suspected the FPR it appears more likely that the killing was the work of Hutu hardliners opposed to the conciliatory approach of the President.

(2) For discussions of the Rwandan tragedy see Martin Plaut, 'Rwanda: Looking Beyond the Slaughter', *The World Today*, August-September 1994, pp.149-153: Stephen D. Goose and Frank Smyth, 'Arming Genocide in Rwanda', *Foreign Affairs*, Vol.73, No.5, September-October 1994, pp.86-96: Alain Destexhe, 'The Third Genocide', *Foreign Policy*, No.97, Winter 1994-1995, pp.3-17.

(3) For an outstanding study of this history see Rene Lemarchand, *Burundi: Ethnocide as Discourse and Practice*, Cambridge, Cambridge University Press, 1994.

(4) For a detailed analysis of the elections see Filip Reyntjens, 'The Proof of the Pudding is in the Eating: The June 1993 Elections in Burundi', *The Journal of Modern African Studies*, Vol.31, No.4, 1993, pp.563-583.

(5) Ibid. p.582.

(6) Cited in Lemarchand (1994), op. cit. p.xviii.

(7) For a detailed study of the 1970 elections see Khaketla (1971), op. cit.

(8) For details of the election see Southall (1994), op. cit.: *The General Election in Lesotho 27 March 1993: The Report of the Commonwealth Observer Group*, London, Commonwealth Secretariat, 1993.

(9) For an account of the confused nature of the revolt see the report 'Lesotho: What Rebellion', *Focus on Africa*, Vol.5, No.2, April-June 1994, p.23.

(10) The politics of the Basotho monarchy represent a major topic in its own right. King Letsie was installed in 1991 by the military who deposed his father King Moshoeshoe. This continued to be a matter of conflict and in December 1994 it was announced that Letsie would stand down in favour of his father.

(11) For accounts of these events see the reports in *New African*, November

1994, p.32 and in *Focus on Africa*, Vol.5, No.4, October-December 1994, p.19.

(12) Historically the Roman Catholic church had played an extremely reactionary role in the politics of Lesotho. See L. B. B. J. Machobane, *Government and Change in Lesotho 1800-1966*, Basingstoke, Macmillan, 1990.

(13) Southall op. cit. p.115.

(14) For a discussion of the background to the situation in Mali and Niger see Richard L. Sklar and Mark Strege, 'Finding Peace Through Democracy in Sahelian Africa', *Current History*, Vol.91, No.565, 1992, pp.224-229.

(15) See, for example, *Nomads of the Sahel*, Minority Rights Group Report No. 33, London, 1977.

(16) Reported in *West Africa*, No.4020, 17-23 October 1994, pp.1782-1783.

(17) The full results of the June 1993 presidential elections were never officially announced. Following the release of the results in just under half the states of the federation the military banned the release of the remainder. However, it is clear from the results that were announced that Abiola was going to emerge as the clear winner. In the 15 states where the results are known Abiola won a majority (often a large one) in 12. Most impressively, given that Abiola is a southern Yoruba, he was able to win majorities in several northern states such as Borno, Kano, and Kaduna. For details see Joseph C. Okoroji, 'The Nigerian Presidential Elections', *Review of African Political Economy*, No.58, November 1993, pp.123-131.

(18) It is not possible to calculate the total number detained but for a list of some of the better known political prisoners see Olu Oguibe ed. *Democracy in Nigeria: The June 12 Mandate*, London, Africa Research and Information Bureau (ARIB), 1993.

(19) Maja-Pearce op. cit.

(20) Ochereome Nnana, 'Fewehimini's Crusade', *New African*, January 1995, p.32.

(21) For another view stressing the strength of civil society in Nigeria see Joel D. Barkan, 'Resurrecting Modernization Theory and the Emergence of Civil Society in Kenya and Nigeria', in Apter and Rosberg (eds) op. cit. pp.87-116. Barkan concludes that 'although Nigeria remains under military rule, civil society is alive, resilient and growing' (p.109).

(22) Pini Jason, 'Nigeria's Real Dilemma', *New African*, April 1994, p.8.

(23) Wole Soyinka, 'The Last Despot and the End of Nigerian History?', *Index on Censorship*, No.6, 1994, pp.67-75.

(24) For an assessment of the coup see Wiseman and Vidler (1995), op. cit.

(25) In 1981 an earlier coup attempt had been defeated and the country had rapidly returned to democratic rule. See Arnold Hughes, The Attempted

Gambian Coup d'Etat of 27 July 1981' in Highes ed., *The Gambia: Studies in Society and Politics*, Birmingham University African Studies Series No.3, 1991, pp.92-106.

(26) See John Mukum Mbaku, 'Political Democracy, Military Expenditures and Economic Growth in Africa', *Scandinavian Journal of Development Alternatives*, Vol.12, No.1, 1993, pp49-64.

(27) See, for example, 'Kaunda Bounces Back', *New African*, October 1994, p.33.

7 The Uncertain Future of Democracy in Africa: The Grounds for Cautious Optimism

The myriad changes brought about by the struggle for democracy in sub-Saharan Africa in the period since 1989 cannot be viewed as collectively coalescing to form a readily definable outcome in terms of constituting a specified political trajectory for the states of the continent, democratic or otherwise. Instead it is possible to identify a fairly extreme example of the general rule that all political outcomes at any particular point in time are uncertain and quite probably impermanent. The extent to which democracy will play a significant role in the future of the political systems of Africa is inherently unpredictable. This being the case one could argue that the only sensible answer to the question of the future of democracy in Africa would be a resounding 'don't know'. This may be the most sensible answer but it is also the least interesting and the most unambitious, as well as being one which would produce a remarkably short concluding chapter to this book. Any discussion of possibilities and probabilities must inevitably be regarded as tentative and speculative but it should at least serve to focus attention on the sorts of factors which will shape the future of Africa.

Optimism or Pessimism?

For the political analyst who wishes to retain academic credibility pessimism is a much safer bet than optimism: as Francis Fukuyama has observed 'a naive optimist whose expectations are belied appears foolish, while a pessimist proven wrong maintains an aura of profundity and seriousness'[1]. Even if the predicted pessimistic scenario fails to materialise the inherently flawed nature of all human systems inevitably means that the pessimist will be able to point to a wide range

156

of unresolved problems, defects, and inequities in any 'real world' political system and suggest that his/her earlier pessimism was not, in essence, misplaced. An example of this would be those people who rejected the possibility of a democratic transition in South Africa and predicted that the elections would either not take place or would collapse into violent anarchy if they did. When these predictions proved inaccurate such people then insisted that we should focus more on the unresolved tensions in South African politics, the extreme disparities in wealth which remained, the legacy of past violence within the system, and so on.

Over the past few years it has become commonplace to dichotomise observers of African democratisation into 'demo-optimists' and 'demo-pessimists' depending mainly on their assessments of the prospects for the creation and/or persistence of democratic rule in a significant number of African states. For the most part I have been identified by others[2] as a 'demo-optimist'. Whilst I have no desire to disavow this label I do feel that it reflects a relative position: that is, my views are optimistic if compared with the sort of extreme demo-pessimism which sees democratic rule in Africa as a virtual impossibility. Clearly it would be ludicrous, or at least unconvincingly over-optimistic, to suggest that all, or even most, of the states of Africa are likely to emerge as stable, consolidated, perfectly functioning democracies in the forseeable future. If this is the case what sort of 'demo-optimist' position might be regarded as plausible by all but the most resolute pessimists? Firstly, it would reflect the relatively minimalist conception of democracy discussed in the opening chapter of this book and not some 'perfect society' type of maximalist conception which has not been realised anywhere in the world. Secondly, it would probably apply to a minority of African states, albeit a larger minority than in the past. Thirdly, it would allow for ambiguous cases which did not fully reflect democracy or dictatorship: the type of 'liberalised authoritarianisms' existing in Kenya, Cameroon, or Togo at the time of writing might be seen as an examples. Fourthly, it would incorporate the possibility of reversal: I must admit that my own 'demo-optimism' received a dent when in, July 1994, a small group of not particularly well organised soldiers overthrew the long-established, rough and ready, democratic system of The Gambia whilst the international community sat around and tut-tutted its disapproval. Clearly the optimism being proposed here is of a limited and cautious variety based on assessment of what is likely to occur in Africa rather than on what one would like to occur (or what many Africans would wish for).

The Limited Value of Global Comparison

In view of the claims of political science to be an essentially comparative discipline it would be logical to pose the question as to what extent the past experience of democratisation in other parts of the world might provide some guidance to future developments in Africa. A reading of the relevant comparative literature[3] suggests that this line of enquiry has a relatively limited utility: as Jennifer Widner has commented in a recent book 'political openings have taken place in settings where social science theory suggests they were least likely to occur'[4]. For a number of reasons studies of recent redemocratisation in Latin America would appear to be the most relevant, or the least irrelevant, to the African case. Comparisons with Southern Europe seem a little distant: Spain, Portugal, and Greece (now all members of the European Union-EU) have little in common with contemporary Africa beyond a history of authoritarianism. In terms of the movement away from authoritarianism and towards democracy it is possible to identify some parallels between Latin America and Africa. The conclusion that in Latin America this movement is caused predominantly by domestic factors certainly squares with the arguments presented in this book in relation to Africa. In relation to Latin America Abraham Lowenthal argues that 'these cases show that, although international factors, direct and indirect, may condition and affect the course of transition, the major participants and the dominant influences in every case have been national'[5]. Similarly O'Donnell and Schmitter argue that 'domestic factors play a dominant role in the transition'[6]. Such statements would be perfectly at home in Chapter 3 of this book. Again in what they refer to as 'resurrecting civil society' and the 'popular upsurge' the description by O'Donnell and Schmitter of how 'trade unions, grass-roots movements, religious groups, intellectuals, artists, clergymen, defenders of human rights, and professional associations all support each other's efforts toward democratisation, and coalesce into a greater whole which identifies itself as the people'[7] could just as accurately have been written about Africa as Latin America. On the other hand the phenomenon of elite pacting which has been widespread (although not ubiquitous) in Latin America has few echoes in Africa. Such a pact reflects an agreement amongst conflicting elites to seek a solution in which all participants 'agree to forgo or underutilise their capacity to harm each other by extending guarantees not to threaten each others' corporate autonomies or vital interests'[8]. Within Africa the settlement which preceded the 1994 elections in South Africa and structured post-election developments does exhibit significant similarities with Latin American elite pacting. It could be argued that the similarities between South Africa and Latin America go well beyond this issue. In terms of levels of indigenous capitalist industrialisation, relatively developed infrastructures, relatively high levels of per capita GNP (with very uneven distribution of wealth), high levels of urbanisation, and a long history of independent statehood, South Africa is much closer in character to Latin America than is any other African state. By and large Latin America has avoided the legally enforced racism which until very recently characterised South Africa. Elite pacting of the Latin American type has not been a significant feature of democratisation in most of the rest of Africa. Although some similarities exist it would be stretching the notion of pacting to its outer limits to include the Nigerian case even in the period before the military unilaterally renegued on the agreement they had made with civilian political elites.

Although it is possible to identify some common features in the recent democratic transitions in Africa and Latin America the possibility of using the experience of the latter as a guide to future developments in the former is doubtful. Most scholars of Latin American politics would regard the future of democracy in that part of the world as reflecting uncertainty. However, even if it were possible to confidently predict the future trajectory of Latin American democracy such predictions would be difficult to apply in Africa with any degree of confidence. With the very partial exception of South Africa (and even here it is important not to exaggerate similarities) the economic, political, social, and historical contexts of democratisation are very different in Africa from those existing in Latin America. Broadly speaking African states have (1) shorter histories as independent national units and greater problems over the identity of those units (no Latin American state faces the possibility of significant secessionist demands) (2) different experiences of types of authoritarian rule: as a generalisation the highly personalised neo-patrimonialism of Africa is not the same as the bureaucratic authoritarianism experienced in Latin America (3) considerably lower levels of economic development and industrialisation leading to greater dependence on the export of primary (mainly agricultural) commodities (4) lower levels of education and literacy (5) higher levels of cultural heterogeneity arising from ethnic, linguistic, and religious pluralism (6) a much less clearly articulated class structure (7) a much weaker corporatist element in social organisation. Whilst structural determinism can be regarded as an unrewarding approach to political analysis one cannot ignore the considerable structural differences between Africa and Latin America which are likely to affect the democratisation process in both cases.

Although it has been argued here that the Latin American experience offers few clues as to future developments in Africa it would be unwise to exclude the possibility that a re-evaluation of this view could become necessary at some time in the future. When I lived in Nigeria in the mid-1970s, in the period of the oil boom, there was a great deal of local discussion over the possibility of Nigeria becoming what was referred to as the 'new Brazil' and even of the potential development of some form of Atlantic economic axis linking the two. Twenty years on this scenario looks decidedly improbable but perhaps one should not preclude totally the possibility of some analagous development at some future date.

There is no Alternative to Democracy?

Such a bold statement obviously requires explanation. In suggesting that there is no alternative to democracy in Africa I am most definitely not saying that other types of political outcome will not occur: in fact the evidence suggests overwhelmingly that they will. The question really is whether or not the alternatives to at least a rough and ready type of democracy can provide can provide the basis for sustainable central government in African states. The period since 1989 has been one of extremely rapid change within African political systems but the future direction of that change remains uncertain. However, it can be argued that the nature of recent change itself precludes, to a greater or lesser extent, the possibility of a simple return to the status quo ante: there is, in an important sense, no going back.

An examination of the choices available to political elites in African states should help to underpin the arguments of the preceding paragraph. To what extent might an attempt to resurrect the single-party state provide a viable alternative to democracy? Such a scenario would suggest a re-run of the early post-independence period when, in many states, the competitive party systems which had been introduced in the terminal colonial period to facilitate the transfer of power were abrogated by incumbent ruling groups in the belief that this would ensure their continuation in office (in practice it frequently failed to achieve this and simply meant that the leaders were ousted violently rather than peacefully). Certainly some single-party states achieved, for a time at least, a reasonable degree of stability and those individuals who did well in that period might find the idea of returning to it an attractive idea. However, to assume that this is a workable proposition would be to assume that nothing has changed and that the circumstances which permitted this development still persist. In several important respects this is not the case. Firstly, the claims to legitimacy of the single-party model, in terms of its promises of development, nation-building, unity, equitable distribution of resources, and even a type of democracy, have been so thoroughly discredited by the experience of its operation that they appear beyond retrieval. This applies not just to the Marxist-Leninist variants but also to the more nationalistic and populistic types of justification for single-party rule. It is difficult to know how much these justifications were believed first time around by all those involved. Certainly they received intellectual support from some western scholars who because of ideological preference, or perhaps in some cases naivety, gave credence to altruistic explanations for the banning and jailing of political opposition. It is difficult to see how any sustainable system of government could be constructed on such a discredited system of beliefs. Secondly, the widespread mass struggle which has produced the level of democratisation achieved so far is itself a new factor in the equation. Having struggled so hard, and risked so much, to create a democratic momentum it is hard to envisage the vast numbers of people who participated accepting with equanimity the revival of the single-party state. Having achieved full or partial victory in the struggle against authoritarianism those sharing the collective experience of the recent period will act in a way which is informed by that experience. Thirdly, unlike the first time around little external support for the single-party state, based then on superpower rivalry, is likely to be forthcoming.

So far no state in Africa has attempted the resurrection of the formal single-party state. However, a variation on the same theme would be the strategy of trying to give the impression of running a democracy whilst at the same time evading the possible consequences of electoral competition (ie. losing power). This would involve camouflaging what was essentially a single-party state with some of the trappings of a multi-party state. To achieve this would require extensive rigging of elections, considerable suppression of opposition targetted carefully at its strongest representatives, and control of the media, combined with some tokens of democracy to try and convince people it did exist. This would appear a more likely scenario for a number of African states than the re-establishment of the full-blown single-party model: indeed some might argue that it is already being pursued in places like Burkina Faso, Kenya, Togo, and Zaire. However, this strategy shares some of the same defects as the preceding one and is likely to be difficult to sustain in the medium to longer-term. The experience of, for example, Liberia in the 1980s indicates the difficulty of maintaining such a system for anything but a short time. The equilibrium of a liberalised authoritarianism is difficult to keep in place. Almost inevitably either available political space increases, so producing a more genuine democracy, or it decreases to such an extent that the democratic camouflage falls away to reveal the authoritarian reality, with all the problems that that is likely to bring for ruling elites.

It could be argued that, in spite of a legitimacy deficit, it might be possible to sustain single-partyism (disguised or not) simply through the use of force, most probably supplied by the military. However, as Barbara Grosh points out, 'to retain one-partyism in the current era would require far more political repression than it previously did, precisely at a moment when regimes in Africa are weak due to economic collapse and cannot afford a larger security apparatus'[9]. The same set of difficulties can be seen in relation to full-blown military rule. It is one of the safest predictions that one can make about the future of African politics (and also one of the bleakest) to forecast that in a number of cases new democracies will be overthrown by a military coup d'etat: indeed the evidence in the previous chapter showed that this was already beginning to happen. However, all past evidence suggests that military rule rarely, if ever, produces stable government: the most likely result of a coup is another coup because of the rather fragmented nature of most African armies. Whilst there is no reason to believe that military rule is likely to prove more stable than it has in the past there are good reasons to suggest that it could lead to even greater instability than it has done previously. The same set of factors making single-party rule difficult to sustain in the changed Africa of the 1990s (collapse of legitimacy, reduced popular tolerance of authoritarian rule producing widespread opposition to it, and the absence of external support) can be seen in the case of military rule. Although in the past authoritarian states in Africa have often been rather weak states the state itself has by and large persisted. Recent evidence suggests that this can no longer be taken for granted and that authoritarian rule instead of producing state oppression is more likely to produce state fragmentation and collapse. In such cases central government lacks the capacity to exercise control over most of the territory of the supposed state and power at the local level passes to local warlords through the privatisation of the means of violence. Many observers would claim that this has already happened in states like Angola, Chad, Liberia, Sierra Leone, Somalia, and (in a slightly different form) Rwanda.

To present the alternatives facing African states as representing a dichotomised choice between democracy and warlordism is obviously rather too stark and simplistic. However, the point of examining the question in this fashion is to raise doubts regarding the credibility of a stable authoritarian alternative to democracy in the light of recent changes in Africa. It would be possible to imagine a less cataclysmic type of instability which stopped short of total state collapse but this implies only a difference of degree. In view of the probability of many African states not succeeding in sustaining democratic rule these conclusions regarding the alternatives may be regarded as decidedly pessimistic.

Democracy and Economic Development

The existence of a strong positive correlation between democratic rule and successful economic development has been universally accepted at least since Seymour Martin Lipset's seminal work on the subject was published in 1959[10]. Although there are a number of exceptions to this 'general rule' a global comparison clearly shows that most states with high per capita GNP are democratically run whilst most states with very low per capita GNP are not. What is less clear, and certainly more arguable, is the causal relationship between the two factors (assuming that there is one)[11]. To put the question in its crudest form one could ask whether economic development causes democracy or whether democracy causes economic development, or indeed whether both are caused by some other factors altogether. To put the question in this crude form is

162

not to suggest that one might be looking for a simple 'right' answer but to point out the complexity of the issue.

At various points in this book the relationship between democracy and development has received attention. In particular it has been argued that authoritarian rule has had a negative effect on economic development and that, even more importantly, it is the indigenous perception of this outcome that has provided one of the major motivating factors in producing the struggle for democracy. Economic failure, approaching total economic collapse in extreme cases, has critically eradicated the legitimacy of the authoritarian state and created the intellectual climate in which the democratic alternative is widely perceived as providing the only viable solution to Africa's economic ills. An inherent danger in this situation is that it may have led to an exaggerated view of the restorative powers of democratic rule and produced heightened expectations that simply cannot be met. Without at least moderate economic improvement the sustainment of democratic rule will be exceptionally difficult.

The precise measurement of economic variables in Africa is fraught with difficulty because the sort of macro-economic data on which such measurements are based are either absent or of dubious reliability. One reason for this is that the administrative infrastructure needed for the collection of reliable economic statistics simply does not exist. There are perhaps only a handful of African states with the capacity to produce dependable statistics on the national economy. An even more difficult problem relates to what macro-economic statistics actually measure. By definition official statistics measure (not necessarily accurately) the performance of the formal sector of the economy: put simply they reflect 'what hits the books'. In recent years it has been widely recognised by many scholars who have chosen a more in-depth approach to the study of African economies[12] that in many states the informal economy (alternatively referred to as the 'second economy' or the 'parallel economy', or even the 'black economy'!) massively outstrips the formal economy as a productive and distributive mechanism. By definition there are no official statistics relating to the unofficial economy. In the light of this it is astonishing how many scholarly observers of the political economy of Africa still base their judgements entirely on discredited 'official' statistics which, at very best, give only a partial picture of economic activity. Because of this situation it would be unwise to base any assessment of the relationship between democracy and development in Africa solely, or even mainly, on official statistics. However, one has only to visit Africa and open one's eyes to realise the undeniable levels of poverty and hardship which exist. Whilst precise measurement of the effects of democracy on African economies may be problematic, to say the least, what really matters is the perception of African people regarding change and how it affects them.

The question which follows from this is whether or not there are credible grounds for expecting that democracy will actually improve the lot of significant numbers of African people in economic terms. Whilst democracy offers no economic panacea a plausible case can be made to suggest that, on balance, its effects will be economically beneficial. Democracy will allow for a more free and open discussion of government policies, and their implementation, including discussion in the newly liberated media. In such circumstances the adoption of totally unsound, and deeply unpopular, economic projects becomes less likely. It would be difficult to imagine, for example, a strategy like the forced villigisation programme adopted in Tanzania in the 1970s, and now universally recognised as a disaster, occurring in a democratic state. Had Tanzanian opposition parties been permitted to exist in the 1970s one imagines that they would have campaigned vigorously against forced villigisation, even if only for self-interested reasons of increasing their popular support. The possibility of open criticism of government policy does not exclude mistakes in economic policy but it does make them less likely, and certainly increases the incentive to rectify them if they occur. The opportunity to criticise should help to reduce the extent of government corruption (but probably not eliminate it) which has been so damaging to economic development whether it has manifested itself in the guise of state socialism or crony capitalism (it is often difficult to distinguish between the two). The fact of being democratically elected serves to enhance the legitimacy of the government and increase its ability to implement its policies, at least in the short term. Conversely, a democratic system provides mechanisms whereby a government which has suffered a decline in its legitimacy can be replaced through peaceful means and without recourse to the sort of violence which is harmful to economic development.

The above observations on the mutually reinforcing relationships between democratic accountability and economic development in Africa remain, for the moment, hypothetical and unproven due to the fact that the movement towards democracy is still very recent. This does not make them worthless but only time will make possible a realistic evaluation of the relationship between the two. It also has to be remembered that many important factors relating to future African economic development are not susceptible to domestic democratic accountability. Factors such as the rise or fall of world commodity prices, growth or recession in the economies of trading partners, or even the arrival or non-arrival of 'good rains', are important economic determinants which lie outside the influence of African governments. Whilst it is possible to retain a cautious optimism in relation to the chances of moderate economic improvement in Africa, and the beneficial effects of this on democratic legitimacy, one could not put it more strongly than that.

Democracy and Political Leadership

To all but the most obdurate structuralist human agency is a crucial factor in shaping political life. The characteristics of individual leaders are extremely relevant in determining political outcomes and this holds as true in relation to democratisation as it does to any other political developments. Samuel Huntington makes the point simply and effectively when he writes that 'democracy will spread in the world to the extent that those who exercise power in the world and in individual countries want it to spread'[13]. To argue in this way is not to suggest that political leaders have perfect freedom to select any political outcome they wish. In the real world they are always constrained by a whole range of factors but within those constraints they do have real choices to make and what they choose to do has important consequences for the political systems in which they operate. This is especially so in relation to political systems which are of recent origin and weakly institutionalised. Given the plasticity of the democratisation process in contemporary Africa key decisions taken by leaders at key points in the process have a great impact in enhancing or weakening the prospects for democracy.

Certainly the evidence from the relatively limited number of examples of cases where democracy has survived for long periods in Africa suggests that the question of political leadership was extremely important. The roles of Seretse Khama (Botswana), Dawda Jawara (The Gambia: for nearly thirty years before the coup), and Seewoosagur Ramgoolam (Mauritius), in sustaining democratic political systems during periods when democracy was on the wane in Africa were of crucial importance[14]. More recent developments also indicate the importance of leadership[15], perhaps nowhere more clearly than in South Africa where the contribution of Nelson Mandela has been critical in the transition from authoritarianism to democracy. In a different way the willingness of defeated incumbents in regime changing elections to accept loss of office can be regarded as a positive development.

It would be mistaken to see the willingness of political leaders to behave in a manner consistent with the principles of democracy as necessarily resulting from a high level of altruism on the part of the individual (although some degree of altruism is certainly useful). Recently published evidence[16] strongly suggests that the development of an authoritarian political system is not only hazardous for regime opponents but also for those imposing authoritarianism. This is because authoritarian rule precludes the possibility of peaceful succession and thus creates the likelihood of violent change in which the incumbent authoritarian leaders are likely to suffer severely negative consequences. Since independence roughly between one half and two thirds of political leaders in the, predominantly authoritarian, systems of Africa have ended up in prison, in exile, or being killed by political opponents[17]. Because democracy reduces the extreme zero-sum aspects of political competition it can be seen as serving the interests of leaders who, one must assume, have some regard for their personal safety. The arguments presented earlier regarding the unsustainability of authoritarian rule in the changed political environment of Africa reinforce the relevance of such calculations. If it is near impossible to retain power through authoritarian means it is less risky to attempt to retain it through democratic means.

Although there are grounds for optimism that the nature of political leadership, and the style of leaders, is changing in a way more supportive of democracy, it is nevertheless the case that there are a number of states in which authoritarian leaders have continued to act in ways which are highly obstructive in relation to democratic progress. Currently ruling leaders in states such as Zaire, Togo, Burkina Faso, Sudan, Nigeria, and Kenya, can be seen to different degrees to belong to this category. In general terms only a cautious optimism is, again, suggested.

Assistance from Outside for African Democracy?

If I really thought that the success of the democratic experiment in Africa was going to depend on high levels of assistance from foreign, presumably Western, powers I would be the most convinced 'demo-pessimist' around. As was argued in chapter 3, political conditionality played a small role in the struggle for democracy by giving some support to pro-democratic movements in Africa. Since then very little help has been forthcoming from the west to increase assistance to states which have made reasonable progress towards democracy. The 'stick' of cutting aid to authoritarian regimes has not been complemented by the 'carrot' of aid to democratic ones except in very small ways in a few limited cases. The strategic and economic marginalisation of Africa in the post-cold war period has produced a primarily non-interventionist policy in the west as regards Africa. Events like the catastrophe of Rwanda cause embarrassment amongst the western powers but do not appear to promote the sort of far-ranging policies which might help to avert the possibilities of repetition elsewhere in Africa. Before the 1992 presidential election in the USA Bill Clinton talked of 'leading a global alliance for democracy' with Africa as a central concern[18]. Whilst the victory of Clinton raised a degree of optimism over the possibility of a new agenda for American foreign policy in relation to Africa, which would place African interests at the forefront, very little of significance actually materialised. The victory of the Republicans in the November 1994 congressional elections in the USA must further reduce the prospects for any meaningful American assistance for African democracy, especially if it costs money.

166

The gloomy comments above could only be seen to undermine the case for 'demo-optimism' if the arguments for the latter perspective were based in large part on external assistance being a precondition for sustaining democracy in Africa. As was argued in chapter 3, the most important factors supporting the initial struggle for democracy were internal to Africa. For the future the most important factors determining the future of democracy will also be primarily internal. No doubt many Africans would welcome assistance from abroad but they would be very unwise to rely on it being forthcoming in any significant way, however much one might wish that the situation was different. The crucial balance of power will be that between Africans supporting democracy and those opposing it and the relative capacities of both groups to mobilise the support necessary to secure victory. The future of African democracy depends on Africans which, in my opinion, is how it should be.

Regional Considerations

It is abundantly clear that the recent democratisation process in Africa has affected different African states in different ways and that there is every reason to expect that this pattern of variation will continue. Every African state has its own particular history, social and economic composition, culture, and leadership style, all of which will continue to shape its distinct identity. However, I would suggest that it is also worth considering the question of the future of democracy at a level that lies between the individual state and the continental totality. From the evidence available so far is it possible to detect the emergence, even if only in embryonic form, of regional patterns of variation in the role of democracy? Whilst it would be unrealistically simplistic to search for internally homogeneous regional patterns (such that all states in a particular region would be expected to behave in identical ways) it is still useful to examine the prospects for regional factors impacting on processes of democratisation in such a way that the prospects for democratic consolidation might be viewed as better in one region than in another.

For a number of reasons the Southern African region appears the most likely to demonstrate such a regional pattern. Historically the individual states of the region have exhibited more far-reaching levels of interaction than has been evident in other regions. For several decades, until very recently, the dominant factor structuring these interactions was the existence in the dominant state of the region of a political system which was unacceptable to the other states. The racial domination of the apartheid system in South Africa produced severe tensions within the region as the South African government sought to prevent its neighbours from providing support for its domestic opponents, most notably the

ANC, and the other states struggled to limit the economic and military threats posed by the incomparably greater power of the South African state. This threat led to the development of regional organisations, which inevitably excluded South Africa, designed to offer some mutual protection to the weaker states of the region. On the political and diplomatic level the most important of these was the Frontline States[19] organisation which included most states of the region (fKhad). On the economic level the most important was the Southern African Development Co-ordination Conference (SADCC) which changed its name to the Southern African Development Community (SADC) in 1992. The participation of Tanzania, which would not normally be regarded as 'Southern' African, in both of these organisations resulted from the personal commitment of Julius Nyerere to the anti-apartheid struggle rather than to any great Tanzanian economic or historical role in the region. The states of Southern Africa thus already have an established tradition of structured interaction which sets them apart from other regions of Africa and makes Southern Africa a region in ways that go far beyond a mere geographical expression. The replacement of apartheid with non-racial democracy in South Africa can be expected to produce dramatic changes in the region because it has eliminated the main barrier to the peaceful participation in regional affairs of the regionally dominant power.

The above analysis clearly suggests that Southern African is very likely to exhibit a regional dimension with the individual states of the region influencing each other's affairs, although still seeking to operate the principle of state sovereignty. Having established the element of 'regionality' one is now in a position to attempt to answer the question as to whether or not the prospects for democracy in this region are better than in other parts of Africa. Provided that it is understood that the idea of 'regional prospects' cannot imply that all states will act in the same way I would suggest that it is reasonable to argue that the prospects for democracy are better in Southern Africa than elsewhere.

On balance the recent experience of democracy in the region appears promising. Of central importance, of course, was the transition in South Africa but other states complemented this positive development. Botswana is Africa's longest surviving democracy and might be viewed as having already achieved consolidation. Although more recently established Namibia's democracy appears to be functioning well. Zambia, Malawi, and Lesotho, have all recently experienced democratic regime changing elections, although post-election developments in Lesotho give cause for concern. The expected demise of democracy in Zimbabwe in 1990 did not materialise and although the democratic credentials of some members of the ruling party may appear less than totally convincing the country has a thriving and dynamic civil society determined to avoid any move towards a more authoritarian form of rule. Swaziland still retains an undemocratic form of 'traditional' monarchy but with a record of political stability and increasing internal pressure for democratisation it may not remain immune from changes in the region. The Lusophone states of Angola and Mozambique remain more problematic from the point of view of democratic rule. Mozambique did enjoy a relatively democratic election in late 1994 but the situation there remains tense. The prospects for democracy in Angola are the worst of any state in the region following Jonas Savimbi's unilateral abandonment of the electoral process in 1992. At the time of writing eight out of ten of the states of the region are ruled by governments which can reasonably claim to have been democratically elected.

To what extent can these states be seen to be influencing each other in ways which are supportive of democracy other than by contributing their own example to a more democratic balance in the region? In general, communications within the region are easier than within other regions of Africa. Communications infrastructure is relatively developed over most of the region and, with the exceptions of Angola and Mozambique, the English language provides a futher facilitating factor. Again with the exception of the Lusophone cases (and Mozambique may join soon), all the states of the region are members of the Commonwealth which has itself adopted a supportive position in relation to democracy in its member states over the past few years. In addition to providing a regional environment which is conducive to democracy the regional factor also reflects specific instances of pro-democracy influences. When Nelson Mandela visited Zimbabwe in 1990 and spoke passionately in favour of multi-party democracy he made a significant contribution in support of Zimbabweans opposed to President Mugabe's plans at the time to introduce a single-party state. Whilst it is difficult to estimate exactly how important this was in bringing about the abandonment of this scheme it was certainly influential. The revered status of Mandela spreads far beyond the borders of South Africa and is a factor which is favourable to democracy. In the previous chapter it was shown how a combination of neighbouring states assisted in defeating two major threats to democracy in Lesotho in January and August 1994. In some ways Lesotho presents a 'soft target' for neighbouring states which wish to apply pressure for democracy because of its weakness and vulnerability. Positive results were relatively easy to obtain without any great expenditure of effort or resources on the part of Lesotho's more powerful neighbours. If the potential costs of intervention had been higher the latter might well have been far more reluctant to intervene in what was essentially a Basotho problem which carried little or no threat to anybody else. The South African government is obliged through its own democratic accountability to place its own domestic constituency at the top of its priorities and would almost certainly be unwilling to devote significant levels of resources to sorting out the problems of its neighbours. Suggestions that the South African military might become involved in trying to restore peace in

Angola have received a cool response in Pretoria. Pragmatism may well ensure that aiding democracy in the region is limited to relatively low cost exercises but these might be expected to have some positive effects. In October 1994, following a meeting of the FLS in Harare, diplomatic pressure from South Africa (especially from Vice President Thabo Mbeki) and Zimbabwe was important in persuading the RENAMO leader Afonso Dhlakama to abandon his plans to boycott the first multi-party elections in Mozambique and then in persuading him to accept the results, which he did rather grudgingly.

At a regional level the prospects for democracy appear fairly promising in Southern Africa. A possible potential weakness of this situation is that it is rather heavily dependent on South Africa continuing to develop a stable and democratic system. Although the nightmare scenario of South Africa collapsing into major civil war and anarchy now looks less likely than it has ever done it remains the case that if such a development were ever to take place the effect on the rest of the region would be devastating.

In the other regions of Africa the regional dimensions of democratisation are likely to be less pronounced and the future of democracy more dependent on what happens at state level. Other regions simply do not have the level of regionality that exist, and have existed for a long time, in Southern Africa. In West Africa, for example, the states of the region have not experienced the levels of interaction seen in Southern Africa. Even the establishment of the Economic Community of West African States (ECOWAS), which has now been in existence for twenty years, has failed to achieve any significant levels of integration. Certainly individual states may be influenced by developments in neighbouring states relating to democracy but this is not likely to occur at a regional level. The only state potentially capable of exercising the role of regional superpower in West Africa, in the way that South Africa does in Southern Africa, is Nigeria but here incapacitation through internal conflict and instability (including civil war), combined with economic chaos, has prevented this from happening. For obvious reasons it would be totally implausible to suggest that Sanni Abacha might be able to play the sort of regional role that Nelson Mandela has been exercising in Southern Africa.

The Eastern African region and the Central African region also cannot be seen as replicating the regionality of Southern Africa. Because of this a specific regional dimension to democratisation seems unlikely to occur. To suggest the absence of a strong regional dimension of democratisation is not to suggest that democratisation has not, or will not, take place in other African regions apart from Southern Africa but rather to suggest that democratic success or failure in individual states will depend more on local domestic factors. It is grounds for some optimism that in the only region where a regional dimension can be clearly identified the effects of that dimension appear to be supportive of democracy.

170

Population Size

All regions of Africa contain a mixture of states with relatively large populations and states with relatively small populations. Irrespective of the geographical location of an African state it is useful to ask if population size is a relevant consideration when attempting to predict the possibilities and probabilities of creating and sustaining democratic rule. The evidence would seem to suggest that a small population is positively advantageous to democracy but that the advantages so accruing may be offset by other factors which are also related to size. A small population may be defined, in an admittedly arbitrary fashion, as one of one and a half million or less. Applying this to the whole post-independence period it is noticeable that the states with the best record of sustaining democracy, Botswana, The Gambia (the 1994 coup notwithstanding), and Mauritius, all fall into the small population category. Equally if the same is done in relation to more recent democratisation it is noticeable that some of the more successful cases, for example Cape Verde, Sao Tome and Principe, and Seychelles, also fall into the same category. In a state with a small population the number of people who may be considered to be part of the political elite will be correspondingly small. Because there are so few of them they will tend to know each other fairly well and this intimacy can be seen as a factor facilitating the sort of compromise approach to political life on which democracy depends.

Although it is reasonable in the light of the above to argue that states with small populations are better positioned to develop consolidated democracies this view is in need of qualification. Several African states with small populations have very poor records of democracy and, in part at least, this might also be explained by population size. Equatorial Guinea, for example, has one of the very poorest records of democracy and human rights in Africa and there is little hope that this will improve in the foreseeable future[20]. One of the problems facing Equatorial Guinea has been the development of a culture of political violence within its small political elite which has many of the characteristics of a vicious family feud The country has had only two national leaders since independence: in 1979 the brutal dictator Macias Nguema Biyogo Negu Ndong was overthrown and killed by Teodoro Obiang Nguema Mbasago who was his nephew. In 1986 there was a violent attempt to overthrow the latter in a coup led by his uncle Fructuoso Mba Onana Nchama. Apart from domestic conflicts small states, perhaps especially island states, are extremely vulnerable to interference from some very dubious outsiders. For most of the post-independence period The Comoros (since 1992 officially entitled the Federal Islamic Republic of the Comoros) was effectively ruled by a group of European mercenaries, led by the infamous Frenchman Colonel Robert (Bob) Denard, which installed and deposed Comoran presidents more or less at will. Only the despatch of a French naval task force to Comoros in 1989 finally persuaded Denard and his gang to withdraw. Although Comoros represents an extreme case it does illustrate the vulnerability of very small states.

Looking towards the future it would seem that the prospects for sustained and consolidated democracy are better in states with small populations than they are in states with large populations. It must be emphasised that this is not to suggest political uniformity in relation to size: there will no doubt be large democracies and small dictatorships as well as the reverse. Outside of Africa one need only remember the case of India, with a population of around 850 million (more than the whole African continent), to see the actualisation of democracy within a massive Third World state over an extended period. However, the extent to which one may expect states with small populations to be disproportionately overrepresented in any future invoice of successful democratisation in Africa creates something of a paradox because whilst significantly increasing the number of states which are ruled democratically it has a very much smaller effect on the number of African people living under democratic rule.

Luck, Accident, and 'Chaos'

As a body professional social scientists tend to be very uneasy when dealing with phenomena such as luck and accident in their attempts to analyse occurrences in human societies. For dedicated structuralists, with their focus on the deterministic nature of macro economic and social forces, any discussion of luck or accident comes close to heresy. Even for others such issues appear to be less than substantial in analytical terms. Some historians[21] feel more at ease in laying stress on the role of historical accident and good, or bad, fortune in their attempts to explain events and outcomes, partly because they are less driven by the imperative to be 'scientific'. However, I would argue that there is nothing inherently 'unscientific' about suggesting that in many ways luck and accident will most likely have a role to play in shaping the success and the failure of democracy in some African states. In many cases the situation remains delicately balanced so that relatively small variations in the course of events, such as would be caused by fortune or misfortune, could significantly affect outcomes. This line of argument appears entirely consistent with the branch of theoretical physics known as 'chaos theory' which specialises in dealing with complex systems in the natural world. The physicist James Gleick points out how 'tiny differences in input could quickly become overwhelming differences in output'[22]. Chaos theorists refer to this as the 'Butterfly Effect' which reflects the notion that a butterfly stirring the air today in Peking can transform storm systems next month in New York.

In terms of the debate between 'demo-optimism' and 'demo-pessimism' luck and accident fulfill a neutral role because, by definition, they remain unpredictable (or, at least, beyond our powers of prediction). Their unpredictability precludes specific discussion here but at least it is possible to give some indication of the types of phenomena which might be important. Having stressed the importance of leadership it would appear logical to suggest that what happens to individual leaders could have a significant effect. Political leaders are as subject to the misfortunes of sickness, fatal disease, and accidental death as the rest of us. The untimely death of a popular leader who was committed to democracy could easily have severely negative consequences for a fragile new democracy. Equally one could think of some African leaders whose departure from the scene in this manner might well lead to more positive consequences. The same could be applied to deliberate attempts on the lives of leaders: sometimes the assassin's bullet just misses and sometimes it doesn't[23]. The success or failure of democratisation will inevitably be affected by a large number of individual decisions taken by a large number of individuals: none of these decisions is completely predetermined and a wide range of factors determine the choices which will be made and whose advice will be listened to. Gary Marks highlights this point when he argues that 'the implantation of democratic institutions and practices is notoriously a chaotic affair, full of sudden and unpredictable shifts in behaviour and decisive watersheds where decisions made at particular moments in time appear to shape the possibilities of democracy for years to come'[24]. Even if one assumed that individuals wished to make a decision favourable to democracy (which is certainly not always true) the possibility of a decision being shaped by the bad luck of error, miscalculation, or misinformation, is always present. Once taken, decisions inevitably provoke reactive decisions from other political actors which compound the original decision and shape future developments in a way which could easily have been different if the original decision had been different. In the confusion and uncertainty of the real world, which is enhanced by the plasticity of the transitional context, the observer must be careful not to ascribe a retrospective inevitability to decisions which could quite easily have been different. Luck and accident can stretch beyond the scope of human agency. A catastrophic drought, or similar environmental disaster, can place impossible stress on a fragile political system by undermining its, predominantly agrarian, economic base. Conversely, propitious climatic conditions can provide welcome relief from hardship by enhancing the conditions for domestic food supply and increasing export crop production.

It has been reported, perhaps apocryphally, that when it was time for Napoleon Bonaparte to appoint a new general his most important question was 'is he lucky?': for Napoleon a lucky general was more likely to win battles than was a good one. It could be suggested that what Africa needs is lucky democratic leaders. Clearly the accidents of fortune cannot provide a complete explanation of success and failure but equally an awareness of such factors cannot be avoided.

Conclusions

For those who genuinely care about what happens in Africa observing political change on the continent provides an emotional roller coaster of alternating euphoria and depression. The emotional high produced by the conduct of the South African elections is offset by the emotional low occasioned by the collapse into catastrophic anarchy in Rwanda: the peaceful ousting through the ballot box of dictators like Kerekou (in Benin) and Banda (in Malawi) is counteracted by the actions of Mobutu (in Zaire) and Abacha (in Nigeria) who appear determined to cling to power whatever the costs to the nation.

Euphoria and depression may be inescapable but neither provide a sound basis for reaching realistic conclusions about the new struggle for democracy in Africa. Viewed objectively this struggle can be seen as having produced a mixture of success and failure and a large ambivelant and uncertain middle ground where success and failure intermingle in, as yet, undetermined ways. A few years ago (before the most recent struggle began) I wrote a book on democracy in Africa in which I concluded that 'the future of African democracy is likely to be patchy and changeable but persistent'[25]. Since then the 'new struggle' has placed democracy more firmly on the African political agenda than was previously the case. Although enormous obstacles to democratic consolidation remain, the markedly increased role played by democracy in African politics over the last few years is unlikely to dissipate or become atrophied in the future. Cautious optimism is justified.

Notes

(1) Fukuyama (1992), op. cit., p.70.
(2) See, for example, Rob Buijtenhuijs and Elly Rijnierse, *Democratisation in Sub-Saharan Africa (1989-1992): An Overview of the Literature*, Leiden, Afrika-Studiecentrum, 1993, and Peter Woodward, 'Democracy and Economy in Africa: The Optimists and the Pessimists', *Democratization*, Vol.1, No.1, Spring 1994, pp.116-132.
(3) Because I cannot claim expertise on the non-African world I have relied heavily on the secondary literature. Of particular importance is the four volume set edited and/or written by Guillermo O'Donnell, Philippe

Schmitter and Laurence Whitehead: (1) O'Donnell, Schmitter and Whithead (eds), *Transitions from Authoritarian Rule: Southern Europe* (2) O'Donnell, Schmitter and Whitehead, *Transitions from Authoritarian Rule: Latin America* (3) O'Donnell, Schmitter and Whitehead, *Transitions from Authoritarian Rule: Comparative Perspectives* (4) O'Donnell and Schmitter, *Transitions from Authoritarian Rule: Tentative Conclusions about Uncertain Democracies:* all Baltimore and London, Johns Hopkins University Press, 1986.

Other important books in this field are: Kenneth E. Bauzon (ed,), *Development and Democratization in the Third World: Myths, Hopes and Realities*, Washington, Crane Russak, 1992: Larry Diamond and Marc F. Plattner (eds.), *The Global Resurgence of Democracy*, Baltimore and London, Johns Hopkins University Press, 1993: Charles Guy Gillespie, *Negotiating Democracy: Politicians and Generals in Uruguay*, Cambridge, Cambridge University Press, 1991: Alex Hadenius, *Democracy and Development*, Cambridge, Cambridge University Press, 1992: David Held (ed.), *Prospects for Democracy*, Cambridge, Polity Press, 1993: John Higley and Richard Gunther, *Elites and Democratic Consolidation in Latin America and Southern Europe*, Cambridge, Cambridge University Press, 1992: Gary Marks and Larry Diamond (eds.), *Reexamining Democracy: Essays in Honour of Seymour Martin Lipset*, London, Sage, 1992: Tatu Vanhanen, *The Process of Democratization: A Comparative Study of 147 States*, 1980-88, Washington, Crane Russak, 1990: Geraint Parry and Michael Moran (eds), *Democracy and Democratization*, London, Routledge, 1994. See also Huntington (1991) op. cit. and Fukuyama (1992) op. cit. already cited several times in this volume. For a most useful review of some of these (and some others) see, David Beetham, 'Conditions for Democratic Consolidation', *Review of African Political Economy*, No. 60, 1994, pp.157-172.

My own understanding of Latin American democratisation was enhanced when I participated, as an invited guest Africanist, in the Latin American workshop organised by the European Consortium for Political Research (ECPR), in Rimini in 1988.

(4)   Widner (ed.), 1994, op. cit., p.3

(5)   Abraham Lowenthal, 'Foreword' in O'Donnell and Schmitter, 1986, op. cit., p.ix.

(6)   O'Donnell and Schmitter, 1986, op. cit., p.19.

(7)   Ibid. p.54.

(8)   Ibid. p.38.

(9)   Barbara Grosh, 'Through the Structural Adjustment Minefield: Politics in an Era of Economic Liberalization', in Widner (ed.) op. cit. p.36.

(10) Seymour Martin Lipset, 'Some Social Requesites of Democracy: Economic Development and Political Legitimacy', *American Political Science Review*, No.53, 1959, pp.69-105. For a more recent exposition see Seymour Martin Lipset, Kyoung-Ryung Seong and John Charles Torres, 'A Comparative Analysis of the Social Requesites of Democracy', *International Social Science Journal*, No.136, 1993, pp.155-175.

(11) For a recent useful discussion of this debate see Larry Diamond, 'Economic Development and Democracy Reconsidered' in Marks and Diamond (eds), (1992), op. cit., pp.93-139. In a recent article two scholars argue that 'what the literature has considered in the past to be preconditions of democracy may be better conceived in the future as the outcomes of different types of democracy'. See Terry Lynn Karl and Philippe C. Schmitter, 'Modes of Transition in Latin America, Southern and Eastern Europe', *International Social Science Journal*, No.128, 1991, pp.269-284.

(12) An outstanding example of this approach is Janet MacGaffey, *The Real Economy of Zaire*, London, James Currey, 1991. See also T. L. Maliyamkono and M. S. D. Bagachwa, *The Second Economy in Tanzania*, London, James Currey, 1990.

(13) Huntington, (1991), op. cit., p.316.

(14) For discussions of these leaders see Wiseman (1990), op. cit.

(15) See, for example, Jennifer Widner, 'Two Leadership Styles and Patterns of Political Liberalization', *African Studies Review*, Vol.37, No.1, April 1994, pp.151-174.

(16) John A. Wiseman 'Leadership and Personal Danger in African Politics', *The Journal of Modern African Studies*, Vol.31, No.4, 1993, pp.657-660.

(17) Ibid. p.659. Of 485 leaders examined 288 had suffered negative outcomes.

(18) See Bill Clinton 'Election '92: The Democratic Agenda', *Africa Report*, Vol.37, No.5, September-October 1992, pp.18-20.

(19) For a major recent study of the Frontline States see Gilbert M. Khadiagala, *Allies in Adversity: The Frontline States in Southern African Security*, 1975-1993, Athens Ohio, Ohio University Press, 1994.

(20) See Liniger-Goumaz, (1988), op. cit.

(21) The eminent historian A. J. P. Taylor is a good example of a scholar who frequently stressed the roles played by luck and accident. See, for example, his *The Origins of the Second World War*, London, Hamish Hamilton, 1961, or *The First World War*, London, Hamish Hamilton, 1963.

(22) James Gleik, *Chaos: Making a New Science*, London, Heinemann, 1988, p.8.

(23) To see the possible consequences of such accidents one could imagine the following, purely hypothetical, scenario. Just suppose that Nelson Mandela were to be assassinated by a white far right fanatic. This could easily

provoke an upsurge of support for black organisations opposed to the current settlement and consequent attacks on white civilians. In turn this could provoke attacks on black civilians by an enlarged white rejectionist front. In such circumstances the fragile unity of the security forces could break down with inter-racial conflict within the army and police rapidly leading to virtual civil war. Whilst this was going on Buthelezi could announce the secession of Kwazulu from South Africa so producing a further type of conflict. The collapse of South Africa could then have serious negative consequences for other states in the region. NB the above is a purely hypothetical scenario imagined to emphasise the point and is most definitely not a prediction of likely future developments.

(24) Gary Marks, 'Rational Sources of Chaos in Democratic Transition', in Marks and Diamond (eds), (1992), op. cit., p.48.
(25) Wiseman, 1990, op. cit. p.191.

Bibliography

Adamolekun, Ladipo, *Politics and Administration in Nigeria*, London, Hutchinson, 1986.

Adepoju, Aderanti (ed.), *The Impact of Structural Adjustment on the Population of Africa*, London, James Currey, 1993.

Agbaje, Adigun A.B., *The Nigerian Press: Hegemony and the Social Constitution of Legitimacy 1960-1983*, New York, Edwin Mellen Press, 1992.

Agbese, Pita Ogaba, 'With Fingers on the Trigger: The Military as Custodian of Democracy in Nigeria', *Journal of Third World Studies*, Vol.9, No.2, 1992, pp.220-253.

Ahluwalia, D. Pal, 'Democratic Transition in African Politics: The Case of Kenya', *Australian Journal of Political Science*, Vol.28, 1993, pp.499-514.

Ajulu, Rok, 'The 1992 Kenya General Elections: A Preliminary Assessment', *Review of African Political Economy*, No. 56, March 1993, pp.98-102.

Ake, Claude, 'The Unique Case of African Democracy', *International Affairs*, Vol.69, No.2, 1993, pp.239-244.

Akinola, Anthony A., 'Manufacturing the Two-Party System in Nigeria, *The Journal of Commonwealth and Comparative Politics*, Vol.28, No.3, November 1990, pp.309-327.

Allen, Chris, Michael S. Radu and Keith Somerville, Benin, *The Congo, and Burkina Faso: Politics, Economics and Society*, London, Pinter Publishers, 1988.

Allen, Chris, 'Restructuring an Authoritarian State: Democratic Renewal in Benin', *Review of African Political Economy*, No.54, 1992, pp.42-58.

Allison Jr., Graham T. and Robert P. Beschel, 'Can the United States Promote Democracy?', *Political Science Quarterly*, Vol.107, No.1, 1992, pp.81-98.

Apter, David E., and Carl G. Rosberg (eds.), *Political Development and the New*

Realism in Sub-Saharan Africa, Charlottesville and London, University Press of Virginia, 1994.

Arat, Zehra F., *Democracy and Human Rights in Developing Countries*, Boulder and London, Lynne Rienner, 1991.

Bandele-Thomas, 'Biyi, 'Interview with Wole Soyinka', *Index on Censorship*, No.8-9, 1993, pp.32-33.

Barkan, Joel D., 'Kenya: Lessons from a Flawed Election', *Journal of Democracy*, Vol.4, No.3, July 1993, pp.85-99.

Bates, Robert H., *Unions, Parties and Political Development: A Study of the Mineworkers in Zambia*, New Haven, Yale University Press, 1971.

Bauzon, Kenneth E. (ed.), *Development and Democratization in the Third World: Myths, Hopes and Realities*, Washington, Crane Russak, 1992.

Bayart, Jean-Francois, *The State in Africa: The Politics of the Belly*, London, Longman, 1993.

Baylies, Caroline and Morris Szeftel, 'The Fall and Rise of Multi-Party Politics in Zambia', *Review of African Political Economy*, No.54, July 1992, pp.75-91.

Baynham, Simon, 'Geopolitics, Glasnost and Africa's Second Liberation: Political and Security Implications for the Continent', *Africa Insight*, Vol.21, No.4, 1991, pp.263-268.

Beetham, David, 'Conditions for Democratic Consolidation', *Review of African Political Economy*, No.60, June 1994, pp.157-172.

Bienen, Henry, 'Leaders, Violence, and the Absence of Change in Africa', *Political Science Quarterly*, Vol.108, No.2, pp.271-282.

Bjornland, Eric, Michael Bratton and Clark Gibson, 'Observing Multi-Party Elections in Africa: Lessons from Zambia', *African Affairs*, Vol.91, No.364, July 1992, pp.405-431.

Boahen, Adu, 'Military Rule and Multi-Party Democracy: The Case of Ghana', *Africa Demos*, Vol.1, No.2, January 1991, p.5.

Bowman, Larry W., *Mauritius: Democracy and Development in the Indian Ocean*, London, Dartmouth, 1991.

Bratton, Michael, 'Zambia Starts Over', *Journal of Democracy*, Vol.3, No.2, April 1992, pp.81-94. .

Bratton, Michael and Nicolas van de Walle, 'Popular Protest and Political Reform in Africa', *Comparative Politics*, Vol.24, No.4, July 1992, pp.419-442.

Bratton, Michael and Nicolas van de Walle, 'Neopatrimonial Regimes and Political Transitions in Africa', *World Politics*, Vol.46, July 1994, pp.453-489.

Buijtenhuijs, Rob, and Elly Rijnierse, *Democratisation in Sub-Saharan Africa (1989-1992): An Overview of the Literature*, Leiden, Afrika-Studiecentrum, 1993.

Callaghy, Thomas M., *The State-Society Struggle: Zaire in Comparative Perspective*, New York, Columbia University Press, 1984.

Callaghy, Thomas, 'Africa: Back to the Future', *Journal of Democracy*, Vol.5, No.4, October 1994, pp.133-145.

Caron, B., A Gboyega and E. Osaghae (eds), *Democratic Transition in Africa*, Ibadan, Centre For Research, Documentation and University Exchange (CREDU), 1992.

Chabal, Patrick, 'Democracy and Daily Life in Black Africa', *International Affairs*, Vol.70, No.1, 1994, pp.83-91.

Chalker, Linda, 'Development and Democracy: What Should the West be Doing?', *The Round Table*, No.329, 1994, pp.23-26.

Chan, Stephen and Chanda L.J. Chingambo, 'Democracy in Southern Africa: The 1990 elections in Zimbabwe and 1991 Elections in Zambia', *The Round Table*, No.322, 1992, pp.183-201.

Charlick, Robert B., *Niger: Personal Rule and Survival in the Sahel*, Boulder, Westview Press, 1991.

Charlick, Robert B., 'Corruption in Political Transition: A Governance Perspective', *Corruption and Reform*, Vol.7, No.3, 1993, pp.177-187.

Charlton, Roger, 'The Politics of Elections in Botswana', *Africa*, Vol.63, No.3, 1993, pp.330-370.

Chazan, Naomi, 'Africa's Democratic Challenge', *World Policy Journal*, Vol.9, No.2, Spring 1992, pp.279-307.

Cheater, Angela P., 'The University of Zimbabwe: University, National University, State University, or Party University?', *African Affairs*, Vol.90, No.359, 1991, pp.189-205.

Cherry, Janet, 'Development, Conflict and the Politics of Ethnicity in South Africa's Transition to Democracy', *Third World Quarterly*, Vol.15, No.4, 1994, pp.613-631.

Chikwanda, A.B., 'Zambia: The Challenge Posed Starkly', *International Review of Administrative Sciences*, Vol.59, pp.579-583.

Clapham, Christopher, *Transformation and Continuity in Revolutionary Ethiopia*, Cambridge, Cambridge University Press, 1988.

Clapham, Christopher, 'Democratisation in Africa: Obstacles and Prospects', *Third World Quarterly*, Vol.14, No.3, 1993.

Clark, John F., 'Theoretical Disarray and the Study of Democratisation in Africa', *The Journal of Modern African Studies*, Vol.31, No.3, 1993, pp.529-534.

Cliffe, Lionel, with Ray Bush, Jenny Lindsay, Brian Mokopakgosi, Donna Pankhurst, and Balefi Tsie, *The Transition to Independence in Namibia*, Boulder and London, Lynne Rienner, 1994.

Cohen, Robin, and Harry Goulbourne, (eds), *Democracy and Socialism in Africa*, Boulder, Westview Press, 1991.

180

Cornia, Giovanni Andrea, Rolph van der Hoeven and Thandika Mkandawire (eds), *Africa's Recovery in the 1990s: From Stagnation and Adjustment to Human Development*, Basingstoke, Macmillan, 1992.

Dahl, Robert A., *Democracy and its Critics*, New Haven and London, Yale University Press, 1989.

Dale, Richard, 'The UN and African Decolonization: UNTAG in Namibia', *TransAfrica Forum*, Fall 1991, pp.31-48.

Danopoulos, Constantine P. (ed.), *Civilian Rule in the Developing World: Democracy on the March?*, Boulder, Westview Press, 1992.

Davidson, Scott, *Human Rights*, Buckingham, Open University Press, 1993.

Decalo, Samuel, 'Towards Understanding the Sources of Stable Civilian Rule in Africa: 1960-1990', *Journal of Contemporary African Studies*, Vol.10, No.1, 1991, pp.66-83.

Decalo, Samuel, 'The Process, Prospects and Constraints of Democratization in Africa', *African Affairs*, Vol.91, No.362, January 1992, pp.7-35.

Destexhe, Alain, 'The Third Genocide', *Foreign Policy*, No.97, Winter 1994-1995.

Diamond, Larry, *Class, Ethnicity and Democracy in Nigeria: The Failure of the First Republic*, Basingstoke, Macmillan, 1988.

Diamond, Larry, Juan J. Linz, Seymour Martin Lipset (eds), *Democracy in Developing Countries: Volume Two, Africa*, Boulder, Lynne Rienner, 1988.

Diamond, Larry, 'Nigeria's Third Quest for Democracy', *Current History*, Vol.90, No.555, pp.201-204 and 229-231.

Diamond, Larry (ed.), *The Democratic Revolution: Struggles for Freedom and Pluralism in the Developing World*, New York, Freedom House, 1992.

Diamond, Larry, and Marc F. Plattner (eds.) T*he Global Resurgence of Democracy*, Baltimore and London, Johns Hopkins University Press, 1993.

Diamond, Larry (ed.), *Political Culture and Democracy in Developing Countries*, Boulder and London, Lynne Rienner, 1993.

Diamond, Larry, 'Towards Democratic Consolidation', *Journal of Democracy*, Vol.5, No.3, July 1994, pp.4-17.

Doornbos, Martin, Lionel Cliffe, Abdel Ghaffar M. Ahmed and John Markakis (eds), *Beyond Conflict in The Horn*, London, James Currey, 1992.

Duignan, Peter, and Robert H. Jackson (eds), *Politics and Government in African States, 1960-1985*, London, Croom Helm, 1986.

Dundas, Carl W., 'Transparency in Organising Elections', *The Round Table*, No.329, 1994, pp.61-65.

Dzimbiri, Lewis B., 'The Malawi Referendum of June 1993', *Electoral Studies*, Vol.13, No.3, 1994, pp.229-234.

Egero, Bertil, *Mozambique: A Dream Undone*, Uppsala, Scandinavian Institute of African Studies, 1987.

Ellis, Stephen, 'Tuning in to Pavement Radio', *African Affairs*, Vol.88, No.352, July 1989, pp.321-330.

Ellis, Stephen, 'Rumour and Power in Togo', *Africa*, Vol.63, No.4, 1993, pp.462-476.

Eshete, Andreas, 'Implementing Human Rights and a Democratic Constitution in Ethiopia' *Issue*, Vol.21, No.1-2, 1993, pp.8-13.

Fatton Jr., Robert, *The Making of a Liberal Democracy: Senegal's Passive Revolution, 1975-1985*, Boulder and London, Lynne Rienner, 1987.

Fatton,Jr., Robert, 'Liberal Democracy in Africa', *Political Science Quarterly*, Vol.105, No.3, 1990, pp.455-473.

Fatton Jr., Robert, 'Democracy and Civil Society in Africa', *Mediterranean Quarterly*, Vol.2, No.4, Fall 1991, pp.83-95.

Fatton Jr., Robert, *Predatory Rule: State and Civil Society in Africa*, Boulder and London, Lynne Rienner, 1992.

Faure, Yves, 'Democracy and Realism: Reflections on the Case of Cote d'Ivoire', *Africa*, Vol.63, No.3, 1993, pp.313-329.

Forster, Peter G., 'Culture, Nationalism and the Invention of Tradition in Malawi', *The Journal of Modern African Studies*, Vol.32, No.3, 1994, pp.477-497.

Fukuyama, Francis, *The End of History and the Last Man*, London, Penguin Books, 1992.

Gann, L.H. and Peter Duignan, *Hope for South Africa?*, Stanford, Hoover Institution Press, 1991.

Garber, Larry, 'The OAU and Elections', *Journal of Democracy*, Vol.4, No.3, 1993, pp.55-59.

Geisler, Gisela, 'Fair? What has Fair got to do with it. Vagaries of Election Observations and Democratic Standards', *The Journal of Modern African Studies*, Vol.31, No.4, 1993, pp.613-637.

Gibbon, Peter and Yusuf Bangura (eds), *Authoritarianism, Democracy and Adjustment: The Politics of Economic Reform in Africa*, Uppsala, Scandinavian Institute of African Studies, 1992.

Gifford, Paul, *Christianity and Politics in Doe's Liberia*, Cambridge, Cambridge University Press, 1993.

Gifford, Paul (ed.) *The Christian Churches and the Democratisation of Africa*, Leiden, E.J. Brill, 1995.

Gillespie, Charles Guy, *Negotiating Democracy: Politicians and Generals in Uruguay*, Cambridge, Cambridge University Press, 1991.

Gleik, James, *Chaos: Making a New Science*, London, Heinemann, 1988.

Glickman, Harvey, 'Frontiers of Liberal and Non-Liberal Democracy in Tropical Africa', *Journal of Asian and African Studies*, Vol.23, No.3-4, 1988, pp.234-254.

Goose, Stephen D. and Frank Smyth, 'Arming Genocide in Rwanda', *Foreign Affairs*, Vol.73, No.5, September-October 1994, pp.86-96.

Guie, Honore Koffi, 'Organizing Africa's Democrats', *Journal of Democracy*, Vol.4, No.2, 1993, pp.119-129.

Guyer, Jane I., 'Representation Without Taxation: An Essay in Democracy in Rural Nigeria, 1952-1990', *African Studies Review*, Vol.35, No.1, April 1992, pp.41-79.

Gyimah-Boadi, E., 'Ghana's Uncertain Political Opening', *Journal of Democracy*, Vol.5, No.2, April, 1994, pp.75-86.

Hadenius, Alex, *Democracy and Development*, Cambridge, Cambridge University Press, 1992.

Hamalengwa, Munyonzwe, *Class Struggles in Zambia 1889-1989 and the Fall of Kenneth Kaunda 1990-1991*, Lanham, University Press of America, 1992.

Harbeson, John W., Donald Rothchild, Naomi Chazan (eds), *Civil Society and the State in Africa*, Boulder and London, Lynne Rienner, 1994.

Harrison, Graham, 'Mozambique: An Unsustainable Democracy', *Review of African Political Economy*, Vol.21, No.61, 1994, pp.429-440.

Harsch, Ernest, 'Accumulators and Democrats: Challenging State Corruption in Africa', *The Journal of Modern African Studies*, Vol.31, No.1, 1993, pp.31-48.

Hamill, James, and J.E.Spence, 'South Africa's Watershed Election' *The World Today*, July 1994, pp.128-132.

Hatchard, John, 'Re-Establishing a Multi-Party State: Some Constitutional Lessons from Seychelles', *The Journal of Modern African Studies*, Vol.31, No.4, 1993, pp.601-612.

Haynes, Jeff, 'Sustainable Democracy in Ghana? Problems and Prospects', *Third World Quarterly*, Vol.14, No.3, 1993, pp.451-467.

Haynes, Jeff, 'The State, Governance, and Democracy in Sub-Saharan Africa', *The Journal of Modern African Studies*, Vol.31, No.3, 1991, pp.535-539.

Healey, John, and Mark Robinson, *Democracy, Governance and Economic Policy: Sub-Saharan Africa in Comparative Perspective*, London, Overseas Development Institute, 1992.

Heilbrunn, John R., 'Social Origins of National Conferences in Benin and Togo', *The Journal of Modern African Studies*, Vol.31, No.2, 1993, pp.277-299.

Held, David (ed.), *Prospects for Democracy*, Cambridge, Polity Press, 1993.

Hicks, John F., 'Supporting Democracy in Africa', *TransAfrica Forum*, Vol.9, No.2, Summer 1992, pp.69-77.

Higley, John, and Richard Gunther, *Elites and Democratic Consolidation in Latin America and Southern Europe*, Cambridge, Cambridge University Press, 1992.

Hughes, Arnold (ed.), Marxism's Retreat from Africa, Special Issue of *The Journal of Communist Studies*, Vol.8, No.2, 1992.

Hughes, Arnold (ed), *The Gambia: Studies in Society and Politics*, Birmingham University African Studies Series No.3, 1991.

Huntington, Samuel P., *The Third Wave: Democratization in the Late Twentieth Century*, Norman and London, University of Oklahoma Press, 1991.

Huntington, Samuel P., 'How Countries Democratize', *Political Science Quarterly*, Vol.106, No.4, 1991-1992, pp.579-616.

Husain, Ishrat, 'Results of Adjustment in Africa: Selected Cases', *Finance and Development*, June 1994, pp.6-9.

Hyden, Goran, 'The Efforts to Restore Intellectual Freedom in Africa', *Issue*, Vol.20, No.1, Winter 1991, pp.5-14.

Hyden, Goran, and Michael Bratton (eds.), *Governance and Politics in Africa*, Boulder and London, Lynne Rienner, 1992.

Ihonvbere, Julius O., 'Structural Adjustment and Nigeria's Democratic Transition', *TransAfrica Forum*, Vol.8, No.3, Fall 1991, pp.61-83.

Imanyara, Gitobu, 'Kenya: Indecent Exposure', *Index on Censorship*, Vol.21, No.4, April 1992, pp.21-22.

Iyob, Ruth, *The Eritrean Struggle for Independence: Domination, Resistance, Nationalism 1941-1993*, Cambridge University Press, 1995.

Jackson, Robert H. and Carl G. Rosberg, *Personal Rule in Black Africa: Prince, Autocrat, Prophet, Tyrant*, Berkeley, University of California Press, 1982.

Jackson, Robert H. and Carl G. Rosberg, 'Democracy in Tropical Africa: Democracy Versus Autocracy in African Politics', *Journal of International Affairs*, Vol.38, No.2, 1985, pp.292-305.

Kasfir, Nelson, 'Popular Sovereignty and Popular Participation: Mixed Constitutional Democracy in the Third World', *Third World Quarterly*, Vol.13, No.4, 1992.

Jason, Pini, 'Nigeria's Real Dilemma', *New African*, April 1994, p.8.

Jawara, Alhaji Sir Dawda Kairaba, 'The Commonwealth and Human Rights', *The Round Table*, No.321, 1992, pp.37-42.

Jeffries, Richard, and Clare Thomas, 'The Ghanaian Elections of 1992', *African Affairs*, Vol.92, No.365, July 1993, pp.331-366.

Johnston, Alexander, 'South Africa: The Election and the Emerging Party System', *International Affairs*, Vol.70, No.4, 1994, pp.721-736.

Jones, Christine and Miguel A. Kiguel, 'Africa's Quest for Prosperity: Has Adjustment Helped?', *Finance and Development*, June 1994, pp.2-5.

Joseph, Richard A., *Democracy and Prebendal Politics in Nigeria: The Rise and Fall of the Second Republic*, Cambridge, Cambridge University Press, 1987.

Joseph, Richard A. 'Africa: The Rebirth of Political Freedom', *Journal of Democracy*, Vol.2, No.4, 1991, pp.11-24.

Karl, Terry Lynn, and Philippe C. Schmitter, 'Modes of Transition in Latin America, Southern and Eastern Europe', *International Social Science Journal*, No.128, 1991, pp.269-284.

Karikari, Kwame, 'Africa: The Press and Democracy', *Race and Class,* Vol.34, No.3, 1993, pp.55-66.

Khadiagala, Gilbert M., *Allies in Adversity: The Frontline States in Southern African Security, 1975-1993*, Athens Ohio, Ohio University Press, 1994.

Khaketla, B.M., *Lesotho 1970: An African Coup Under the Microscope*, London, C. Hurst, 1971.

Kimenyi, Mwangi S., 'Interest Groups, Transfer Seeking and Democratization', *American Journal of Economics and Sociology*, Vol.48, No.3, July 1989, pp.339-349.

Klein, Martin A., 'Back to Democracy: Presidential Address to the 1991 Meeting of the African Studies Association', *African Studies Review*, Vol.35, No.3, December 1992, pp.1-12.

Knight, Virginia Curtin, 'Growing Opposition in Zimbabwe', *Issue*, Vol.20, No.1, 1991, pp.23-30.

Komisar, Lucy, 'The Claws of Dictatorship in Zaire', *Dissent*, Summer 1992, pp.325-330.

Kpundeh, Sahr J., and Stephen P. Riley, 'Political Choice and the New Democratic Politics in Africa', *The Round Table*, No.323, 1992, pp263-271.

Kraus, Jon, 'Building Democracy in Africa', *Current History*, Vol.90, No.553, May 1991, pp.209-212.

Kuria, Gibson Kamau, 'Confronting Dictatorship in Kenya', *Journal of Democracy*, Vol.2, No.4, 1991, pp.115-126.

Lancaster, Carol, 'Democracy in Africa', *Foreign Policy*, No.85, Winter 1991-1992, pp.148-165.

Lancaster, Carol, 'New Direction in U.S. Foreign Aid', *TransAfrica Forum*, Vol.9, No.2, Summer 1992, pp.53-67.

Lancaster, Carol, 'Democratisation in Sub-Saharan Africa', *Survival*, Vol.35, No.3, Autumn 1993, pp.38-50.

Landell-Mills, Pierre, 'Governance, Cultural Change, and Empowerment', *The Journal of Modern African Studies*, Vol.30, No.4, 1992, pp.543-567.

Leftwich, Adrian, 'States of Underdevelopment: The Third World State in Theoretical Perspective', *The Journal of Theoretical Politics*, Vol.6, No.1, 1994, pp.55-74.

Legum, Colin, 'The Coming of Africa's Second Independence', *The Washington Quarterly*, Winter 1990, pp.129-140.

Lemarchand, Rene, 'African Transitions to Democracy: An Interim (and

Mostly Pessimistic) Assessment', *Africa Insight*, Vol.22, No.3, 1992, pp.178-185.

Lemarchand, Rene, 'Africa's Troubled Transitions', *Journal of Democracy*, Vol.3, No.4, October 1992, pp.98-109.

Lemarchand, Rene, *Burundi: Ethnocide as Discourse and Practice*, Cambridge, Cambridge University Press, 1994.

Lemon, Anthony, *Apartheid in Transition*, Aldershot, Gower, 1987.

Lerche, C.O., 'Social Strife in Nigeria 1971-78', *Journal of African Studies*, Vol.9, No.1, 1982, pp.2-12.

Leslie, Winsome J., *Zaire: Continuity and Political Change in an Oppressive State*, Boulder, Westview Press, 1993.

Lewis, Peter M., 'Endgame in Nigeria? The Politics of a Failed Democratic Transition', *African Affairs*, Vol.93, No.372, July 1994, pp.323-340.

Lijphart, Arend, *Democracy in Plural Societies*, New Haven, Yale University Press, 1977.

Liniger-Goumaz, Max, *Small is not always Beautiful: The Story of Equatorial Guinea*, London, C. Hurst and Co., 1988.

Lipset, Seymour Martin, 'Some Social Requesites of Democracy: Economic Development and Political Legitimacy', *American Political Science Review*, No.53, 1959, pp.69-105.

Lipset, Seymour Martin, Kyoung-Ryung Seong and John Charles Torres, 'A Comparative Analysis of the Social Requesites of Democracy', *International Social Science Journal*, No.136, 1993, pp.155-175.

Lodge, Tom, 'Post-Modern Bolsheviks: South African Communists in Transition', *South Africa International*, April 1992, pp.172-179.

Lodge, Tom, and Bill Nasson, *All Here and Now: Black Politics in South Africa in the 1980s*, London, C. Hurst and Co., 1992.

Luckham, Robin, 'The Military, Militarization and Democratization in Africa: A Survey of Literature and Ideas', *African Studies Review*, Vol.37, No2, September 1994, pp.13-75.

Lungu, Gatian F., 'The Church, Labour and the Press in Zambia: The Role of Critical Observers in a One-Party State', *African Affairs*, Vol.85, No.340, July 1986, pp.385-410.

Lwanda, John Lloyd, *Kamuzu Banda of Malawi: A Study in Promise, Power and Paralysis*, Glasgow, Dudu Nsomba Publications, 1993.

MacGaffey, Janet, *The Real Economy of Zaire*, London, James Currey, 1991.

Machobane, B.B.J., *Government and Change in Lesotho 1800-1966*, Basingstoke, Macmillan, 1990.

Magang, David, 'A New Beginning: The Process of Democratization in Africa', *The Parliamentarian*, No.4, October 1992, pp.235-239.

Maina, Kaniaru wa, 'The Future of Democracy in Kenya', *Africa Today*, 1st and 2nd Quarters 1992, pp.122-127.

Maja-Pearce, Adewale, 'The Press in Nigeria', *Index on Censorship*, No.6, 1994, pp.209-227.

Makinda, Samuel M., 'Kenya: Out of the Straitjacket, Slowly', *The World Today*, October 1992, pp.188-192.

Maliyamkono, T.L., and M.S.D. Bagachwa, *The Second Economy in Tanzania*, London, James Currey, 1990.

Mamdani, Mahmood, 'Africa: Democratic Theory and Democratic Struggles', *Dissent*, Summer 1992, pp.312-318.

Mandaza, Ibbo and Lloyd Sachakonye (eds), *The One Party State and Democracy*, Harare, Southern Africa Political Economy Series Trust, 1991.

Manor, James (ed), *Rethinking Third World Politics*, London, Longman, 1991.

Marks, Gary, and Larry Diamond (eds), *Reexamining Democracy: Essays in Honour of Seymour Martin Lipset*, London, Sage, 1992.

Mbaku, John Mukum, 'Political Democracy and the Prospects of Development in Post-Cold War Africa', *The Journal of Social, Political and Economic Studies*, Vol.17, Nos.3-4, Fall/Winter 1992, pp.345-371.

Mbaku, John Mukum, 'Political Democracy, Military Expenditures and Economic Growth in Africa', *Scandinavian Journal of Development Alternatives*, Vol.12, No.1, 1993, pp.49-64.

Mbeki, Govan, *Learning from Robben Island: The Prison Writings of Govan Mbeki*, London, James Currey, 1991.

McFerson, Hazel M., 'Democracy and Development in Africa', *Journal of Peace Research*, Vol.29, No.3, 1992, pp.241-248.

Meyns, Peter, and Dani Wadada Nabudere, *Democracy and the One-Party State in Africa*, Hamburg, Institute for African Studies, 1989.

Michaels, Marguerite, 'Retreat From Africa', *Foreign Affairs*, Vol.72, No.1, 1993, pp.93-108.

Milimo, John T., 'Multiparty Democracy in Africa: Lessons from Zambia', *International Journal of World Peace*, Vol.10, No.1, March 1993, pp.35-42.

Mills, Greg, 'Zambia and the Winds of Change', *The World Today*, January 1992, pp.16-18.

Minogue, Martin, 'Mauritius: Economic Miracle or Developmental Illusion', *Journal of International Development*, Vol.4, No.6, 1992, pp.643-647.

Mkhondo, Rich, *Reporting South Africa*, London, James Currey, 1993.

Moore, Mick (ed.) 'Good Government', special issue of *IDS Bulletin*, Vol.24, No.1, January 1993.

Moore, Robert C., *The Political Reality of Freedom of the Press in Zambia*, Lanham, University Press of America, 1992.

Moyo, Jonathan N., *Voting for Democracy: Electoral Politics in Zimbabwe*, Harare, University of Zimbabwe Publications, 1992.

Muigai, Githu, 'Kenya's Opposition and the Crisis of Governance', *Issue*, Vol.21, No.1-2, 1993, pp.26-34.

Munslow, Barry, 'Democratisation in Africa', *Parliamentary Affairs*, Vol.46, No.4, October 1993, pp.478-490.

Muravchik, Joshua, *Exporting Democracy: Fulfilling America's Destiny*, Washington, AEI Press, 1991.

Mwansasu, Bismark U., and Cranford Pratt (eds.), *Towards Socialism in Tanzania*, Dar es Salaam, Tanzania Publishing House, 1979.

Nannan, Sukhwant Singh, 'Africa: The Move Towards Democracy', *Strategic Analysis*, Vol.14, No.10, 1992, pp.1221-1232.

Ndue, Paul Ntungwe, 'Africa's Turn Towards Pluralism', *Journal of Democracy*, Vol.5, No.1, January 1994, pp.45-54.

Newbury, Catharine, 'Paradoxes of Democratization in Africa', *African Studies Review*, Vol.37, No.1, April 1994, pp.1-8.

Ngasongwa, Juma, 'Tanzania Introduces a Multi-Party System', *Review of African Political Economy*, No.54, 1992, pp.112-116.

Ninalowo, Bayo, 'On the Structures and Praxis of Domination, Democratic Culture and Social Change: With Inferences from Africa', *Scandinavian Journal of Development Studies*, Vol.9, No.4, December 1990, pp.107-117.

Nwajiaku, Kathryn, 'The National Conferences in Benin and Togo Revisited', *The Journal of Modern African Studies*, Vol.32, No.3, 1994, pp.429-447.

Nwokedi, Emeka, 'Nigeria's Democratic Transition: Explaining the Annulled 1993 Presidential Election, *The Round Table*, No.330, April 1994, pp.189-404.

Nyang'oro, Julius E., 'Reform Politics and the Democratization Process in Africa', *African Studies Review*, Vol.37, No.1, April 1994, pp.133-149.

Nyong'o Peter Anyang', 'Africa: The Failure of One-Party Rule', *Journal of Democracy*, Vol.3, No.1, January 1992, pp.90-96.

Nyong'o, Peter Anyang', (ed.), *30 Years of Independence in Africa: The Lost Decades*, Nairobi, African Association of Political Science, Academy Publishers, 1992.

Nzouankeu, Jacques Mariel, 'The African Attitude to Democracy', *International Social Science Journal*, No.128, May 1991, pp.373-385.

Nzouankeu, Jacques Mariel, 'The Role of the National Conference in the Transition to Democracy: The Cases of Benin and Mali', *Issue*, Vol.21, No.1-2, 1993, pp.44-50.

Nzouankeu, Jacques Mariel, 'Decentralization and Democracy in Africa', *International Review of Administrative Sciences*, Vol.60, 1994, pp.213-227.

Nzomo, Maria, 'The Gender Dimension of Democratization in Kenya: Some International Linkages', *Alternatives*, Vol.18, No.1, Winter 1993, pp.61-73.

Odedokun, M.O., 'Factors Responsible for the Poor Economic Growth Performance of Africa in 1970s and 1980s: A Cross-Sectional Evidence from 42 Countries' *African Development Review*, Vol.5, No.1, June 1993, pp.32-61.

O'Donnell, Guillermo, Philippe Schmitter and Laurence Whitehead (eds), *Transitions from Authoritarian Rule: Southern Europe*, Baltimore and London, Johns Hopkins University Press, 1986.

O'Donnell, Guillermo, Philippe Schmitter and Laurence Whitehead (eds.), *Transitions from Authoritarian Rule: Latin America*, Baltimore and London, Johns Hopkins University Press, 1986.

O'Donnell, Guillermo, Philippe Schmitter and Layrence Whitehead (eds,), *Transitions from Authoritarian Rule: Comparative Perspectives*, Baltimore and London, Johns Hopkins University Press, 1986.

O'Donnell, Guillermo, and Philippe Schmitter, *Transitions from Authoritarian Rule: Tentative Conclusions about Uncertain Democracies*, Baltimore and London, Johns Hopkins University Press, 1986.

Okoroji, Joseph C., 'The Nigerian Presidential Elections', *Review of African Political Economy*, No.58, November 1993, pp.123-131.

Olagunju, Tunji, Adele Jinadu and Sam Oyovbaire, *Transition to Democracy in Nigeria (1985-1993)*, Ibadan, Spectrum Books Limited, 1993.

Olukoshi, Adebayo O. (ed.), *The Politics of Structural Adjustment in Nigeria*, London, James Currey, 1993.

Omara-Otunnu, Amii, 'The Struggle for Democracy in Uganda', *The Journal of Modern African Studies,* Vol.30, No.3, 1992, pp.443-463.

Owusu, Maxwell, 'Democracy and Africa: A View from the Village', *The Journal of Modern African Studies*, Vol.30, No.3, 1992, pp.369-396.

Oyugi, Walter O., E.S. Atieno Odhiambo, Michael Chege, and Afrifa K. Gitonga (eds), *Democratic Theory and Practice in Africa*, London, James Currey, 1988.

Panter-Brick, Keith (ed.), *Soldiers and Oil: The Political Transformation of Nigeria*, London, Frank Cass, 1978.

Panter-Brick, Keith, 'Prospects for Democracy in Zambia', *Government and Opposition*, Vol.29, No.2, 1994, pp.231-247.

Parry, Geraint, and Michael Moran (eds), *Democracy and Democratization*, London, Routledge, 1994.

Phiri, Bizeck Jube, 'Zambia: The Myth and Realities of One-Party Participatory Democracy', *Geneve-Afrique*, Vol.24, No.2, 1991, pp.9-24.

Plaut, Martin, 'Rwanda: Looking Beyond the Slaughter', *The World Today*, August-September 1994, pp.149-153.

Pool, David, 'Eritrean Independence: The Legacy of the Derg and the Politics of Reconstruction', *African Affairs*, Vol.92, No.368, pp.389-402.

Raftopoulos, Brian, 'Beyond the House of Hunger: Democratic Struggle in Zimbabwe', *Review of African Political Economy*, No.54, 1992, pp.59-74.

Rakner, Lise, 'Political Transition and Economic Reform: The Role of Labour in Zambian National Politics', *Forum for Development Studies*, Vol.3, No.2, 1993, pp.131-147.

Reynolds, Andrew (ed.), *Election '94 South Africa: The Campaigns, Results and Future Prospects*, London, James Currey, 1994.

Reyntjens, Filip, 'The Winds of Change: Political and Constitutional Evolution in Francophone Africa, 1990-1991', *Journal of African Law*, Vol.35, No.1-2, 1991, pp.44-55.

Reyntjens, Filip, 'The Proof of the Pudding is in the Eating: The June 1993 Elections in Burundi', *The Journal of Modern African Studies*, Vol.31, No.4, 1993, pp.563-583.

Riggs, Fred W. 'Fragility of the Third World's Regimes', *International Social Science Journal*, No.136, May 1993, pp.199-243.

Riley, Stephen P., *The Democratic Transition in Africa: An End to the One-Party State?*, London, Research Institute for the Study of Conflict and Terrorism, 1991.

Riley, Stephen P., 'Political Adjustment or Domestic Pressure: Democratic Politics and Political Choice in Africa', *Third World Quarterly*, Vol.13, No.3, 1992, pp.539-551.

Riley, Stephen P., 'Post-Independence Anti-Corruption Strategies and the Contemporary Effects of Democratization', *Corruption and Reform*, Vol.7, No.3, 1993, pp.249-261.

Rimmer, Douglas (ed.), *Action in Africa*, London, James Currey, 1993.

Robinson, Pearl T., 'Democratization: Understanding the Relationship between Regime Change and the Culture of Politics', *African Studies Review*, Vol.37, No.1, April 1994, pp.39-67.

Rose, Laurel L., *The Politics of Harmony: Land Dispute Strategies in Swaziland*, Cambridge, Cambridge University Press, 1992.

Rotimi, Ajayi Ola, and Julius O. Ihonvbere, 'Democratic Impasse: Remilitarisation in Nigeria', *Third World Quarterly*, Vol.15, No.4, 1994, pp.669-689.

Rudebeck, Lars (ed.), *When Democracy Makes Sense: Studies in the Democratic Potential of Third World Popular Movements*, Uppsala, Working Group for the Study of Development Strategies, 1992.

Sachikonye, L.M., 'The Debate on Democracy in Contemporary Zimbabwe', *Review of African Political Economy*, No.49, Winter 1990, pp.117-125.

Sahn, David E. and Alexander Sarris, 'The Evolution of States, Markets, and

Civil Institutions in Rural Africa, *The Journal of Modern African Studies*, Vol.32, No.2, 1994, pp.279-303.

Sandbrook, Richard, 'Liberal Democracy in Africa: A Socialist-Revisionist Perspective', *Canadian Journal of African Studies*, Vol.22. No.2, 1988, pp.240-267.

Sandbrook, Richard, *The Politics of Africa's Economic Recovery*, Cambridge, Cambridge University Press, 1993.

Sangmpam, S.N., *Pseudocapitalism and the Overpoliticized State*, Aldershot, Avebury, 1994.

Scarlett, Prunella, 'The Ndwedwe Experience', *The Round Table*, No.331, 1994, pp.299-301.

Schatzberg, Michael G., *The Dialectics of Oppression in Zaire*, Bloomington, Indiana University Press, 1988.

Schmitz, Gerald J. and Eboe Hutchful, *Democratization and Popular Participation in Africa*, Ottawa, The North-South Institute, 1992.

Schoeman, Stan, 'Swaziland: The Changing Political Climate', *AI Bulletin*, Vol.32, No.8, 1992, pp.1-2.

Schraeder, Peter J., 'Elites as Facilitators or Impediments to Political Development? Some Lessons from the "Third Wave" of Democratization in Africa', *The Journal of Developing Areas*, Vol.29, No.1, October 1994, pp.69-90.

Searle, Chris, 'Agony and Struggle in Northern Somalia', *Race and Class*, Vol.34, No.2, 1992, pp.23-32.

Serpa, Eduardo, 'Madagascar: Change and Continuity', *Africa Insight*, Vol.21, No.4, pp.233-245.

Shapiro, Ian, 'Democratic Innovation: South Africa in Comparative Context', *World Politics*, Vol.46, No.1, October 1993, pp.121-150.

Shaw, Timothy M., *Reformism and Revisionism in Africa's Political Economy in the 1990s*, Basingstoke, Macmillan, 1993.

Shaw, William H., 'Towards the One-Party State in Zimbabwe: A Study in African Political Thought', *The Journal of Modern African Studies*, Vol.24, No.3, 1986, pp.373-394.

Shillington, Kevin, *Ghana and the Rawlings Factor*, London Macmillan, 1992.

Shivji, Issa G. (ed.) *State and Constitutionalism: An African Debate on Democracy*, Harare, Southern Africa Political Economy Series Trust, 1991.

Simon, David, *Independent Namibia One Year On*, London, Research Institute for the Study of Conflict, 1991

Sithole, Masipula, 'Is Zimbabwe Poised on a Liberal Path?: The State and the Prospects of the Parties', *Issue*, Vol.21, No.1-2, 1993, pp.35-43.

Sklar, Richard L. and Mark Strege, 'Finding Peace Through Democracy in Sahelian Africa', *Current History*, Vol.91, No.565, 1992, pp.224-229.

Smith, Patrick, 'Angola: Free and Fair Elections', *Review of African Political Economy*, No.55, November 1992, pp.101-106.

Somerville, Keith, 'Africa Moves Towards Party Pluralism', *The World Today*, Vol.47, No.8-9, August/September 1991, pp.152-155.

Somerville, Keith, 'The Failure of Democratic Reform in Angola and Zaire', *Survival*, Vol.35, No.3, Autumn 1993, pp.51-77.

Somerville, Keith, 'Africa: Is there a Silver Lining?', *The World Today*, November 1994, pp.215-218.

Southall, Roger, 'The 1993 Lesotho Election', *Review of African Political Economy*, No.59, 1994, pp.110-118.

Soyinka, Wole, 'The Last Despot and the End of Nigerian History', *Index on Censorship*, No.6, 1994, pp.67-75.

Sparks, Donald L. and December Green, *Namibia: The Nation after Independence*, Boulder and Oxford, Westview Press, 1992.

Spence, J.E., 'Everybody has Won, So All Must Have Prizes: Reflections on the South African General Election', *Government and Opposition*, Vol.29, No.4, Autumn 1994, pp.431-444.

Stamp, Patricia, 'The Politics of Dissent in Kenya', *Current History*, Vol.90, No.555, May 1991, pp.205-208 and 227-229.

Starr, Harvey, 'Democratic Dominoes: Diffusion Approaches to the Spread of Democracy in the International System', *Journal of Conflict Resolution*, Vol.35, No.2, June 1991, pp.356-381.

Strauss, Annette, 'The 1992 Referendum in South Africa', *The Journal of Modern African Studies*, Vol.31, No.2, 1993, pp339-360.

Szeftel, Morris, 'Ethnicity and Democratization in South Africa', *Review of African Political Economy*, Vol.21, No.60, 1994, pp.185-199.

Szeftel, Morris, 'Negotiated Elections in South Africa, 1994', *Review of African Political Economy*, Vol.21, No.61, September 1994, pp.457-470.

Tandon, Yash, 'Political Economy of Struggles for Democracy and Human Rights in Africa', *Economic and Political Weekly* (Bombay), June 22, 1991, pp.1554-1561.

Taylor, A.J.P., *The Origins of the Second World War*, London, Hamish Hamilton, 1961.

Throup, David, 'Elections and Political Legitimacy in Kenya', *Africa*, Vol.63, No.3, 1993, pp.371-396.

Tordoff, William (ed.), *Politics in Zambia*, Manchester, Manchester University Press, 1974.

Tordoff, William, *Government and Politics in Africa*, London, Macmillan, 1993.

Turrittin, Jane, 'Mali: People Topple Traore', *Review of African Political Economy*, No.52, November 1991, pp.97-103.

Tvedten, Inge, 'The Angolan Debacle', *Journal of Democracy*, Vol.4, No.2, April 1993, pp.108-118.

van Donge, Jan Kees, 'Kamuzu's Legacy: The Democratisation of Malawi', paper presented to the African Studies Association (UK) conference, University of Lancaster, September 1994.

van Hoek, F. and J. Bossuyt, 'Democracy in Sub-Saharan Africa: The Search for a New Institutional Set-Up', *African Development Review*, Vol.5, No.1, June 1993, pp.81-93.

Vanhanen, Tatu, *The Process of Democratization: A Comparative Study of 147 States, 1980-88*, Washington, Crane Russak, 1990.

Vengroff, Richard, 'Governance and the Transition to Democracy: Political Parties and the Party System in Mali', *The Journal of Modern African Studies*, Vol.31, No.2, 1993, pp.277-299.

Vengroff, Richard, 'The Impact of the Electoral System on the Transition to Democracy in Africa: The Case of Mali', *Electoral Studies*, Vol.13, No.1, 1994, pp.29-37.

Venter, Albert and Michele Oliver, 'Human Rights in Africa: Nyerere and Kaunda', *International Journal of World Peace*, Vol.10, No.1, March 1993, pp.21-33.

Villalon, Leonardo A., 'Democratizing a (Quasi) Democracy: The Senegalese Elections of 1993', *African Affairs*, Vol.93, No.371, April 1994, pp.163-193.

Vivekananda, Franklin and Ibrahim James, 'Militarism and the Crisis of Democracy in Africa 1980-85', *Scandinavian Journal of Development Alternatives*, Vol.9, No.4, December 1990, pp.79-93.

Volman, Daniel, 'Africa and the New World Order', *The Journal of Modern African Studies*, Vol.31, No.1, March 1993, pp.1-30.

Wamala, A.S., 'The Role of Workers in the Struggle towards Multi-Party Democracy: Africa's Colonial and Post-Colonial Experience', *Eastern Africa Social Science Research Review*, Vol.8, No.1, January 1992, pp.46-61.

Weiner, Myron and Ergun Ozbudun, *Competitive Elections in Developing Countries*, Duke University Press, 1987.

Welch, Claude E. Jr., 'The Single Party Phenomenon in Africa', *TransAfrica Forum*, Fall 1991, pp.85-94.

Welch, Claude E. Jr., 'The Organisation of African Unity and the Promotion of Human Rights', *The Journal of Modern African Studies*, Vol.29, No.4, 1991, pp.535-555.

Whitaker, C.S., *The Politics of Tradition: Continuity and Change in Northern Nigeria 1946-1966*, Princeton New Jersey, Princeton University Press, 1970.

White, Landeg, *Magamero: Portrait of an African Village*, Cambridge, Cambridge University Press, 1987.

Widner, Jennifer A., 'The 1990 Elections in Cote d'Ivoire', *Issue*, Vol.20, No.1, 1991, pp.31-40.

Widner, Jennifer A., *The Rise of the Party State in Kenya: From Harambee to Nyao*, Berkeley, University of California Press, 1992.

Widner, Jennifer A., 'Kenya's Slow Progress Toward Multiparty Politics', *Current History*, Vol.91, No.365, 1992, pp.214-218.

Widner, Jennifer A., 'Two Leadership Styles and Patterns of Political Liberalization', *African Studies Review*, Vol.37, No.1, April 1994, pp.151-174.

Widner, Jennifer A. (ed), *Economic Change and Political Liberalization in Sub-Saharan Africa*, Baltimore and London, Johns Hopkins University Press, 1994.

Wignaraja, Ponna (ed.), *New Social Movements in the South: Empowering the People*, London, Zed Books, 1993.

Williams, Gavin, 'Why Structural Adjustment is Necessary and Why It Doesn't Work', *Review of African Political Economy*, No.60, 1994, pp.214-225.

Windrich, Elaine, 'Media Coverage of the Angolan Elections', *Issue*, Vol.22, No.1, 1994, pp.19-23.

Wiseman, John A., 'Urban Riots in West Africa, 1977-1985', *The Journal of Modern African Studies*, Vol.24, No.3, 1986, pp.509-518.

Wiseman, John A., *Democracy in Black Africa: Survival and Revival*, New York, Paragon House, 1990.

Wiseman, John A., 'Early Post-Redemocratisation Elections in Africa', *Electoral Studies*, Vol.11, No.4, 1992, pp.279-291.

Wiseman, John A., 'Democracy and the New Political Pluralism in Africa: Causes, Consequences and Significance', *Third World Quarterly*, Vol.14, No.3, 1993, pp.439-449.

Wiseman, John A., 'Leadership and Personal Danger in African Politics', *The Journal of Modern African Studies*, Vol.31, No.4, 1993, pp.657-660.

Wiseman, John A. and Elizabeth Vidler, 'The July 1994 Coup d'Etat in The Gambia: The End of an Era', *The Round Table*, No.333, 1995, pp.63-65.

Woodward, Peter, 'Democracy and Economy in Africa: The Optimists and the Pessimists', *Democratization*, Vol.1, No.1, Spring 1994, pp.116-132.

World Bank, *Adjustment in Africa*, Oxford, Oxford University Press, 1994.

Yohannes, Okbazghi, 'Eritrea: A Country in Transition', *Review of African Political Economy*, No.57, July 1993, pp.7-28.

Young, Crawford, *Ideology and Development in Africa*, New Haven, Yale University Press, 1982.

Young, Crawford, *The Rise and Decline of the Zairian State*, Madison, University of Wisconsin Press, 1985.

Young, Crawford, 'Zaire: The Shattered Illusion of the Integral State', *The Journal of Modern African Studies*, Vol.32, No.2, 1994, pp.247-263.

Young, Tom, 'The Politics of Development in Angola and Mozambique', *African Affairs*, Vol.87, No.347, April 1988, pp.165-184.

Young, Tom, 'Elections and Electoral Politics in Africa', *Africa*, Vol.63, No.3, pp.299-312.

Zack-Williams, A. and Stephen Riley, 'Sierra Leone: The Coup and its Consequences', *Review of African Political Economy*, No.56, March 1993, pp.91-98.

Zartman, I. William (ed.) *Collapsed States: The Disintegration and Restoration of Legitimate Authority*, Boulder, Lynne Rienner, 1995.

Zolberg, Aristide R., 'The Specter of Anarchy: African States Verging on Dissolution', *Dissent*, Vol.39, No.3, 1992, pp.303-311.

Zunes, Stephen, 'Unarmed Insurrections Against Authoritarian Governments in the Third World: A New Kind of Revolution', *Third World Quarterly*, Vol.15, No.3, 1994, pp.403-426.

Reports of the Commonwealth Observer Group: All Commonwealth Secretariat, London.

Presidential and National Assembly Elections in Zambia 31 October 1991
Elections to the Constitutional Commission in Seychelles 23-26 July, 1992
The Presidential Election in Ghana 3 November 1992
Referendum on the Draft Constitution in Seychelles 12-15 November 1992
The Presidential, Parliamentary and Civic Elections in Kenya 29 December 1992
The General Election in Lesotho 27 March 1993

Newspapers and Magazines
Africa Confidential (London)
Africa Events (London)
Africa Forum (London)
Africa South (Johannesburg)
African Business (London)
African Topics (London)
Daily Champion (Lagos)
Daily Nation (Nairobi)
Daily Times (Blantyre)
Keesings Archives (London)
Focus on Africa (London)

Malawi Democrat (Blantyre)
Mayibuye (Journal of the African National Congress), Marshalltown
New African (London)
New Nigerian (Kaduna)
The News (Lagos)
Newswatch (Lagos)
Nigerian Tribune (Lagos)
Society (Nairobi)
Southern African Economist (Harare)
Tell (Lagos)
The Week (Lagos)
Uganda Today (Croydon)
West Africa (London)

Index

199